MASS POLITICS IN THE PEOPLE'S REPUBLIC

POLITICS IN ASIA AND THE PACIFIC
Interdisciplinary Perspectives

Haruhiro Fukui
Series Editor

MASS POLITICS IN THE PEOPLE'S REPUBLIC

State and Society in Contemporary China

Alan P.L. Liu

UNIVERSITY OF CALIFORNIA–SANTA BARBARA

WestviewPress

A Division of HarperCollins*Publishers*

To
Alex S. Edelstein
Mentor and Friend
and to the memory of my sister
Donna H.C. Liu

Politics in Asia and the Pacific: Interdisciplinary Perspectives

Copyright © 1996 by Westview Press, Inc., A Division of HarperCollins Publishers, Inc.

Published in 1996 in the United States of America by Westview Press, Inc., 5500 Central
Avenue, Boulder, Colorado 80301-2877, and in the United Kingdom by Westview Press,
12 Hid's Copse Road, Cumnor, Oxford, OX2 9JJ

Library of Congress Cataloging-in-Publication Data

Liu, Alan P. L., 1937–
    Mass Politics in the People's Republic : state and society in contemporary China /
Alan P.L. Liu.
        p.   cm.   —   (Politics in Asia and the Pacific)
    Includes bibliographical references.
    ISBN 0–8133–1334–1 (alk. paper). —ISBN 0–8133–1335–X (pbk. alk. paper).
    1. Political participation—China.   2. Political culture—China.   3. Public opin-
    ion—China.   4. China—Politics and government—1949–I. Title.   II. Series.
JQ1516.L54 1996
323'.042'0951–dc20   96–6850
                                                                                CIP

The paper used in this publication meets the requirements of the American National
Standard for Permanence of Paper for Printed Library Materials Z39.48–1984.

10   9   8   7   6   5   4   3   2   1

CONTENTS

TABLES AND ILLUSTRATIONS

Figures

Maps

ACKNOWLEDGMENTS

I would like to thank Haruhiro Fukui for including this book in his series. I also wish to express my great appreciation to Nancy Lynch for her careful editing. I am indebted to the librarians at the Oriental Collection of the University of California at Santa Barbara.

Additional thanks go to Senior Editor Susan McEachern of Westview Press and an anonymous reader of the first version of this book.

Alan P.L. Liu

ACRONYMS

ACFTU	All-China Federation of Trade Unions
CCP	Chinese Communist Party
CPPCC	Chinese People's Political Consultative Conference
GNP	Gross National Product
NIC	Newly Industrializing Countries
NPC	National People's Congress
PRC	People's Republic of China
SMO	Social Movement Organizations

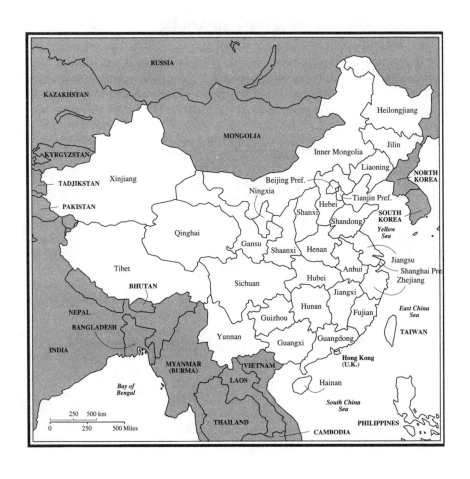

1

INTRODUCTION: RISE OF THE MASS IN CHINESE POLITICS

The first interesting fact is, as is seldom suspected, that the Chinese are great critics of their rulers, perhaps even more so than western people. What makes the Chinese such great critics of their government is the fact that they are consistently and thoroughly cynical about most of their officials all the time—a fact which is often superficially ignored through the apparent quiet submission of the people to their oppressors.

—Lin Yutang (c1937)[1]

On April 5, 1976, a mass demonstration occurred at the Tian'anmen Square in Beijing. The size of the crowd at the height of the protest was estimated to be about 100,000.[2] One of the impromptu poems circulating among the demonstrators described the popular mood as follows: "China is no longer the China of yore, and the people are no longer wrapped in sheer ignorance; gone for good is Chin Shih Huang's feudal society."(Before the death of Mao Zedong in September 1976, the name of Qin Shi Huang, (Chin Shih Huang), the despotic emperor of the Qin dynasty, 221–206 B.C., was used by ordinary Chinese as the pseudonym for Mao.)[3] This demonstration served notice to Chinese leaders and the outside world that the mass age in Chinese politics had arrived. Until then, the Chinese seemed to have played mainly the role of subjects; they were "reformed," "led," or "moved" *(yundong qunzhong)* by the Communist Party-dominated state in endless mass campaigns. The demonstration of April 5 changed all that. It was the first populistic campaign initiated by the Chinese masses themselves after the birth of the People's Republic of China (PRC) in 1949. Since then, scarcely a year has passed by without a variety of mass protests in Beijing or some other major Chinese cities. The "Democracy Wall" movement in 1978–1980, student demonstrations throughout the 1980s, and unrest among peasants and workers in the 1990s are examples.

The dawn of the mass age in China meant that the Chinese political system from now on cannot simply be the expression of one charismatic ruler's will as it was under Mao. Public opinion must be taken into account. The various post-Mao reforms were the Communist Party's long-delayed reactions to the general sentiments and demands of the public in China. Nowadays, the pent-up feelings of ordinary Chinese threaten to erupt like a live volcano that might destabilize, if not dethrone, the Communist Party. Lowell Dittmer argued that the strife among the Chinese elite is significantly affected by the scale of social unrest.[4] It is thus time to inquire into the cultural, political, social, and economic roots of Chinese mass behavior.

Until recently, U.S. scholars specializing in China paid episodic attention to Chinese mass sentiments. The concept of public opinion did not appear in the lexicon of contemporary U.S. Sinology until the 1980s. Prior to that, China specialists studied Chinese public views and reactions largely in connection with government-initiated campaigns such as the Hundred Flowers movement in 1957 and the Cultural Revolution of 1966–1969. These works tended to concentrate on the intellectuals, "intellectuals-in-waiting"(students), or urban occupational groups.[5] In the late 1970s and early 1980s, several scholarly works on industrial workers and peasants appeared, focusing mainly on their economic and social lives.[6] But, on the whole, Sinologists (until quite recently) paid more attention to Chinese elites than the masses.[7] Even for scholars who recognized the important role that the masses played in the Chinese political process, their concern was still with the lower elites. Lynn White, for example, wrote: "We need a new kind of political science—one that takes seriously not just reactions to state coercion by 'weak' leaders in many small collectives, but also their own sovereign initiatives—to explain major political events."[8] After the student pro-democracy movement at Tian'anmen Square in April–June 1989, scholars' interest in Chinese mass behavior increased, although much of the attention seemed to revolve around the alleged emergent "civil society" (more on this topic in the concluding chapter).[9] Curiously, proponents of the idea of Chinese "civil society" did not extend their analyses to the core of civil society—public opinion. The few scholars who paid singular attention to public opinion concentrated on opinion polls in the post-Mao period and did not frame their analyses in the "civil society" context. Moreover, these polls were taken almost entirely among urban groups such as cadres, staff members, workers, and students. Only a limited number of surveys were done among peasants or ethnic minorities.[10]

My study focuses on the sentiments and reactions of four nonelite groups: peasants, workers, educated youths, and ethnic minorities. In my view, the opinions of these four groups constitute the Chinese public opinion. I shall endeavor to prove that public opinion, as the concept is generally understood in the West, has existed in the PRC since its inception. More important, public opinion in China, as in the United States, has played an influential role in shaping major political outcomes. I shall employ a developmental and comparative perspective to analyze the views of these four groups. In this chapter I will explain the presuppositions that inform subsequent analyses.

The analytical framework of my work may be set forth simply and briefly: The workings of Chinese public opinion are significantly affected by the Party-state structure, the segmented Chinese social structure, and an environment of conflict. But first let me clarify the meaning of public opinion in the Chinese context.

Public Opinion

When one ventures into scholarly definitions of public opinion in the United States, one quickly comes across a number of dualities. First, public opinion may be defined restrictively or broadly. The former defines public opinion exclusively in a democratic political context. In his classic essay "The Historical Development of Public Opinion," Hans Speier said that public opinion refers to "opinions on matters of concern to the nation freely and publicly expressed by men outside of the government who claim a right that their opinions should influence or determine the actions, personnel, or structure of their government."[11] According to Speier, public opinion therefore does not exist if a government denies that the opinions of the citizens have any role to play in policymaking or if a government prevents free and public expression of such opinions. Jurgen Habermas interpreted public opinion in an even more restricted sense than Speier. Habermas restricted public opinion to that of the powerful exponents of public debate in Western democratic societies. He thus "limits the treatment of public opinion to countries of Western Europe and North America in the last two centuries."[12]

But surely opinions on governmental matters exist beyond the Habermasian limits or Speier's democratic systems. A broader definition of public opinion is both more realistic and fruitful for comparative analysis. Bernard Berelson defined public opinion as "people's response (that is, approval, disapproval, or indifference) to controversial political and social issues of general attention."[13] Ithiel de Sola Pool viewed public opinion as having three constitutive elements: (1) the opinions referred to are publicly expressed, (2) the opinions referred to are about public affairs, and (3) the opinion is held by the general public instead of by some small group.[14] It is evident that public opinion as defined by Berelson and Pool exists in all types of societies, although the working of public opinion differs across states. A general definition of public opinion is more intellectually meaningful and fruitful than a restricted one because public opinion is "system-sensitive." Public opinion does not exist in a vacuum. It is significantly affected by the overall cultural, political, social, and economic environment. Psychologist Daniel Katz wrote:

> The public opinion process is one phase of the influencing of collective decisions, and its investigation involves knowledge of channels of communication, of the power structures of a society, of the character of mass media, of the relation between elites, factions, and masses, of the role of formal and informal leaders, of the institutionalized access to officials.[15]

Once over the hurdle of definition, there is another duality of public opinion concerning types of opinion. Walter Lippmann wrote profusely about pathologies of public opinion such as the public's lack of information, use of stereotypes, or moralizing, but he implicitly recognized two generic types of public opinion. One type is "where the grievance is so plain that virtually without leadership the same reaction takes place in many people."[16] Apparently, Lippmann did not regard this first type of opinion pathological. It is the second type of public opinion, which deals with distant issues, that Lippmann deemed problematic. Lippmann was not alone in distinguishing types of public opinion. Pool also wrote about two kinds of public opinion: (1) on matters that personally affect the believer, for example, unemployment or juvenile delinquency; and (2) on matters known only through mediated experience.[17] Presumably, in Pool's classification, the latter type is more prone to Lippmann's opinion pathology than the first type.

This book is primarily concerned with the first type of opinion in China: public opinion on matters which affect the Chinese masses at first hand. Opinion of this type is relatively unencumbered by the "screening" phenomenon. This is largely due to the status of the four groups, particularly the peasants, workers, and the minorities (somewhat less so with the educated youths). Peasants and workers, engage daily in practical activities, having little time for or interest in the theoretical (or ideological) aspects of life. Swedish sociologist Ulf Himmelstrand pointed out that

> nonverbal activity often has the property of bringing the actor directly in touch with things, a property which verbal activity in itself has not. Being directly confronted with the things about which he talks regularly gives the actor an opportunity to benefit from feedback of unanticipated information regarding the things concerned.[18]

In contrast with the masses, the elite of a society tends to live in an environment of symbols (or, in Pool's terms, "mediated experience") as the latter has relegated to themselves the responsibility of integration.

Himmelstrand said that those who deal mostly with symbols tend to neglect the objective or conceptual referents of the symbols and react to any attempt to change their political, social, or economic formulations with "aggressive responses." In other words, it is the elite whose opinions are more prone to Lippmann's pathology than the masses.

There is yet one more duality of public opinion that must be clarified. This one deals with the way public opinion presents itself. Philip Converse referred to this third duality as the "two faces of public opinion."[19] One face of it is seen in the results of opinion surveys and the other, in the public opinion "atmospherics" as presented in daily news media. The latter often assumes the form of a campaign or social movement. Converse called the first, populist opinion and the second, effective public opinion (effective in actual political outcomes). The key to these two faces of public opinion, according to Converse, is differential mobilization, the effective public opinion being mobilized opinion. Russell Neuman commented on the same two-faced appearance of public opinion in the United States: "Public opinion has been characterized as a sleeping giant. Most of the time it is passive and unresponsive. But when aroused, it has effects on the polity that are significant and immediate."[20]

Chinese public opinion also has two faces. I refer to them as general and specific public opinions. The former refers to the people's response (approval, disapproval, or indifference) to controversial state policies that affect their daily lives. The latter is mobilized public opinion in the form of a social movement. For the specific public opinion in China, I use Neidhardt and Rucht's definition of a social movement: "an organized and sustained effort of a collectivity of inter-related individuals, groups and organizations to promote or to resist social change with the use of public protest activities."[21] The general and specific public opinions in China are closely related. The latter, exemplified by the April 5, 1976, protest at Tian'anmen Square, is the concluding act of a developing general opinion. At the same time, the two types of opinions may be seen as alternates. When a specific opinion such as that manifested by the 1976, demonstration meets with state repression, people revert to the general public opinion. Over a period, if the Party-state persists in ignoring public opinion, then general public opinion will gather intensity and be precipitated into specific opinion. In 1993, signifying the Communist elite's recognition of the rising importance of public opinion, a high-ranking propagandist of the Chinese Communist Party (CCP) expounded a new theory on the mass behavior of the Chinese.[22] Although his theory applied mainly to ethnic minorities, it has general validity and is very close to my notion of general and specific public opinion. This Party official said that the ethnic minorities' reactions to the CCP policies and programs were characterized, sequentially, by accumulation (of discontent), sudden eruption, contagion, mutation, and (after meeting state repression) "sedimentation" (going underground). "Sedimentation," feeds on

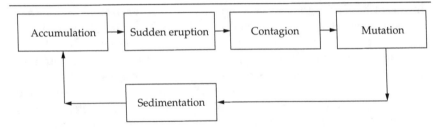

Figure 1.1   A Chinese propagandist's view of the "contradictions" between the
state and the ethnic minorities

accumulation and so the five characteristics are actually phases of a circular sequence as shown in Figure 1.1.

In other words, discontent among the masses increases, gathers strength underneath the surface, and precipitates into open protests after a period of time. Open protests are likely to spread among the masses. During this process, conflicts between the state and the masses undergo a mutation in which new conflicts are added to old ones. The degree of antagonism between the masses and the state thus intensifies. The state would then be compelled to repress the protests. The masses would withdraw and hide their discontent, only to gather strength beneath the surface once more and in time be precipitated into another sudden eruption. It is clear that the phases of "sedimentation" and "accumulation" correspond to my idea of general public opinion, while "sudden eruption," "contagion," and "mutation" are parts of my concept of specific public opinion.

To clarify further the two faces of Chinese public opinion, Tables 1.1 and 1.2 contrast and compare (where possible) the general and specific opinions in the PRC with that of the United States. The fundamental difference between the two countries is whether public opinion is institutionalized. All other differences are derived from that. General public opinion in China is uninstitutionalized. Hence, Chinese public opinion is articulated through what Weber referred to as amorphous social action,

Table 1.1   General Public Opinion in China and the United States

	China	**United States**
Style of articulation	Uninstitutionalized	Institutionalized
Means of articulation	Undifferentiated from productive conduct	Differentiated
Substance	Condensed and negative	Diverse and both positive and negative
Effect	Long-term aggregation	Long- and short-term

Table 1.2　Social Movement in China and the United States

	China	United States
Status	Unconventional	Unconventional
Context	Severe repression	Free of repression
Variables	Social strain	Resource mobilization
	Precipitants	
	Diffused collectivities	Organization
	Ecology	
	Assembling dynamics	

such as workers' grumbling or slowdowns.[23] In China expression of opinion is not differentiated from daily productive conduct since the CCP has preempted all formal channels of communication and representation. John Burns wrote an informative essay on the various means of peasant-interest articulation. Among these, Burns mentioned formal institutions such as the bureaucracy, meetings, mass organizations, and elections. But most peasant articulation, Burns noted, "occurs outside of formal institutions" and "is an indication of the failure of the party successfully to institutionalize effective formal channels."[24]

Paraphrasing Marx's allegation on capitalism's simplifying the class structure in society, it can be said that totalitarian control simplifies public opinion. General public opinion concentrates on fewer basic issues dealing with subsistence in contrast to the great number of issues that Americans are called upon to deliberate. Moreover, concerning the judgmental nature of public opinion, Chinese opinion tends to be more negative than positive. That is, Chinese opinion is more about resisting the state's various policies than advocating new ones. (I shall have more to say later about this aspect of general opinion in connection with the nature of the Chinese state.) Finally, general public opinion in China, much more than in the United States, relies on a long period of resisting and pressuring the state to produce any major political outcome in the direction of the opinion. The totalitarian state of China tends to sharpen the demarcation between the state and society as the masses are relegated to a structurally similar position. Under such a circumstance, seemingly amorphous social action is transformed into a public formed without deliberate direction that is capable of producing aggregative effect over a long time.[25]

Just as in the case of general public opinion in China, specific opinion (social movement) may also be systematically compared and contrasted with its U.S. counterpart as presented in Table 1.2. In both countries, social movement as a vehicle of public opinion is regarded as unconventional. In Weberian terms, social movements are also amorphous social actions since they are intermittent and the number of their participants fluctuates.[26] The similarity of social movements between those in China and in the United States, however, does not extend beyond their unconventional status. A fundamental difference is the certainty of state repression in China. In the United States, social movements occur in an environment relatively free of political repression. Consequently, U.S. studies on social movements tend to emphasize technical and tactical matters. U.S. scholars also play down psychological factors such as grievances and social strains because the latter are regarded as social constants. The real keys to social movement, in the U.S. perspective, are organization and strategy. The most important school of thought in U.S. social movements is known as the "resource mobilization" school.[27] With painstaking efforts, U.S. and some West European scholars dissect the social movements into fine components of "sponsoring ideological packages," "consensus mobilization," "frame alignment," and "collective identity." However, another group of U.S. scholars pointed out that the poor and ethnic minorities in the United States have little organizational resources and their movements are often met with local political repression. These scholars' insights into social movements of the poor and the socially marginal (minorities and students) are relevant to the understanding of social movements in China, particularly their stresses on social strains and spontaneous mobilization.[28] Recent studies on the social movements in Eastern Europe that brought about the collapse of all Communist regimes there also contribute to my thinking about social movements in China.[29]

Due to severe state repression, social movements in China must rely on spontaneous factors. The psychological factor of social strain in China cannot and should not be played down, as U.S. or Western European scholars do. For any social movement to start in China, the amount of grievances in Chinese society must be such that the people momentarily disregard state repression. For mobilization to happen in China, any movement must count on a series of precipitants that add to the strain and alienation between the state and the masses. Since the Communist state proscribes any attempt at organizing by the people themselves, Chinese movements have to use "diffused collectivities" as organizational substitutes. According to Pamela Oliver, "Diffuse collectivities are made of informal or primary groups linked by ties of acquaintanceship and the casual conversations of strangers. Individuals form their ideas and behaviors within these diffuse collectivities."[30] Since the Chinese cannot openly mobilize, they must employ "existing ecological units" such as the village, market place, or public square as substitutes for conscious mobilization to rally participants.

The most difficult theoretical point in my dual view of Chinese public opinion is the transition from general to specific opinion. This is the problem of threshold. As Timur Kuran observed, in connection with the revolutions in Eastern Europe in 1989, people have different thresholds of tolerating regime repression. Whether a critical mass will rise up to confront or even topple a regime depends on "distribution of thresholds" among the people but that can at best be imperfectly observed.[31] It is, however, not my intention to predict a revolution in China but to analyze the different ways Chinese express opinions in the face of severe state repression. I shall simply note two facts. First, when the tension level in the general opinion is sufficiently high, outbreaks of specific opinions are inevitable. Rick Fantasia wrote that people's subjective attitudes, such as feelings and cognitions, "sometimes cause [them] to throw caution to the winds and act in the face of great or unknown odds."[32] Second, no matter how repressive a state is, its control strength cannot be uniform, especially in a highly segmented society such as China. Mass outbursts will occur at the weakest links of the state's repressive system, such as in the peripheral areas or among some groups whose associational potentiality is strong.

The State

It is the state that primarily determines the status of public opinion: institutionalized or uninstitutionalized. The basis of political legitimacy also affects public opinion significantly, especially in issue formulation. Pool wrote: "The more eclectic and pragmatic the system, the more often decisions will be conceived of as defined by small discrete issues, each standing on its own feet. The more ideological the system, the more all issues will be felt to hang together."[33] Above all, the character of the state decides the way public opinion influences policy. Thus, the Chinese state system must be described in order to understand the workings of Chinese public opinion.

The relationship between the Chinese Communist state and public opinion is dominated by one fundamental fact: The Chinese state itself evolved from a revolutionary social movement. The social-movement origin of the state puts a stamp on virtually every aspect of its interaction with society. The second fundamental fact about the Chinese state is that, at least in Mao's time (possibly also at present), the state is more often than not the leader's personal tool. In the West, the state has developed into a permanent institution that is largely free of individual idiosyncrasies.[34] In China the state, even in the post-Mao period, is not yet free from idiosyncratic influences; thus, in subsequent discussions on the state, Mao's views will occupy a prominent place.

To delineate the relationship between the Chinese state-and-public opinion relationship in a systematic way, three aspects of the Chinese state must be dealt with: its self-perception, past experience, and reference groups. The CCP was victorious only after a long and bitter civil war. The

Party, including Mao in particular, perceived itself as the embodiment of the general will of Chinese society. In Mao's mind, his personality, the CCP, and "the people" were virtually one and the same. Dittmer wrote that "Mao seemed to take it for granted that his interests were identical with those of the masses."[35] Mao equated his or the Party's views with Chinese public opinion. When Mao was confronted with incontrovertible evidence of differences of opinions between the CCP and the general Chinese public, his standard response was to portray the CCP (himself) as a "cross-bearing" prophet, so to speak. In the face of rising popular discontent in the mid-1950s as a result of collectivization in the countryside and political repression in the cities, Mao made the following statement at a gathering of regional Party officials: "From time immemorial, nothing progressive has ever been favorably received at first and everything progressive has invariably been the object of abuse. Marxism and the Communist Party have been abused from the very beginning. Even ten thousand years hence, things progressive will still be abused at the outset."[36]

On other occasions, Mao often used the metaphor of sailing to describe the CCP and public opinion. After his suppression of free speech during the Hundred Flowers campaign in 1957, Mao said at a Party meeting in May 1958: "The whole Party has gone through a steeling experience last year. After that, we can now sit safely in our fishing boat in spite of the surges of the winds and waves. Such a big wind last year, but our ship did not capsize."[37]

Although oscillating between populism and elitism, Mao had never questioned his belief that he and the masses were of one mind. The masses might be misguided momentarily, according to Mao, but with a little enlightening by the Party, they would see the light and follow the CCP. In March 1959, when Mao was still hopeful that his Great Leap Forward campaign would succeed, he expressed his most basic view about public opinion at a high-level Party conference:

> As I said earlier, in establishing such a complicated and historically unprecedented [institution] as the people's communes [mistakes in implementation] are unavoidable. All we need to do is to tell the people about that, provided we also make corrections of past errors committed in our practical work. After that we shall recover our initiative and the broad masses will stand together with us. We should take into account the laughs and scorns from those opportunists and revanchists. The landlords, rich peasants, counterrevolutionaries, and bad elements will also engage in sabotage. But we must tell our cadres and the masses: When these things happen, we should not fear. We should remain calm, do nothing for a while, and brace [all oppositions]. Let those people expose themselves fully. When such an occasion arises, the broad masses will make a quick and clear judgment, separating right from wrong, and

friend from foe. They will rise to destroy the opportunists who laugh at us and the hostile elements who attack us. After such a period of consolidating the people's communes, our unity with the masses will grow stronger.[38]

In sum, the self-perception of Mao and the CCP, as derived from their interpretation of their victory in the Chinese civil war, virtually excluded any possibility of an autonomous sphere of public opinion in China.

Another manifestation of the influence of the CCP's past experience with revolutionary movements was Mao's literal approach to formal ideological tenets. Those who had closely associated with Mao throughout the long revolution recalled after Mao's death that, in the mid-1950s, he had explicitly declared his intention to realize the aims that Marx and Engels regarded as "utopian socialism." Mao was also reportedly influenced by the ancient Chinese ideal of "the great unity" or "the great harmony" *(datong)*.[39] This seems to be a common trait among those whose lives are bound up with radical social movements. As Ralph Turner and Lewis Killian noted, "If there is a movement-prone configuration, the most promising clue to follow may be the tendency to adopt values in a more literalistic fashion than most people do."[40] Louis Kriesberg also wrote that victory in a revolutionary conflict "may be viewed as imposing new grand responsibilities" for the victor. "Thus, a revolutionary party espousing nationalist goals, mixed with religious or political claims, may increase the religious or political emphases upon victory."[41]

Furthermore, those who have lived through social movements for protracted periods become emotionally attached to the movement as a way of life. According to Turner and Killian, members of a movement derive tremendous emotional satisfaction from their group life. Its collective spirit and like-mindedness become surrogates for reality. "When the movement is a surrogate for reality, experience within it demonstrates the attainability of utopian goals in the community at large."[42] We find ample evidence of this attitude in Mao, especially in his various pronouncements on the "mass line" approach to social change. The "mass line" refers to a specific method of agitation and persuasion that CCP cadres used to promote class hatred among the poor peasants. Specifically, Mao mentioned a seven-step procedure: interview the poor, recruit the active elements, make alliances, solidify the core, stage shows of peasants' pouring out their bitterness, organize the rank and file, and carry out class struggle.[43] To Mao, the mass-line technique established a deep emotional bond between the masses and the CCP. Mao used terms rich in emotional evocations such as *ganqing* (mutual affection) and *yikao* (reliance) to describe the cadre-people relationship.[44] These are terms that ordinary Chinese use to describe feelings among close acquaintances or between parents and children.[45] Mao extended his sense of group solidarity from the revolutionary movement to the relationship between himself (or the CCP) and the masses. It was this perceived solidarity with the masses that made Mao so confident that he could accomplish almost anything. Mao regarded the "mass line" and the cadres as the most unique and valuable assets of the CCP. In the 1950s, Mao often stressed that these two things were responsible for the CCP's being more successful than other Communist parties in East European countries—or even in the Soviet Union–in moving society toward socialism. Mao also believed that these two assets would achieve the ambitious goals of the Great Leap Forward of 1958–1959.[46]

Mao's sense of solidarity with the masses is closely related to his fundamentally polarized view of society—also a very common feeling among members of a social movement. According to Eric Hirsch, polarization performs some vital functions for a social movement. It strengthens the participants' belief that their fate is tied to that of the group. In a polarized environment, consensus within the group increases and participants are more willing to persist in their struggle.[47] But what begins as an adaptation to situational need later becomes an independent attitude. That was the case with Mao, who turned polarization into a formal doctrine. Li Rui, personal secretary to Mao, recalled that a few months before the CCP's complete victory in the Chinese mainland in 1949, Mao received a high-ranking army general. Mao asked the general to define the main task of the revolution after the cities were taken. The general replied: "To develop production." Whereupon Mao sternly corrected the general by saying: "You are wrong. The main task is still class struggle, to solve the problem of struggling with the bourgeoisie."[48] The possibility that Mao derived personal gratification from conflicts, struggles, or polarization cannot and should not be discounted. Kriesberg observed, in connection with social conflict in general, that some people obtain gratification from certain conflict behavior; it enables them to feel solidarity with others and to be a part of an important movement. "People enjoy the excitement of crises and may even help create them or define some events as a crisis in order to increase their own feelings of importance and the significance of their coping with it."[49] Li Rui wrote:

> Mao Zedong was wont to stress his "philosophy of struggle." Early in his life he left us with the famous saying: "I feel boundless joy in struggling with heaven, with earth, and with men." "Activism" and "struggle" formed the vortex of Mao's early philosophy. That was his world outlook and personal motto. In sum, [Mao] loved action and enjoyed struggle, especially putting into practice his own saying: "feeling boundless joy in struggling with men."[50]

The state-society relationship in China had been strongly influenced by Mao and the example set by the former Soviet Union, which the CCP used as its primary reference group. That was perhaps unavoidable. "As for making a transition to socialism and constructing socialism," former secretary Li Rui wrote, "the only things that Mao and the CCP could use as guides were the theories of Marx, Lenin, and Stalin and the concrete examples from the Soviet Union."[51] But note just which aspect of the Soviet system Mao seemed to be attracted to initially: the state.[52] Since 1958, however, Mao became increasingly critical of the Soviet model. But that merely meant that Mao wished to be more radical than the Soviets in "socialist transformation." Mao's critique of the Soviets served as a justification for his Great Leap Forward movement. The Soviet political economic thinking then stressed an evolutionary path that went against Mao's "revolutionary" approach to economic development. Although critical of the Soviet model, Mao still regarded the Soviets as his chief reference, but only as the target for him to surpass.[53]

It is thus instructive to mention what sort of state-society relationship the former Soviet Union had. "One may see totalitarianism," wrote Harry Eckstein, "as a grotesque response to disjunction, for its essence is the absorption of social life by political authority."[54] According to Annie Kriegel, the state-society relationship in the former Soviet Union experienced two phases after revolutionary victory. First, the Communist Party encouraged release of the energy stored up in the masses "and in the most savage and destructive form possible—libertarian anarchism." After that, the new state became another face of the Party, which then "turn[ed] against the masses, against the civil society, serving as the instrument of repression."[55] Under such conditions, "though civil society is not entirely moribund, it is a mere shadow of itself, living in quiet, desperate obscurity, emerging periodically for short, brutal gasps of air—spiritual protest, uprisings or misery, workers' revolts, and nationalist upheavals."[56]

The state-society relationship in China after 1949 bore an unmistakable resemblance to the Soviet pattern.[57] But the collapse of the regimes in the former Soviet Union and Eastern Europe in 1989–1990 should make us rethink about the "short, brutal gasps of air" of civil society under state repression. These gasps of air may represent a larger force—the general public opinion that became the silent counterforce to the Communist state and was the main cause of the Communist system's downfall in Europe.[58] Then we must analyze how the relative power of the state and society undergoes changes and, in the end, society or public opinion reasserts its power.

Since the death of Mao in 1976, the Chinese state-society relationship has conformed closely to the universal pattern of social and political segmentation and anomie following the collapse of a hegemonic regime.[59] In an anomic situation, the state, with its formal rules and institutions, temporarily substitutes for norms.[60] But the state might also use naked force or, going to the other extreme, provide opportunity for participation by the masses. In the latter case, a genuine polity might result, that is, an integration between the state and society in which the prestige of the state is checked and balanced by the prestige of public opinion.

From the perspective of the foregoing, Deng Xiaoping's administration established a mixed state system in which the Maoist element of charisma (albeit transformed into the charisma of the Party oligarchy) coexisted with the formalism and legalism of the state. The new mixed regime of Deng relied heavily on coercion to rule and made little attempt to expand genuine participation. As Burns pointed out, the initial promise of Deng's regime to separate the Party and the state was not followed through.[61] After more than a decade of talks on opening civil service to public participation, the national government in Beijing finally held its first civil service examination in 1994.[62] The state under Deng resembled the traditional Confucian conception of the state. That meant setting aside the fundamental question of political legitimacy and concentrating on (1) conduct of the ruler and officials, and (2) outcomes of the rule.

But in mixed regimes, Robert Dahl said:

> As in hegemonies, when the barriers are lowered, oppositions, interests, and political preferences previously repressed or inhibited spring forth to engage in public contestation. Leaders in these countries of course know this perfectly well—whatever they may say in public. And the presence of these repressed forces creates a genuine danger to the regime for which it can find no easy solution.[63]

These are apt descriptions of post-Mao Chinese state and society. In addition to confronting a surge of pent-up stresses, the post-Mao state of China was faced with the fact that reform itself was anomic and destabilizing. Moreover, just as the social and political disintegration following Mao's death necessitated a strengthening of the state, there was also a need to reduce the state's presence in society. Under Mao, the state had expanded greatly but had contributed little to providing stability and integration. Instead, the Maoist state was faulted primarily for stifling society. To invigorate social life and the economy, Deng's administration was called upon to reduce the state's presence in society and the economy. Meanwhile, the state under Deng's control had formally assumed the welfare function. Deng wished to perform well this new task of the state in order to establish a degree of genuine legitimacy for the CCP, but that would require expanding the state, instead of restraining it. These mutually contradictory forces deepened the degree of segmentation and anomie in post-Mao Chinese politics and society.[64] My analysis of the Chinese public opinion in the post-Mao period must be seen against the foregoing discussion of Deng's state system.

So far I have treated the Chinese state as a single entity. In reality the state in China or elsewhere is a plural phenomenon, having different factions of elite groups, different levels of administration, and, most important of all in China, a heterogeneous lower elite. The policies of a national leader such as Mao or Deng might at best fix broad limitations within which lower elites may act. Still, the latter always have a sphere of free action, especially in such a diverse country as China. Both Mao and Deng themselves manipulated the inherent differences among lower elites for political purposes. Under Mao, some sectors were given preferential treatment such as more funds and materials for the peasants than other sectors.[65] The lower elites might "deviate" either to the "left" or "right" of Mao or Deng. The diversity in the state system, together with the heterogeneous ecological conditions of China, is of vital importance in studying Chinese public opinion. Given the segmented Chinese social structure, to be discussed shortly, local elites and ecology have as much impact on public reactions as the national elites.

Social Structure

That the Chinese public opinion is uninstitutionalized, however, is not entirely due to the political system. The Chinese social structure is equally responsible for that. As a rule, Kurt Back pointed out, "the definition of public opinion . . . is an outcome of the structure of the society in which it is stated."[66] For example, the U.S. definition of public opinion is based on populistic measurements (the polls) and may be attributed to the individualistic character of U.S. society. Back proposed several models of public opinion situated in different social structures. The first two polar types are the highly individualistic and the collectivistic. Between the two are intermediate ones: "A dominant one, which may be represented by only one leader, and the remaining mass, whose opinion is then taken as the public opinion. Another model would consist of several groups of differing power who are concerned with each other's positions."[67] Mao's conception of public opinion closely corresponded to the second model with some revisions. As described earlier, he saw himself or the CCP representing the great majority of the workers and peasants. Theirs was the dominant group—engaging in constant struggles with assorted groups of "class enemies" and political deviants. Mao's conception seemed to stem directly from his experience with the segmented Chinese social structure.

Both the rise of the CCP to power and the present situation of extensive anomie have their roots in the segmented Chinese social structure. The main reason for that has always been a predominance of the rural population. Here I merely wish to present the most essential facts—those that have a direct impact on public opinion. First, the situation in 1949.

A recent study showed that in 1949 about 90 percent of the Chinese population (541,670,000) resided in the countryside.[68] Sociologist C. K. Yang estimated that the rural population then lived in about a million ecological units known as "villages."[69] Chinese peasants had never experienced extensive non-kinship types of organizations. Given the Chinese farms' reliance on human labor and the nuclear family for production, sociologist Fei Xiaotong pointed out in a 1946 essay that "extensive organization in such enterprises gives no appreciable profit but rather complicates human relations."[70] Under Mao, the CCP had aggregated the villages into 54,000 rural communes.[71] After 1982, communes were abolished and disassembled into 190 million peasant households.[72] The experience with collectivization caused the Chinese rural social structure to move from segmentation to the verge of fragmentation. Jonathan Unger wrote that after Deng's order to dissolve the communes was carried out, most peasants "declined to adapt their two decades of experience with socialism to fit present conditions, even where a pooling of resources might have proved profitable to them."[73]

As far as social segmentation is concerned, the situation in the city was not any better than the countryside. Before 1949, aside from the warring CCP and the Guomindang, only two other groups had organized self-consciously for political objectives: university students and the minority parties in politics. The students constituted about 0.23 percent of the urban population and 0.024 percent of the total population then.[74] According to a U.S. diplomatic report, the minority parties "allowed themselves to be divided and were consequently unable to influence the situation [1947–1949]."[75] There was an active labor union movement in Chinese cities then. The total number of union members in 1948 was 16 million, constituting 28 percent of the urban population.[76] They were primarily active in a few large cities along the eastern coast. A 1947 survey by the Chinese Nationalist government found that 70 percent of the factories and 69 percent of the workers were concentrated in the four cities of Shanghai, Tianjin, Qingdao, and Guangzhou.[77] Most of the strikes that occurred in 1946–1948 were for economic reasons. "There was no spontaneous working-class revolt in the cities, and apparently little authentic identification by the Chinese worker himself of the Communist victory with the workers' interests."[78] Although students and workers were the two most militant groups in staging demonstrations before 1949, there was little coordination between them.

The emergent business class was not an assertive group; its number was small. The Nationalist government reported in 1948 that there were 14,078 factories registered with the state. Over half of these were located in Shanghai.[79] The CCP economic planner Chen Yun reported in 1954 that there were 17,000 "relatively large" private businesses in China, the number being close to the last Nationalist count.[80] Under the Nationalist rule, the business class was easily coerced or coopted by the government. In Shanghai during the 1930s, the Chamber of Commerce "was little more than a mere 'cog of local government.'"[81] In 1949 the prominent Chinese sociologist Kuo-heng Shih, collaborating with U.S. scholar Marion J. Levy Jr., published a study on the modern Chinese business class. Shih gives a pessimistic assessment:

> The writer does not think there will be a great future for the modern busi- ness class. If the Kuomintang wins, most of the new industries will be owned and dominated by the government or by officials. Private indus- trialists would become minor partners of high officials. If the Communists win, probably all major new industries will eventually be nationalized and put under party control. In either case there would be not much room for independent industrialists to develop.[82]

One example was sufficient to demonstrate the politically feeble character of the new middle class in the pre-1949 Chinese cities. In 1948 it was only after an appeal by the American ambassador Stuart that a broad association composed of industrialists, professors, financiers, and jour- nalists was organized; this group quickly disclaimed any political ambi- tion.[83] Almost all these urban groups were at best simply organizations independent of the state; there was a paucity, if not total absence, of self- consciously coordinated groups for common political objectives. If by "civil society" we mean independent private associations coordinating self-consciously for common political objectives, then there was no civil society in China before 1949.[84] There was what I would call a "tendency toward civil society"—private organizations making intermittent appeals to the state.

Other information indicated the absence of any real foundation for a civil society before 1949. The Institute of Chinese Public Opinion con- ducted a nationwide poll in 1948 and found that 73 percent of the people were illiterate.[85] The distribution of radio sets was one for every 6,000 people and that of the telephone, one for every 3,238 people.[86] A civil soci- ety *cannot* be built with so few instruments of social communications.

Aside from students and urban workers, the only other social groups that organized themselves into large and cohesive (relatively speaking) associations were perhaps the Christians and Muslims. Most of the Muslims were ethnically non-Chinese. But the Christians, about 3 million Catholics and 700,000 Protestants, were dispersed and not active politi- cally.[87] In 1948 there were about 50 million Muslims in China.[88] Following a time-honored tradition, large ethnic minorities from Tibet to Mongolia were in full-scale rebellion between 1947 and 1948 as they often were in the past when China was politically divided.

It was against this segmented social background that Mao came to power. His perception of himself and the CCP as the incarnations of the will of the masses must be seen against the segmented nature of Chinese social structure. Mao's aggressive destruction of the "tendency toward civil society" in Chinese cities after 1949 has been discussed elsewhere so there is no need to take it up here.[89] What is noteworthy is that in the city as in the countryside, Mao's centralist rule perpetuated Chinese social segmentation. In a survey of daily life in urban China under Mao, sociologists Martin King Whyte and William Parish found that urban Chinese had a weak sense of both the community and the nation. People's social activities revolved around either the nuclear family or work places, which were "self-contained social units."[90]

There are many reasons for continuous social segmentation in China, but the key to the problem is power disparity between the Chinese state and society. The CCP and the state were initially strong because they were highly organized and equipped with a standing army; the rest of Chinese society was segmented and divided. In such a situation, the tendency is for the less powerful to yield to threats of coercion, "but the more powerful may tend to seek further gains because of the tempting weakness of the less powerful."[91] In other words, the seemingly weak and segmented Chinese society tempted Mao to use his great organizational and mobilizational strengths to accomplish deeds that were strongly contrary to the people's wishes. Instead, Mao provoked resistance from individuals and "diffused collectivities" on a massive scale. The results not only defeated Mao's many programs but also left the Chinese society as segmented as ever.

So far, I have been discussing the social structure of China in aggregate terms. As Mao did in the past, the CCP at the present must confront each group. Every social group in China has its own tradition and special characteristics. Moreover, each group occupies a distinct status in the CCP's scheme of things, be it Mao's "utopian socialism" or Deng's "socialism with Chinese characteristics." To analyze the Chinese public's reactions to CCP rule, then and now, one must take into account distinct group traits.

Later chapters will deal with the tradition and reaction of each of the four groups—peasants, workers, educated youths, and ethnic minorities. Here I shall present their modal reactions in broad sketches in order to explain my analytical scheme. I have tentatively analyzed each group's reaction in terms of two types of characteristics: behavioral and structural. The first refers to each group's potentiality and propensity for association for common purposes, which I call solidarity. The second refers to each group's status in the CCP's scheme of "socialist construction." I use the term "included" to refer generally to the CCP's willingness to grant a group a secure and "fair" (in the eyes of the Party elite) share of surplus of the society's total products. In Table 1.3, (+) signifies having the specific characteristic (solidarity or includedness) and (-), not having it. It is very

Table 1.3 Group Characteristics and Forms of Opinion Expression

	Solidarity	Includedness	Modal Reaction
Peasant Ethnic Minorities (1)	−	−	Amorphous social action
Workers	±	+	Amorphous social action, segmentary conflicts
Educated youths	+	±	Movement
Ethnic minorities (2)	+	−	Movement

clear that the CCP has maintained a highly calculating attitude toward the various groups' contributions to the Party's valued goal of industrialization. Those that the Party deems to be essential to such a goal are rewarded with a secure share of the surplus. This is most evident in the Party's differential treatment of workers and peasants.[92]

Table 1.3 presents the modal reactions of the four groups to CCP rule. I have further divided the ethnic minorities into two subgroups. The first subgroup rates low in internal solidarity—as do the numerous small tribes in the southwestern borderlands of China, which have generally reacted to the Chinese state in the same way as did the great peasant masses. The second subgroup rates high in internal solidarity and may be regarded as "nations-in-waiting." This subgroup includes the Tibetans, the Uighurs, the Muslims of the Northwest, and the Mongols in Inner Mongolia. Their reactions to Chinese Communist rule clearly have been different from the small tribes in the Southwest. Table 1.3 also allows a degree of complexity in each group's characteristics (signified by having both plus and minus signs). Chinese workers, for example, have an indeterminate propensity for association as will be explained later. The status of educated youths in the eyes of the CCP, and Mao in particular, has been indeterminate. I shall discuss this topic extensively in Chapter 4.

The reactions of each group are "modal" in nature, that is, reactions other than the ones listed here are also possible but are of secondary importance. One finds a certain degree of "rationalism" in each group's reaction. Peasants, being scattered and unorganized, primarily rely on amorphous social actions. Although urban Chinese workers are securely included in the CCP's scheme of things, they experience other types of strain, especially segmentary conflicts. Thus, some workers resort to amorphous social actions, such as work slowdowns, while a substantial number of workers displace the strain into protracted segmentary conflicts. Students are strong in their associational propensity and suffered from perpetual status anxiety, especially under Mao's rule. Since they are not part of the productive establishment, students can not rely, as the peasants can, on the aggregative impact of productive conduct to pressure the state. Instead, the students organize protest movements. The reactions of ethnic minorities with high solidarity are like the students, with a significant potential for protest movements.

There are other characteristics that seem to be connected closely with modal reactions. For example, students and solidary minorities tend to be more ideological than the other groups which are mostly pragmatic in orientation. Expressed in different terms, conflicts between the state and students and solidary ethnic groups are more dissensual than consensual.[93] Dissensual conflicts involve clashes in cultures and fundamental values, while consensual conflicts deal with a "zero-sum" situation as the state, workers, and peasants all try to acquire a greater share of society's surplus. Students and solidary ethnic groups tend to be less dependent on changes in "opportunity structure" to make their views known than the other groups. "Opportunity structure" means any loosening of social control and elite strength that provides society an opening for articulation of interests.[94] At first almost all four groups are dependent on objective "opportunity structure." But students and solidary ethnic minorities later become self-activating, without waiting for the opportunities granted (wittingly or unwittingly) by the elites.

Finally, each group's reactions to the CCP rule showed an evolutionary pattern. Each group initially attempts to use its pre-Communist ways to deal with the new state. Peasants, for example, stage localized rebellions or religious revivals, but they soon recognize the vast disparity of power between them and the state. Starting in the mid-1950s, peasants and workers shifted to their modal patterns of resistance. Students and solidary ethnic minorities followed more or less the same evolutionary paths as workers and peasants did somewhat later.

Environment of Conflict

In addition to the state system and social structure, the third determinant of Chinese public opinion is the general cultural environment. As Figure 1.2 shows, public opinion may be regarded as the confluence of the state system, the social structure, and the cultural environment. All three interdependent variables also constitute a system.

The cultural environment that has partially fostered Chinese public opinion is marked predominantly by conflict. One might view the Chinese environment of conflict from two levels in terms of structure of social action.[95] At the "high" level of societal integration, environment of conflict means that "social organizations have been in conflict with one another in proposing different rules of the game, split on such fundamental questions

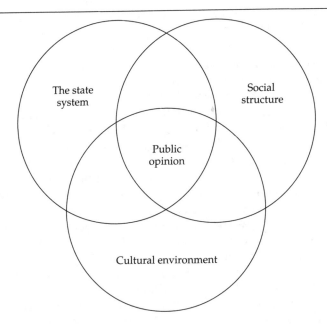

Figure 1.2   Interlinks between the state, social structure, cultural environment, and public opinion.

as what is proper human behavior and how should the society be constituted."[96] At the low or operational level, social conflicts revolve around the question of life chances for various groups. Here, most Chinese have faced a "zero-sum" condition since the mid-nineteenth century; it became even worse under Mao's rule. For the latter period, five conditions have contributed to the environment of conflict.

The first one is the revolutionary origin of the CCP. As noted by a number of scholars, revolutionaries in general tend to rely on force to suppress potential opponents. "It takes a full political generation," wrote Ted Robert Gurr and Jack Goldstone, "to overcome the battle-hardened revolutionaries' habit of relying on force to maintain power."[97] In 1981, the CCP under Deng's direction conceded as much:

> Our party had long existed in circumstances of war and fierce class struggle. It was not fully prepared either ideologically or in terms of scientific study, for the swift advent of the new-born socialist society. . . . We were liable, owing to the historical circumstances in which our party grew, to continue to regard issues unrelated to class struggle as its manifestations when observing and handling new contradictions and problems. . . . And when confronted with actual class struggle under the new conditions, we habitually fell back on the familiar methods and experiences of the large-

scale, turbulent mass struggle of the past, which should no longer have been mechanically followed.[98]

The second condition is a direct result of the "strong state" phenomenon in China in the early 1950s. Being "strong," the Communist Party-state wanted to convert the society totally. Consequently, the state rode roughshod over the mores*and interests of various groups. When the state-imposed new modes of survival (such as collectivization) failed to deliver the promised results, mass disillusionment and resistance rose. Conflicts between the state and society grow intense because a strong state sharpens the boundary between itself and the various groups.

The third condition contributing to the environment of conflict is related to the formality of governing. The Maoist state is essentially centralized corporatism. As such, the state tends to solidify group consciousness and sharpen intergroup rivalries. Take, for example, the Chinese state's policy toward ethnic minorities. June Dreyer wrote that "each effort at integration was apt to be cancelled out by an equal but opposite disintegration and reaction."[99] The Chinese state's promotion of distinct languages and historiography for various ethnic groups encourages separatism. The government's propaganda about equality and programs of industrialization in ethnic areas creates strain in the traditional social structures of these ethnic groups. Similarly, the state's rhetoric about "peasant and worker alliance" and its clear bias in favor of the latter results in peasant resentment and resistance.

The fourth condition concerns the marriage between a highly segmented and rural social structure and an autocratic state, especially under Mao. The first means a paucity of crosscutting ties among the masses, which produces segmentary conflicts in abundance. Autocracy or charismatic rule prevents institutionalized regulations regarding group conflicts. White attributed the widespread and intense conflicts in the Cultural Revolution partly to the proliferation of patron-client relationships in Chinese society under Mao.[100]

Finally, the fifth cause of the conflictual environment in China was Mao's promotion of conflict for strategic and expressive purposes. However, Mao was not as able in containing the dynamics of conflict. Dittmer's analysis was the following:

> Mao tended to redefine events to fit a structure of critical conflict, artificially polarizing the community and casting some in the roles of enemies of the people, some as revolutionary masses, some as temporarily trustworthy allies of convenience. In a crisis atmosphere the leader is justified in calling upon followers to make inordinate sacrifices for the commonweal, and leadership is likely to be more readily obeyed than under normal circumstances. To foster such an atmosphere, objective difficulties are

exaggerated and the magnitude of threat to socialist objectives inflated to the proportions of a "life-or-death struggle."[101]

Mao's tactics, said Dittmer, "created bitter and lasting cleavages that also infected periods of normalcy."

While this is not the place to explore the deep roots of the Chinese environment of conflict, a few words are necessary to put the foregoing interpretation in perspective. The cultural environment of conflict in China is itself enclosed by an even broader environment, which may be labeled "structural environment." The most important characteristics of the latter are war and demographic pressure. Since the mid-nineteenth century, China had experienced one form of devastating war or another. The long-term and systematic effects of war on Chinese culture and society have not yet been studied in contemporary U.S. Sinology. But wars have deep impact on the public opinion of any country. Robert Lane and David Sears wrote in a popular textbook on public opinion: "Historically, popular rationality seems to be reduced by the great traumas of war and depression."[102] Wars tend to enhance social segmentation and political extremism. The various effects of demographic pressure certainly increase social conflicts since they cause a "zero-sum" perspective among the populace.

All the analytical variables for this book and their interrelations are presented in Figure 1.3. In sum, my analysis starts with the state's attempts to convert society. Whether the strains caused by the state-initiated social changes will lead to collective protest or amorphous social action depends on group characteristics (degree of solidarity and status of inclusion) and

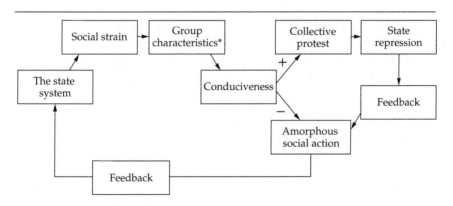

*Solidarity and includedness
"+" Local politics and ecology conducive to protest
"–" Local politics and ecology not conducive to protest

Figure 1.3   The analytical framework

conduciveness (local politics and ecology). Collective protests surely will be met by state repression. Those who never organize themselves and those who do eventually settle on amorphous social actions. The two types of reaction, or public opinion, cause feedback to the state. The reactions of the elite may be varied. Mao's way was typically to meet the popular reactions by aggressively implementing an even more radical program with the hope that the sooner the "socialist transition" was over, the more willing the masses would be in accepting socialism. That, in turn, builds up even more strain in society. Another consequence of the feedback to the elite is a long-term internal factionalization, as has happened to the CCP over the past decades.

Sources

Before I turn to the chapters on each social group, a few points are in order concerning my sources. I relied primarily on publications from China, especially the print media. The natural question from the reader would be on the reliability of the Chinese media, which, as is well known, are part of the state's propaganda machinery. However, even official propaganda contain some genuine information about society.

First, the Chinese press is used partly by the national elite to communicate with the lower elite on policy matters and also on how to deal with popular reactions. One may then gather a general idea of the trend of popular reactions and even specific examples of the views of the masses from the press. Over the years, some important works on Chinese society has been done by combing through the press, such as Ezra Vogel's study of Guangdong [Canton].[103] The Chinese media are also capable of independent articulations, sometimes contrary to the wishes of the national elite. As Jeffrey Goldfarb demonstrated, news and cultural media in Communist states in general often engage in "independent public expressions."[104] Mao, for example, was critical of the Chinese press for publishing too much of what he perceived to be negative news. In 1959, while launching the people's commune movement, Mao complained at the famous Lushan Conference: "There are 700,000 production teams and if you publish 700,000 errors, it will take more than a year to do it. . . . The newspapers that specialize in publishing bad news will be destroyed [by the people] within a week."[105] Here it is noteworthy that some of the most prominent Chinese dissidents were formerly journalists, such as the student leader Lin Xilin in 1957 and the writer Liu Binyan. It seems that a modern profession such as journalism has a universalistic credo that not even the powerful propaganda machinery of a Communist regime can destroy entirely. The CCP implicitly affirms and uses this universal journalistic credo by publishing several confidential journals and papers that contain uncensored news reports by Chinese journalists. Mao was reported to have said that he disliked these confidential publications as they printed only "the dark side" of society.[106]

Second, the capability for independent expression by the Chinese media in general fluctuated from period to period. The political atmosphere of China under Mao and Deng alternated between "tighten up" (*shou*) and "let go" (*fang*). In the latter periods, such as those from 1956 through mid-1957, 1963–1965, and 1978–1980, the press and all information media enjoyed a higher degree of freedom of expression than in other periods.

Third, as has been noted before, the Chinese state is not a singular entity. The lower elites control a great segment of the media in China. Whether the media reflect the genuine public opinion also depends on the attitudes of the lower elites. The Chinese press, for example, revealed a great deal about peasant reactions to the collectivization in the mid-1950s because a substantial number of regional Party officials were opposed to the collectivization. Although Mao continuously purged the "rightist" cadres from the Party-state, it was simply not possible for him to impose a single voice throughout China. In the 1970s, local broadcasting records from China became available for researchers in the United States and they provided information on local conditions that the national media did not cover. In sum, the "totalitarian" communication media of China are more diverse and informative than one usually assumes.

Fourth, the media are especially valuable for my study since I aimed at a moving target—the changing climate of public opinions in China. As discussed earlier, public opinion has two faces: one shown in populistic measurements and the other in the "atmospherics" of daily news media. The latter deals with mobilized public opinion. Opinion polls, said Sidney Tarrow, are like taking still photographs; they cannot capture a moving phenomenon.[107] The limitations of polls are also evident in narrowly constructed interviews with former residents of China.

Fifth, I have insured a degree of reliability of printed sources by consulting a wide variety of them. These included the Chinese national press, the provincial press, specialized journals, local radio broadcasting records, classified documents, wall posters, unofficial publications, interviews with Chinese refugees in Hong Kong, and memoirs by former residents of China. The diversity of my sources serves the purpose of cross-checking and validating the information. The long-time span of my study also serves as a check.

The post-Mao period greatly expanded my sources. In particular, six new types of information became available: foreign correspondents' dispatches from China, polls conducted by Chinese scholars, memoirs by Chinese leaders on Mao's role in policymaking in the 1950s (especially on rural collectivization), writings by Chinese dissidents, field research by

U.S. scholars, and reports from visitors to China. I have also done some limited interviewing myself over the years. My informants included students, professors, workers, and peasants. During the crisis months of April to June 1989 I happened to be teaching at Beijing University and was able to observe students' movements not only in Beijing but also in two cities in the western region. However, I have never had a chance to talk to a member of an ethnic minority from China.

In contemporary U.S. Sinology, some fine works on the Chinese society have been done chiefly through the interview method. Former residents from China were interviewed in Hong Kong on various aspects of life in China under Mao's rule. These studies enable us to understand better the specifics of life in China. But at the same time the works based on interviews also illuminate some major problems. They typically present what Fred Greenstein referred to as "phenomenology"—overt behavior of individuals—but neglect the underlying "dynamics," particularly the "genesis" of behavior. At best the interviews tell us how the Chinese adapt to new modes of life imposed by the state. However, some authors tend to mistake adaptation for genuine acceptance. One study of a village in Guangdong Province in the early 1970s, for example, concluded that (1) the CCP's collectivization was a success, (2) the Chinese state and the peasants had arrived at a modus vivendi, and (3) the collectivized system of farming in China was looking forward to a long life.[108] Within three years of the publication of the study, collectivization in China ended and the villages in Guangdong embarked on a rapid development based on individual household farming, combined with business entrepreneurship.[109]

There are essentially two problems with these interview-based works. First, their analysis is too exclusively based on interviews. If the two U.S. sociologists who conducted the Guangdong study had consulted documentary sources from China and had followed long-term reactions of the peasants, they would have discovered enduring peasant resistance to collectivization in Guangdong and elsewhere in China. Second, the interviews, if not handled with care, might become "imperial scholarship." Scholars impose a set of questions on interviewees, who then present to the former a picture of life taken out of context in order to fit what the scholars want. The deeper aspects of peasant life, which require inquiries into peasants as feeling and thinking human beings and into community mores and habits, were neglected in the aforementioned study of Guangdong villages. But it is these deeper aspects of peasant life that determine whether the state-imposed modes of survival will last.[110]

The same U.S. scholars who did the Guangdong village study also published a major book on Chinese urban life, again relying primarily on interviews.[111] Like their village study, the book on urban China is informative on the daily lives of the people but is short on the deeper aspects of social life. They, for example, could detect no generational conflict between the youth and the older generation or any sign of a culture of poverty among the working population. But in the early 1980s, generational conflict became one of the most talked-about topics in the Chinese media, and the wall posters in Beijing exposed cases of the culture of poverty among workers. I shall deal with these topics in later chapters. My point here is simply that the fashionable interview method, if not combined with a variety of other sources, can misrepresent reality, just as an exclusive reliance on any single source can. In the final analysis, whether the sources of this book and its conceptual scheme are useful and valid for studying Chinese public opinion ultimately depends on the analysis itself, to which I now turn.

Notes

1. Lin Yutang, *A History of the Press and Public Opinion in China* (New York: Greenwood Press, 1968), p. 20. This book was originally published by S. Hamilton most probably in 1937 (see the reference to the current events on page 136 of the book).

2. *Peking Review* 15 (April 9, 1976): 4.

3. Ibid., p. 5.

4. Lowell Dittmer, "Patterns of Elite Strife and Succession in Chinese Politics," *China Quarterly*, no. 123 (September 1990):405–430.

5. Major works include three by Merle Goldman: *Literary Dissent in Communist China* (Cambridge, Mass.: Harvard University Press, 1967); *China's Intellectuals: Advise and Dissent* (Cambridge, Mass.: Harvard University Press, 1981), and *Chinese Intellectuals and the State: In Search of a New Relationship* (Cambridge, Mass.: Council on East Asian Studies, Harvard University, 1987). See also Andrew J. Nathan, *Chinese Democracy* (New York: Knopf, 1985); Lynn T. White III, *Policies of Chaos: The Organizational Causes of Violence in China's Cultural Revolution* (Princeton: NJ: Princeton University Press, 1989); and Martin King Whyte and William L. Parish, *Urban Life in Contemporary China* (Chicago: University of Chicago Press, 1984).

6. I shall refer to these works in Chapters 2 and 3 on peasants and workers.

7. One of the best books on post-Mao reforms is by Harry Harding, *China's Second Revolution: Reform After Mao* (Washington, D.C.: Brookings Institution, 1987), but it gives public opinion short shrift and dwells almost entirely on elite politics. European specialists took the first tentative steps in studying Chinese mass behavior; see the path-breaking work by David S. G. Goodman, ed., *Groups and Politics in the People's Republic of China* (Cardiff, U.K.: University College Cardiff Press, 1984).

8. White, *Policies of Chaos. The Organizational Causes*, p. 308.

9. Perry Link, Richard Madsen, and Paul G. Pickowicz, eds., *Unofficial China: Popular Culture and Thought in the People's Republic* (Boulder: Westview Press, 1989); Arthur Lewis Rosenbaum, ed., *State and Society in China: The Consequences of Reform* (Boulder: Westview Press, 1992); and Jeffrey N.

Wasserstrom and Elizabeth J. Perry, eds., *Popular Protest and Political Culture in Modern China* (Boulder: Westview Press, 1992).

10. Stanley Rosen is probably the leading U.S. China specialist in studying post-Mao Chinese opinion polls. I will refer to Rosen's works in subsequent chapters. See also Stanley Rosen and David Chu, "Survey Research in the People's Republic of China," a typewritten report prepared for the U.S. Information Agency, December 1987. I am grateful to my colleague M. Kent Jennings for bringing to my attention this paper by Rosen and Chu.

11. Hans Speier, *Social Order and the Risks of War: Papers in Political Sociology* (New York: George W. Stewart, 1952), p. 323. This essay was originally published in the *American Journal of Sociology*, 55 (January 1950): 376–388.

12. See the review by Kurt Back on Habermas' works in *Public Opinion Quarterly* 56, no. 2 (Summer 1992): 257–258. See also Jurgen Habermas, *The Structural Transformation of the Public Sphere: An Inquiry into a Category of Bourgeois Society*, trans. Thomas Burger with the assistance of Frederick Lawrence (Cambridge, Mass.: MIT Press, 1989).

13. Bernard Berelson, "Communication and Public Opinion," in *The Process and Effects of Mass Communication*, ed. Wilbur Schramm (Urbana: University of Illinois Press, 1955), p. 342.

14. Ithiel de Sola Pool, "Public Opinion," in *Handbook of Communication*, ed. Ithiel de Sola Pool et al. (Chicago: Rand McNally College Publishing, 1973), p. 781.

15. Daniel Katz, "The Functional Approach to the Study of Attitudes," *Public Opinion Quarterly* 24, no. 2 (Summer 1960): 163.

16. Walter Lippmann, *Public Opinion* (New York: Macmillan, 1961), p. 230.

17. Ithiel de Sola Pool, "Public Opinion and the Control of Armaments," *Daedalus* (Fall 1960):985.

18. Ulf Himmelstrand, *Social Pressures, Attitudes, and Democratic Processes* (Stockholm, 1960), as quoted in Murray Edelman, *The Symbolic Uses of Politics* (Urbana: University of Illinois Press, 1967), p. 10.

19. Philip E. Converse, "Changing Conceptions of Public Opinion in the Political Process," part 2, *Public Opinion Quarterly* 51, no. 4 (Winter 1987): S19–S24.

20. W. Russell Neuman, *The Paradox of Mass Politics: Knowledge and Opinion in the American Electorate* (Cambridge, Mass.: Harvard University Press, 1986), p. 7.

21. Friedhelm Neidhardt and Dieter Rucht, "The Analysis of Social Movements: The State of the Art and Some Perspectives for Further Research," in *Research on Social Movements. The State of the Art in Western Europe and the USA*, ed., Dieter Rucht (Boulder: Westview Press, 1991), p. 450.

22. Ye Xiaowen, "Luelun Xinxingshixia Minzu, Zongjiaofangmiandi Renmin Naibumaodun" [The internal contradictions among the people in the areas of ethnic groups and religions under the new situation], *Xinhua Wenzhai* [New China Digest], no. 9 (1993): 10–13.

23. Max Weber, *Economy And Society: An Outline of Interpretive Sociology*, vol. 2, ed. Guenther Roth and Claus Wittich (New York: Bedminster Press, 1968), p. 929.

24. John P. Burns, "Chinese Peasant Interest Articulation," in Goodman, *Groups and Politics*, p. 145.

25. Xueguang Zhou, "Unorganized Interests and Collective Action in Communist China," *American Sociological Review* 58, no. 1 (February 1993):54–73.

26. Weber deemed the neighborhood as one form of amorphous social action because of these two characteristics. See Weber, *Economy and Society*, p. 362.

27. Charles Tilly, *From Mobilization to Revolution* (Reading, Mass.: Addison-Wesley Publishing, 1978); Bruce Fireman and William A. Gamson, "Utilitarian Logic in the Resource Mobilization Perspective," in *The Dynamics of Social Movements*, ed. Mayer N. Zald and John D. McCarthy (Cambridge, Mass.: Winthrop Publishers, 1979), pp. 8–44; Bert Klandermans and Sidney Tarrow, "Mobilization into Social Movements: Synthesizing European and American Approaches," in *From Structure to Action: Comparing Social Movement Research Across Cultures*, ed. Bert Klandermans, Hanspeter Kriesi, and Sidney Tarrow (Greenwich, Conn. JAI Press, 1988), pp. 1–38; and Bert Klandermans, "New Social Movements and Resource Mobilization: The European and the American Approach revisited," in *Research on Social Movements*, ed. Rucht, pp. 17–44.

28. Clark McPhail and David Miller, "The Assembling Process: A Theoretical And Empirical Examination," *American Sociological Review* 38, no. 6 (December 1973): 721–735; David Snyder and William R. Kelly, "Strategies for Investigating Violence and Social Change: Illustrations from Analyses of Racial Disorders and Implications for Mobilization Research," in *The Dynamics of Social Movements*, eds., Zald and McCarthy; David Snyder, "Collective Violence Processes: Implications for Disaggregated Theory And Research," in *Research in Social Movements, Conflicts and Change*, vol. 2, ed. Louis Kriesberg (Greenwich, Conn.: JAI Press, 1979), pp. 35–62; Anthony Oberschall, "Loosely Structured Collective Conflict: A Theory and an Application," in *Research in Social Movements, Conflicts, and Change*, vol. 3, ed. Kriesberg pp. 45–68; and Pamela E. Oliver, "Bringing the Crowd Back in: The Nonorganizational Elements of Social Movements," in *Research in Social Movements, Conflicts, and Change*, vol. 11, ed. Kriesberg, pp. 1—30.

29. Timur Kuran, "Now Out of Never: The Element of Surprise in the East European Revolution of 1989," *World Politics* 44, no. 1 (October 1991): 7–49; and Karl-Dieter Opp and Christiane Gern, "Dissident Groups, Personal Networks, and Spontaneous Cooperation: The East German Revolution of 1989," *American Sociological Review* 58, no. 5 (October 1993): 659–680.

30. Oliver, "Bringing the Crowd," p. 24.

31. Kuran, "Now Out of Never."

32. Rick Fantasia, *Cultures of Solidarity: Consciousness, Action, and Contemporary American Workers* (Berkeley: University of California Press, 1988), p. 173.

33. Pool, "Public Opinion," p. 809.

34. For a general discussion on the evolution of Western states, see Harry Eckstein, "On the 'Science' of the State," in *The State*, ed. Stephen R. Graubard (New York: W. W. Norton and Co. 1979), pp. 1–20.

35. Lowell Dittmer, "The Legacy of Mao Zedong," *Asian Survey* 20, no. 5 (May 1980): 555.

36. Mao Tse-tung, *Selected Works of Mao Tse-tung*, vol. 5 (Beijing, Foreign Languages Press, 1977), p. 380.

37. *Mao Tsetung Ssu-hsiang Wan-sui*, [*Wan-sui* hereon] no. 2 (Beijing, 1969; reprint, Washington, D.C.: Center for Chinese Research Materials, 1969), p. 207.

38. *Wan-sui*, no. 2, p. 288.

39. Xie Chuntao, *Dayaojin Kuanglan* [The raging waves of the big leap forward] (Henan: Henan Renmin Chubanshe, 1991), pp. 111–114; Li Rui, *Mao Zedongdi Gongguoshifei* [Mao Zedong's merits and demerits], chapter 8 (Hong Kong: Cosmos Books, 1993). Mao mentioned his wish for "the Great Harmony" as early as June 1949 in the speech "On the People's Democratic Dictatorship,"

Selected Works of Mao Tse-tung, vol. 4, (Beijing: Foreign Languages Press, 1967), p. 412. For an excerpt of the text, see William Theodore de Bary, Wing-tsit Chan, and Burton Watson, comps. *Sources of Chinese Tradition,* vol. 1 (New York: Columbia University Press, 1965), pp. 175–176.

40. Ralph H. Turner and Lewis M. Killian, *Collective Behavior,* 2d ed. (Englewood Cliffs, N.J.: Prentice-Hall, 1972), p. 364.

41. Louis Kriesberg, *Social Conflicts,* 2d ed. (Englewood Cliffs, N.J.: Prentice-Hall, 1982), p. 300.

42. Turner and Killian, *Collective Behavior,* p. 367.

43. *Wan-sui,* no. 2, p. 329; for a vivid description of such methods in land reform of the early 1950s, see C. K. Yang, *A Chinese Village in Early Communist Transition* (Cambridge, Mass.: MIT Press, 1958).

44. *Wan-sui,* no. 2, p. 199; *Selected Works of Mao,* vol. 5, p. 379.

45. For a discussion of *ganqing* in Chinese lives, see Morton H. Fried, *Fabric of Chinese Society* (New York: Octagon Books, 1969).

46. *Wan-sui,* no. 2, p. 205–206, 222, and 370.

47. Eric L. Hirsch, "Sacrifice for the Cause: Group Processes, Recruitment, and Commitment in a Student Social Movement," *American Sociological Review* 55, no. 2 (April 1990): 245.

48. Li Rui, *Mao Zedongdi,* p. 250.

49. Kriesberg, *Social Conflicts,* p. 185.

50. Li Rui, *Mao Zedongdi,* p. 320.

51. Ibid., pp. 253–254.

52. *Selected Works of Mao,* vol. 5, p. 423.

53. *Wan-sui,* no. 2, pp. 222 and 394.

54. Eckstein, "On the 'Science' of the State," p. 17.

55. Annie Kriegel, "The Nature of the Communist System: Notes on State, Party, and Society," in *The State,* ed. Graubard, p. 141.

56. Ibid., p. 141.

57. Thomas B. Gold, "The Resurgence of Civil Society in China," *Journal of Democracy* 1, no. 1 (Winter 1990):18–31.

58. For a general discussion on the need for "new thinking" about the Communist system, see Peter Zwick, "The Perestroika of Soviet Studies: Thinking and Teaching About the Soviet Union in Comparative Perspective," *PS: Political Science and Politics,* XXIV: 3 (September 1991), pp. 461–466.

59. Robert A. Dahl, introduction to *Regimes and Oppositions,* ed. Robert A. Dahl (New Haven: Yale University Press, 1973), pp. 1–26.

60. Eckstein, "On the 'Science' of the State," p. 14.

61. John P. Burns, "China's Governance: Political Reform in a Turbulent Environment," *China Quarterly,* no. 119 (September 1989):481–518.

62. *China Daily,* August 23, 1994.

63. Dahl, introduction to *Regimes,*" p. 16.

64. David Shambaugh, "Losing Control: The Erosion of State Authority in China," *Current History* (September 1993):253–259.

65. Edward Friedman, Paul G. Pickowicz, and Mark Selden, *Chinese Village, Socialist State* (New Haven: Yale University Press, 1991).

66. Kurt W. Back, "Metaphors for Public Opinion in Literature," *Public Opinion Quarterly* 52, no. 3 (Fall 1988): 278.

67. Ibid., p. 281.

68. Kam Wing Chan and Xueqiang Xu, "Urban Population Growth and Urbanization in China Since 1949: Reconstructing a Baseline," *China Quarterly*, no. 104 (December 1985):583–613.

69. Yang, *A Chinese Village*, p. v.

70. Fei Xiaotong [Fei Hsiao-tung], "Peasantry and Gentry: An Interpretation of Chinese Social Structure And Its Changes," in *Class, Status and Power*, ed. Reinhard Bendix and Seymour Martin Lipset (New York: Free Press of Glencoe, 1964), p. 632.

71. *Renmin Ribao* [People's Daily], November 14, 1986.

72. Ouyang Bolin, "Nongye Hongguan Diaokong Jizhi Ruohuadi Yuanyinjiduice," [The causes and countermeasures of the weaknesses of the macro-control mechanism in agriculture] *Nongye Jingji*, no. 9 (1990): 113.

73. Jonathan Unger, "The Decollectivization of the Chinese Countryside: A Survey of Twenty-eight Villages," *Pacific Affairs* 58, no. 4 (Winter 1985–1986):602.

74. For the total number of university students see, *Jen-min Chiao-yu* [People's Education], October 1952, as cited in *Chung-kung Shih-nien* [Ten Years of Chinese Communism] (Hong Kong: Yu-lien Chu-pan-she, 1960), p. 462.

75. *United States Relations with China* (Washington, D.C.: U.S. Government Printing Office, 1949), p. 214.

76. The Nationalist *China Handbook, 1950* (New York: Rockport Press, 1950), p. 432, gives the figure of 16,130,250 for members in labor unions.

77. Fang Tian-pai, "Wo-kuo Chen-hsiang Kuan-hsi-ti Hsin-fa-chan," [New developments in the urban-rural relationship of our country] *Hsueh Hsi* (June 1956):5.

78. W. W. Rostow, *The Prospects for Communist China* (Cambridge, Mass. and New York: Technology Press of MIT and John Wiley and Sons, 1954), p. 157. For a recent study on the political activism of Shanghai workers in the 1930s, see Elizabeth J. Perry, *Shanghai on Strike* (Stanford, Calif.: Stanford University Press, 1993).

79. Chen Chia-lin, ed., *Wo-kuo Ching-chi-ti Fa-chan* [The economic development of our country] (Taipei: Shih-chieh Shu-chu, 1981), p. 28.

80. Chen Yun, *Chen Yun Wenxuan, 1949–1956* [Selected Works of Chen Yun, 1949–1956] (Zhejiang: Renmin Chubanshe, 1984), p. 269.

81. Betty Peh-T'i Wei, *Shanghai: Crucible of Modern China* (Hong Kong: Oxford University Press, 1987), p. 236.

82. Kuo-heng Shih, "The Early Development of the Modern Chinese Business Class," in *The Rise of the Modern Chinese Business Class* by Marion J. Levy Jr. and Kuo-heng Shih (New York: International Secretariat, Institute of Pacific Relations, 1949), p. 19.

83. *North China Daily News*, March 3, 1948.

84. Reinhard Bendix, John Bendix, and Norman Furniss, "Reflections on Modern Western States and Civil Societies," in *Research in Political Sociology*, vol. 3, ed. Richard G. Braungart and Margaret M. Braungart (Greenwich, Conn.: JAI Press, 1987), p. 14; and Timothy Garton Ash, *The Uses of Adversity* (London: Granta Books, 1989), as cited in David Kelly and He Baogang, "Emergent Civil Society and the Intellectuals in China," in *The Developments of Civil Society in Communist Systems*, ed. Robert F. Miller (North Sydney, Australia: Allen and Unwin, 1992), p. 38.

85. *North China Daily News*, December 16, 1948.

86.   *China Handbook*, p. 637.

87.   The numbers of Christians are from the *New York Times*, April 12, 1989.

88.   *China Handbook*, p. 27.

89.   Gold, "Resurgence of Civil Society," pp. 18–31.

90.   Whyte and Parish, *Urban Life*.

91.   Kriesberg, *Social Conflicts*, p. 13.

92.   The work that has made a focal point of this differentiation is Sulamith Heins Potter and Jack M. Potter, *China's Peasants: The Anthropology of a Revolution* (Cambridge, England: Cambridge University Press, 1990).

93.   For definitions of dissensual and consensual conflicts, see Kriesberg, *Social Conflicts*, chapter 2.

94.   For a fuller definition of the "opportunity structure," see Sidney Tarrow, "Aiming at a Moving Target: Social Science and the Recent Rebellions in Eastern Europe," *PS: Political Science and Politics* 24, no. 1 (March 1991): 12–19.

95.   Concerning levels of social action, see Neil J. Smelser, *Theory of Collective Behavior* (New York: Free Press, 1971), pp. 37–46.

96.   Joel S. Migdal, *Strong Societies and Weak States* (Princeton: Princeton University Press, 1988), p. 29.

97.   Ted Robert Gurr and Jack A. Goldstone, "Comparisons and Policy Implications," in *Revolutions of the Late Twentieth Century*, ed. Jack A. Goldstone, Ted Robert Gurr, and Farrokh Moshiri (Boulder: Westview Press, 1991), p. 344.

98.   "On Questions of Party History," *Beijing Review* 24, no. 17 (July 6, 1981): 10–39.

99.   June Dreyer, *China's Forty Millions* (Cambridge, Mass.: Harvard University Press, 1976), p. 265.

100.   White, *Policies of Chaos*.

101.   Dittmer, "The Legacy of Mao," p. 570.

102.   Robert E. Lane and David O. Sears, *Public Opinion* (Englewood Cliffs, N.J.: Prentice-Hall, 1964), p. 82.

103.   Ezra Vogel, *Canton Under Communism* (Cambridge, Mass.: Harvard University Press, 1969).

104.   Jeffrey C. Goldfarb, "Social Bases of Independent Public Expression in Communist Societies," *American Journal of Sociology* 83, no. 4 (January 1978):920–939.

105.   Li Rui, *Mao Zedongdi*, p. 169.

106.   *Wan-sui*, no. 2, p. 272; Li Rui, *Mao Zedongdi*, p. 177.

107.   Tarrow, "'Aiming at a Moving Target,'" p. 17.

108.   William L. Parish and Martin King Whyte, *Village and Family in Contemporary China* (Chicago: University of Chicago Press, 1978).

109.   Ezra F. Vogel, *One Step Ahead in China: Guangdong under Reform* (Cambridge, Mass.: Harvard University Press, 1989).

110.   Vivienne Shue, *The Reach of the State* (Stanford, California: Stanford University Press, 1988). Other studies on the villages in Guangdong do not repeat the flawed interpretations of Parish and Whyte. See, for example, Anita Chan, Richard Madsen, and Jonathan Unger, *Chen Village* (Berkeley: University of California Press, 1984); and Richard Madsen, *Morality and Power in a Chinese Village* (Berkeley: University of California Press, 1984).

111.   Whyte and Parish, *Urban Life*.

2

STATE AND THE PEASANTRY

Under the planned economic system, for many years the state's view of farmers was mainly to request grain and cotton from them, while the farmers, based on their own needs, wanted to increase their income. This contradiction existed for a long time.[1]

The relationship between the Chinese state and the peasantry has been essentially conflictive whether in Mao's or Deng's time. "A social conflict exists," wrote Kriesberg, "when two or more parties believe they have incompatible objectives."[2] The analysis of peasants' reactions to Communist rule must then start from this basic premise of conflict. This chapter focuses on how the state and the peasantry view each other in the post-Mao period, and the behavioral consequences of their opinions and attitudes. However, a succinct review of the peasant-state relationship under Mao is also necessary because many of the current problems in agriculture, such as marginalization and pauperization, resulted from Mao's policies.[3]

To make sense of the intricacies in the relationship between the Chinese state and peasants, a distinction must be made between political and social revolution. A political revolution is the work of a special interest group—the revolutionists. Their first goal is to seize and change the state institution. Having accomplished that, more often than not, the revolutionists attempt to broaden their political agenda to radically change society. Their actions cannot be considered a genuine social revolution since such sweeping changes are externally imposed. A social revolution is mass participation in changing the mores, habits, customs, and values of a people. A social revolution means essentially abandoning the old mode of survival in exchange for a new one. By nature, a social revolution cannot be as "rapid" as a political revolution. Any definition of social revolutions as "rapid, basic transformations of socio-economic and political institutions" is unrealistic.[4] Unlike a political revolution, a social revolution rarely can be externally imposed. In fact, the second tactic often backfires, strengthening a society's resistance to radical changes. Relatively speaking, a social revolution may be "rapid" only if a vast number of people has been, to use Pool's expression, "psychically initiated." This is exemplified by the rapid social changes in the newly industrializing countries (NIC) in East Asia during the postwar period.[5] The distinction between political and social revolutions is similar to William Graham Sumner's old distinction between *crescive* and *enacted* changes. Crescive changes are relatively autonomous, whereas enacted changes are "conscious decisions or intents of legislators or rulers." Those who enact changes need to take into account the mores of the people and resources at their disposal.[6]

The processes of political and social revolution in the Chinese countryside are summed up in Table 2.1. Peasant reactions are represented as an hourglass to indicate graphically the fluctuations in the form of peasant reactions, which may either be diversity or uniformity.

Initially the character of the Chinese state was "strong," which, based on Joel Migdal's definition, meant that the state was capable of penetrating society, regulating social relationships, extracting resources, and using resources in determined ways.[7] Consequently, the 1950s was the period of political revolution. The CCP imposed collectivization on the peasants through political means. Peasants' reactions were evolutionary in nature, changing from latency to explicitness. Radical collectivization led to the crisis of the Great Leap Forward, which caused serious dissension among the top leaders and famine in the countryside. Peasants' reactions became a uniformly amorphous social resistance since their earlier manifestations of resistance were thoroughly suppressed by the state. The crisis in 1959–1962 led to the period of Thermidor in 1963–1966 in which "small freedoms" (traditional, noncollectivistic activities) were allowed the peasants. The Chinese state began its long segmentation at this point as local state agencies acquired a degree of autonomy in the aftermath of the Great Leap.

The failure of the Great Leap emboldened peasants and they took initiatives to counter the political revolution of the 1950s. Their tactics were a combination of what I call "occasionalism" and a long-term resistance by amorphous social actions. By occasionalism I mean that peasants took whatever opportunity existed to revert to their old and preferred mode of farming and trading, in contravention to the Maoist stress on collectivism. In response to the peasants' resistance (counterrevolution), the Maoist state resumed political revolution in the countryside during the Cultural Revolution and through the 1970s. But this second political revolution, just as the first one in the 1950s, also ended in failure. After the death of Mao, the Chinese political system suffered long-term decay during which local autonomy and corruption became widespread. The Dengist state legitimized the peasants' counterrevolution by dismantling the communes and allowed household farming. Peasants seized this opportunity to start their own social revolution by means of emigration, rebellion, and the abandonment of agriculture for industry. The social

Table 2.1 Evolution of State-Peasant Relationship, 1949–1990

State character	State strategy	Peasant reaction
Strong state	Political revolution, 1949-1958	Latency: Dissimilitude Explicitness: Dissent, migration, religious movement, rebellion
Fractured state	Crisis, 1959-1962	Amorphous social actions
Segmented state	Thermidor, 1963-1966	Counterrevolution Occasionalism, amorphous actions
Political decay	Abortive political revolution, 1966-1976 Counterrevolution, 1977-	Social revolution: Auto-marginalization, Anti-pauperization

revolution by the peasants was specifically directed against their twin fate of marginalization and pauperization. Following T. Shanin, marginalization "implies a decline in the significance of peasant agriculture within the national economy and the peasantry acts primarily as a source of cheap labor, cheap food, and markets for industrial goods." Pauperization is "expressed in the phenomena of 'surplus population,' 'rural underemployment,' the 'shanty towns,' 'culture of poverty,' etc."[8]

Peasant Reactions to Mao's Rule

During the period of political revolution, the Maoist state and the Chinese peasantry seemed to be running on two tracks. Between the two, peasants were the realists and Mao the idealist. On the surface Mao seemed to have achieved one victory after another, all without much difficulty, or so he thought. Actually, Mao's idealism—or ideological-mindedness—masked conflicts escalating underneath between the state and the peasants.

The conflicts between Mao and the peasants, however, did not assume the standard form in which both parties harbored an "inherent bad faith" view of each other as their conflicts grew.[9] Instead, Mao perceived rising peasant support for socialism, from the poor in particular. To the extent Mao had any "inherent bad faith" view toward rural people, he reserved it exclusively and a priori for the former landlords and rich peasants. With perceptions like that, Mao in turn rapidly inflated his goals of collectivizing agriculture and felt justified in suppressing dissent among the high-ranking leaders. That Mao persistently believed he had peasant support for policies, ranging from land reform to collectivization, is due to his overwhelming emphasis on outcomes and a habit of screening every bit of feedback through formal ideological tenets. Mao's all-powerful focus on outcomes is partly due to his strong desire for success at any cost and also partly due to the overall culture of socialist economic planning.

The socialist economy is often referred to in China and elsewhere as "product economy," in contrast to "commodity economy" in a market system. The former puts a premium on gross output instead of cost efficiency and quality. In 1956, despite all the opposition from rural cadres and peasants against Soviet-type collectives, Mao told one of his personal secretaries that he had not anticipated that such a stupendous task—transforming some 500 million peasants—would be accomplished with "just one report and a couple of meetings." "After this success, will there ever be anything more difficult or impossible to resolve?" Mao asked.[10] Mao, as a rule, denigrated any negative feedback on his agricultural programs. Dissent from other CCP leaders and from the peasants themselves was denounced by Mao as "carping" or "exaggerated complaints" by "landlords, rich peasants, and counterrevolutionaries."[11] He thus fractured the top leadership by purging from its ranks one high-ranking member after another. For example, the head of the Central Rural Work Department Teng Tzu-hui and, later, Marshal Peng Te-huai (Peng Dehuai) were among the deposed. In outward form Mao's actions conformed to the general pattern of conflict escalation: hardening of views (ideology), realigning of membership, and increasing the stakes of conflicts.

But among peasants, there was a rapid crystallization of the "inherent bad faith" view toward the Maoist state. At first, peasants' views of the CCP were latent and reserved.[12] Mao apparently interpreted the latency of peasants' opinion toward his agricultural program as tacit support. In retrospect, there are three important developments in the peasant opinion during the period of political revolution. The first one was from latency to explicitness or from general to specific opinion. The second change was reflected in the rising numbers of opposition to the state—from segments among the peasantry to peasants *as a class*. The third development in peasant opinion was a trial-and-error evolution out of which peasants found the safest and most effective ways of resisting the state. Throughout this period, peasants steadily alienated themselves from the state. At the start of collectivization in the early 1950s, they first used the "voice" option to deal with the state. They still had some hopes that the Maoist state might be amenable to communication and persuasion from society. Later, they gave up such hopes, saw their relationship with the state as zero-sum, and mobilized themselves to resist the state in whatever ways were at their disposal.

The latency period of peasant opinion occurred after land reform. The Chinese press then described the prevailing mood of the peasants as "fear of being conspicious" (*pa maojian*). This was simply a carry-over from the traditional days when peasants sought to escape molestation by the authorities through dissimilitude.[13] They became cautious in front of Communist cadres; in production they grew just enough food to get by.[14] Peasants also had their first inkling of the state's policy of marginalizing agriculture by observing the preferential treatment that workers received from the state.

The precipitous collectivizations by the Maoist state in the mid-1950s changed peasants' opinion from latency to explicitness. Peasants voiced their dissent and increased discussions among themselves about collectivization. In response the state launched a campaign of suppression, designed to ferret out "hidden counterrevolutionaries" and stamp out "rumors" in the countryside. But peasants also initiated collective actions to deal with their predicament. The most prominent ones were outmigration, religious movements, and rebellions. These were precursors of similar but larger-scale movements in the post-Mao period thirty years later.

In the mid-1950s, emigration of peasants occurred in populous provinces such as Shandong, Hebei, Henan, Jiangsu, and Anhui; they headed for the cities of the Northeast where state-directed industrialization was being launched.[15] Simultaneously, others in the countryside responded to the strain through religious revivalist movements, which may be regarded as a kind of "internal emigration." From 1955 to the eve of the Great Leap Forward (fall 1958), the Chinese press reported a surge of Daoist activities in the countryside, particularly in the southern periphery of Guangdong.[16]

Even more significant than outmigration and religious movements was a rapid rise in peasant rebellions during this period.[17] These revolts occurred primarily in areas with two distinct ecological characteristics: geographical periphery and/or isolation in mountainous districts or grain-producing districts where one might expect the impact of collectivization to be felt more sharply. Specifically, the former characteristics were evidenced in the reports of peasant "uprisings" in Shanxi, Shaanxi, Gansu, Anhui, Jiangxi, Guangxi, Yunnan, Hainan Island, and Xinjiang. The revolts in grain-producing areas took place in Hubei, Hunan, and Sichuan. Peasants in geographically peripheral areas or in mountainous districts (Anhui and Jiangxi, for example) had, in Eric Wolf's terms, "tactical mobility."[18] The second contributing factor is the historical precedence of revolt. Students of collective violence refer to this as "normative support." A number of the districts where revolts occurred had also been used by the CCP as guerrilla bases before 1949. The third contributing factor is the existence of traditional secret societies, whose membership is cemented with some sort of religious beliefs. In the 1950s, the CCP had not yet effectively suppressed religious secret societies among peasants. The fourth condition is the peasants' perception of unjust conduct by local authorities.[19] Religious and localized rebellions persisted through the 1950s until the eve of the Great Leap Forward in 1958. Although these rebellions were raised by small bands, their numbers were less significant than what they represented. The revolts were simply the specific airing of the peasants' general alienation and resentment of the state.

The rebellions in the mid-1950s signified that peasants were gradually taking *class* action since the participants of the revolts encompassed all segments of peasant society. "Collectivization was not an assault on the rich peasantry," wrote Grant Evans, "it was in fact an attack launched against the whole peasantry."[20] In the 1950s, Chinese peasants finally reached the same conclusion. Middle peasants were the main resisters to the Soviet-type collectives.[21] On the eve of the Great Leap Forward, however, poor peasants joined in the opposition to the state. In late 1957 and early 1958, the Chinese press publicized a number of cases of poor peasants' opposition to the collectives and the CCP. In each case, the poor peasants concerned were accused by the CCP of committing the sin of "forgetting one's class origin" *(wangben)*. That the official press saw fit to publicize these embarrassing cases meant that these were far from being isolated instances.[22] In sum, the membership of the peasant opposition now included all the segments and the peasants were acting as a class, although without conscious coordination. It was the Maoist political revolution that precipitated this spontaneous alliance among the peasants.

Finally, over the years and especially after the state's repression of all the previously mentioned actions, peasants settled on one uniform way of resisting the state: work slowdowns. In 1959 Mao bemoaned the fact that "almost the entire country is afflicted with problems such as hiding and privately distributing grain and loud complaints about 'shortages' of grain, cooking oil, pork, and vegetables. *The scale of the complaints is unprecedented,* surpassing those in 1953 and 1955"(emphasis added).[23]

The escalation of conflicts between the Maoist state and the peasants led to the crisis of the Great Leap Forward. In turn, the Great Leap produced a Thermidorean reaction in that the state compromised with the peasants by restoring some of the traditional ways of survival that peasants preferred: sideline businesses, trade, and the resumption of rural markets. These were known as the "small freedoms."

The Maoist state was clearly on the defensive. For the first time, even Mao abandoned his usual "class analysis" of the peasants; instead, he referred to them as a single class. Mao said that he had "overestimated" the peasants and that "the peasants were after all peasants."[24] Thereafter, the Maoist state no longer had the capability to launch political revolution in the countryside. The state fought a defensive battle against the pressure from the peasants to terminate collectivization as a whole. In the 1960s and 1970s, throughout the Cultural Revolution, the Maoist regime sought to renew its political revolution by organizing a parade of political campaigns such as "socialist education" (propagandizing among the peasants on the importance of class struggle), creating "poor and lower-middle peasants associations," bringing "Culture to the Village" *(wenhua xiaxiang)*, emulating "Da Zhai Commune" (a "model" village in Shanxi, supposedly having followed the Maoist way to prosperity), and "Learning Philosophy" (studying Mao's writings). These campaigns produced one primary outcome: They exposed the fact that there was no social reality to Mao's political revolution in the countryside.[25] In response to that, the Maoist state repeated the tactic used in the mid-1950s. It organized a coercive campaign to terrorize the peasants. In 1955, it was the "Suppression of Hidden Counterrevolutionaries" campaign and in the 1970s the coercive campaign was called "Cut the Tails of Capitalism."[26] However, these campaigns left little or no impact mainly because of the changed attitudes of the peasants.

The catastrophe of the Great Leap produced a degree of "cognitive liberation" among the peasants. Scholars of social movements define "cognitive liberation" as an ability to question authority, behavioral change from passivity to assertion of rights, and a new sense of efficacy.[27] The reactions of the Chinese peasants in the post-Leap period were a clear expression of cognitive liberation. In Fujian in 1962, when local Party cadres gave the credit for improved peasant lives to the "enlightened leadership of the party Central Committee and Chairman Mao," peasants countered the Party propaganda by giving credit to the market mechanism and individual entrepreneurship.[28] In deeds and words, Chinese peasants in the post-Leap period were proving that the mode of survival imposed by the state was now bankrupt. It was the time-honored folkway that is superior to the stateway. Those scholars who believe that a strong state is the key to socioeconomic development need to rethink their theses.[29]

From then on peasants relied on a combination of what I call "occasionalism" and amorphous social actions to pressure the state to cancel collectivization. The peasants, not the state, were on the offensive. Peasant occasionalism is best exemplified by peasants' reactions to the Cultural Revolution. The Chinese press had referred to the current peasant behavior as "economism."[30] In other words, peasants withheld a higher proportion of their produce for their own consumption rather than give it to the collectives. Peasants also quickly resumed the modes of reaction that were prominent in the 1950s: outmigration, assaulting state officials in charge of grain requisition, and rebellions in the peripheral areas. A large number of peasants, for example, entered Shanghai in 1967 and clashed with the workers and students there. On July 13, 1967, the CCP Central Committee specifically appealed to the peasants from the provinces of Anhui, Zhejiang, Henan, Hunan, Hubei, Jiangxi, Shanxi, and

Sichuan to return to their villages.[31] Four of these eight provinces—
Anhui, Henan, Hunan, and Sichuan—had "very high rates of death" during the famine of 1960–1962.[32] Here and there, peasants attacked and
destroyed the offices of the State Monopoly of Purchasing and Marketing.
They also expelled workers and former students who were sent to the
countryside after the Great Leap.[33] Once again, peasants in the periphery
were particularly active. In Inner Mongolia, local radio broadcasters
exposed the serious riots against state trade agencies, rapid rise of private
commerce, and groups specializing in raiding state stores and trafficking
in contraband.[34] Unlike the rebellions in the 1950s, the riots during the
Cultural Revolution were spontaneous affairs without the organizing
roles of religious groups or traditional secret societies. The state had effectively suppressed these traditional intermediary groups. However, the
state had to face diffused mass resistance instead.

The general mode of peasant resistance by amorphous social actions
is evidenced in the peasant mood of the 1970s. Among the peasants, a sort
of resistance ethos grew steadily. The Chinese press coined special terms
for this, the most prominent ones being (1) *Mo yanggong* (dawdling
along in field work), (2) *Wogong* (idleness due to poor organization), and
(3) *Dahulong* (crudeness and carelessness in work).[35] The slowdown
behavior of the peasants was confirmed further by the terms that the
press used to refer to rural cadres' work. Harvesting and planting were
referred to as *qianshou* (rush in the harvest) and *qianzhong* (rush-planting).
In a *Radio Hunan* broadcast in 1972, it was said that "the two 'rush'
processes are filled with struggles between two classes, two roads, and
two thoughts."[36] These words suggested unmistakably a deep alienation
between the peasants and the state. A young Sichuan cadre told the dissident journalist Liu Binyan in 1976: "Peasants said that we and they had
been putting on a rival show for some twenty years. That is quite true. If
peasants are opposed to it, then a question mark must be affixed to [the
state's] so-called socialism."[37]

At the time of Mao's death, it was the Chinese peasants who were
"cutting the tail of socialism." Even in the locality where the Maoist
model of Da Zhai was situated, many peasants deserted the communes to
engage in peddling and crafts. A popular saying there was "Leap over the
gate of farming and you raise yourself tens of thousands of feet high."[38]
In other words, the peasants were consciously revolting against the state-
imposed pauperization. In areas where resistance to collectivization was
strong at the outset, such as in southern Zhejiang, collectivization existed
in name only. In the county of Wenzhou, for example, village cadres and
peasants collaborated to sabotage communes through an ingenious system known as *guahu* (attached household). That is, peasant households
were allowed to go into private business, which was, however, formally

registered as part of the commune establishments.[39] The practice in Wenzhou existed elsewhere in China too. According to Wu Xiang, deputy director of the Rural Policy Research Center of the State Council (the national government of China), secret contracting of land or work to individual households was widespread in China in the late 1970s. "That contracting [farm] production to households," wrote Wu in 1980, "revived itself time and again was, in reality, a reflection of peasant resistance to the leftist policy and line."[40]

Mao's failure in collectivizing Chinese agriculture may be viewed on two levels. On the level of economics, collectivization per se, as pointed out by John Hamer, would have been acceptable to the peasants if it had proven to be superior in providing security.[41] But the Maoist collectives, wrote Victor Nee, were mainly for effective extraction of agricultural surpluses and less for peasant security.[42] "Maoism," said Edward Friedman, "left peasants with nothing."[43] On the level of values, as mentioned earlier, those who enacted changes had to take into account the mores of the people and resources at their disposal. But the Maoist state "treated popular mores and peasant norms as enemy forces," so wrote Friedman, Paul Pickowicz, and Mark Selden.[44] In the final analysis, the failure of Mao's collectivization is testimony to the power of the seemingly powerless. When the latter is psychically initiated, no state, no matter how strong, can defeat them. One finds a precedence of such mass resistance in the Norwegian people's opposition to the Nazi occupation during World War II.[45]

Chinese Peasants Under Deng

On the surface, the state and peasant relationship underwent a major change under Deng Xiaoping's administration. The communes had been formally abolished by 1982 and Chinese peasants finally got what they had been asking for since the mid-1950s: land contracted out to individual households ("the responsibility system"). In reality, until the early 1990s, Deng had merely made a tactical change in the state-peasant relationship. Mao's approach to the peasants may be termed behavioral control. Deng's approach may be called structural control. The state under Deng controlled what I call the "choke points" of rural economy: scarce capital input (chemical fertilizers, petroleum, pesticide, etc.) and the marketing outlets. The Dengist tactic toward the peasants resembles closely Jeffery Paige's description of the tactic used by the U.S. company United Fruit in Central America. United Fruit sold off its banana plantations while maintaining control of the transportation of bananas and, of course, marketing in the United States. Paige wrote: "United Fruit is therefore eliminating the image of 'El Pulpo' (the octopus), which has been a target of left-wing propaganda in Central America for half a century, while maintaining control over the most profitable end of the banana business."[46] The new tactic of the Deng administration changed the state-peasant conflict from one over land to one over distribution of income. The latter, according to Paige, is amenable to economic bargaining. But, in China, conflicts over distribution of income between the state and the peasants did not make the relationship between the two any less problematic than conflicts over land.

In the early 1980s, Deng's new tactic toward the peasants briefly diverted the peasants' attention to competition among themselves. That temporarily masked the "value ambiguity" of the Dengist regime toward the peasants. By value ambiguity I mean Deng's publicly declaring the state's recognition of the importance of agriculture. But, in reality, the Maoist urban bias remained unchanged under Deng. One Chinese politician called the Dengist state's attitude toward agriculture a case of "slogan agriculture."[47] Peasant public opinion in the 1980s and early 1990s was determined by the duration that it took the peasants to be fully conscious of the Dengist state's value ambiguity. In subsequent discussion, I shall divide the peasant reactions into two periods. In the first period, from 1979 to 1984, the peasants were preoccupied with the status quo ante activities; they were less attentive to Deng's urban bias policy. In the second period, from 1985 to the early 1990s, the peasants realized Deng's value ambiguity and initiated a social revolution by themselves.

1979–1984: Occasionalism and Parochial Conflicts

As mentioned earlier, the attitude of peasants became occasionalistic after the Great Leap Forward. Peasants responded in the same way to the new opportunities provided by Deng's reform. They tried their best to do the most for the moment and had no long-term thoughts. They learned from the past that the state was capricious.

The first order of business in the post-Mao period was the dismantling of communes. The general rule seemed to be that the poorer the area, the faster and more thorough decollectivization was carried out. But the overall result was that a vast majority of peasants supported decollectivization.[48] It was certainly ironic for Mao, who thought that poor peasants were the most enduring supporters of the collectives. Moreover, decollectivization extended beyond farming; it included all properties owned collectively in the past. Table 2.2 compares the rates of decollectivization in fixed assets in the rural areas of the eastern, central, and western regions of China from 1978 through 1987. It is now common knowledge that modernization and development in China diminish significantly as one moves from the eastern to the western regions.[49] Table 2.2 shows that in the three regions of China, there was a steady decline in collective ownership of fixed assets and an increase in private ownership from 1978 to 1987. But it was in the less developed central and western provinces that decollectivization was more extensive and moved more quickly than in the eastern provinces. Another interesting revelation from Table 2.2 is that in the East, there was a higher rate of family-owned fixed assets than in the rest of the country. Peasants seemed to be more willing to retain a degree of collectivization if they were not entirely deprived of their personal assets.

In contrast, the country's agricultural areas were concentrated in the provinces of central China. These peasants were the most deprived by Mao's agricultural policy and their decollectivization went much further than did that of the peasants in the East. Furthermore, in some of the poor areas decollectivization threw into relief what Chinese official Du Rensheng (former director of the Rural Policy Research Center) referred to as the "alienation of the productive means" phenomenon.[50] That is, peasants vented their frustration and sense of alienation (for lack of rights and power over production) on the tools for production. Chinese scholars who had done field research among the peasants reported that, in some poor areas, decollectivization was accompanied by wanton destruction of earlier collectively owned machinery and other property. For example, peasants from a poor village in southern Gansu destroyed the valuable communal apple orchard and spice plants that could have earned handsomely in the market. They disassembled what had been the collectively owned seeder and thresher and distributed the spare parts among themselves.[51] Chinese sociologist Fei Xiaotong recounted the reaction of one village in Yunnan Province where the peasants used to supplement their incomes by making fine bamboo utensils with the cuttings taken from abundant bamboo in the the hills surrounding the village. During the decollectivization in 1980, the bamboo hill was at first not included in the process. The peasants then ransacked the hill and indiscriminately razed all the bamboo.[52] But this was just the beginning. In later years, peasants would turn against the productive means that they valued so much in the past: the land. That peasants felt alienated from the land might have been a long-delayed reaction to the stark fact that under Mao, as described by Aiguo Lu and Mark Selden, "the land owned the people," not the other way around.[53]

Underneath the occasionalism of Chinese peasants—or the phenomenon of "alienation of the productive means"—was a fundamental distrust toward the state and its policy. This was known as the "fear of policy change" attitude on the part of peasants in the early 1980s. The headlines in the national press were rather telling: "The peasants urgently need stability to care for their families," as one put it. "Earning peasants' trust is of major importance" was yet another commonly seen headline.[54]

Table 2.2 Percentages of Collective and Family-Owned Fixed Assets in Chinese Villages, 1978–1987

	East region				Central region				West region			
	1978	1980	1984[a]	1987[a]	1978	1980	1984	1987	1978	1980	1984	1987
Family-owned	13.51	14.05	30.9	37.03	1.02	4.97	30.47	62.41	10.06	18.87	72.0	84.21
Collective-owned	86.49	85.95	67.43	58.70	98.98	95.03	36.79	35.53	89.94	81.13	27.96	15.09

[a]There is a printing error in the Chinese text. The percentages in these two columns should be moved down by one line in the Chinese text. Because of other forms of ownership, not provided in the original source, the figures do not total 100 percent.

Source: Nongye Jingji [Agricultural Economy], no. 4 (1989): 60.

Specifically, peasants refused to invest much in the land and, as one newspaper reader's letter put it, "they [the peasants] thought only of *using*, not *cultivating*, the land" (emphasis added).[55] This occasionalist ethos of the peasants seemed to be "rational" for, as Thomas Bernstein explained, "the autonomous sphere of the peasants was not institutionalized, and the party-state continued to claim the right to intervene extensively in peasant life."[56]

The occasionalist mentality of Chinese peasants, however, produced a positive but momentary result. The production of grain in China increased significantly in 1981–1984. The grain yield in 1984 represented a 30 percent increase over that in 1978. The state's excess purchase of the peasants' grain in 1984 (after peasants had sold their assigned quota of grain to the state) increased twofold.[57]

Insofar as the specific public opinion of peasants in this initial period of reform is concerned, it was all conditioned by the decollectivization process and its immediate political consequence. The CCP's influence and control at the two lowest levels of Chinese rural settlements—natural villages (the neighborhood) and administrative villages (first aggregation of natural villages)—were significantly reduced. Rural social segmentation evolved rapidly and the peasants' reactions to the various reforms were more and more diverse.

The most prominent specific reactions of peasants at the time resulted in a precipitous rise in competitive conflict and deviant social behavior. The first was reflected in the rapid increase in civil disputes. The number of civil cases handled by the courts grew fourfold from 1978 to 1985.[58] Most of these disputes concerned conflicting ownership claims over hills, water, fields, forests, roads, and houses.[59] These may be referred to as "status quo ante conflicts"—conflicts stemming from peasants trying to recover their old property. Certainly these disputes were also fueled by the peasants' profit motives, the expanding market mechanism, and the quick revival of clans in the countryside.[60]

The second major form of specific public opinion in this period was deviant social behavior, or anomie, in the villages.[61] It is a striking fact that much of rural China saw a quick social breakdown once the state presence receded. All the deeply rooted social problems that the Maoist state masked with overwhelming state controls were now being exposed gradually. These problems included overpopulation, underemployment, lack of education, and, above all, lack of opportunity for mobility. Underlying the widespread deviant behavior seen in petty crimes, assaults, prostitution, and suicides was a mingling of social and political causes in many villages. Impoverishment was conducive to the political incitement initiated by the national elite under Mao's rule.[62] In turn, political conflicts impeded efforts to improve the socioeconomic conditions of these communities.[63] The Dengist state responded to the rural anomie by organizing a campaign known as "civilized villages," and the peasants in the disorderly villages were urged to sign village compacts.

In 1937, the Chinese scholar Liang Shuming argued against the Maoist stress on class struggles. Liang believed that the village was a corporate entity and that dividing the villagers only impeded effective implementation of rural development.[64] Liang turned out to be one of the first senior Chinese intellectuals disgraced publicly by Mao after the founding of the PRC. Deng's "civilized village" campaign was a tacit admission that Liang was right after all. But the effects of some thirty years of class struggle, together with the long-term consequences of the state's urban-biased economic policy, cannot be overcome by a campaign. As Deng's reform proceeded into the late 1980s, there was a further unfolding of anomie or deviance in the countryside.

Finally, the initial years of Deng's reform also saw resurgent collective protests by peasants. The most serious incident occurred on Hainan Island in July 1979. The protest displayed all the essential qualities of collective action in a highly repressive state. First, like previous peasant revolts elsewhere in China, the Hainan incident took place in a peripheral area. In the present case, physical periphery was strengthened by cultural periphery. Hainan is an island off the coast of Guangdong, which is part of China's southern frontier. The 1979 revolt occurred in a mountainous and isolated community in Tunchang County. It is a multi-racial area, with the Han Chinese living together with two ethnic minority races (the Li and Miao people). Second, the riot in Tunchang showed the importance of a prolonged build-up of strains, diffused collectivities, and spontaneous assembling dynamics (see discussion in Chapter 1 and Table 1.2).

By all accounts, three main groups participated in the riot: local cadres, veterans, and peasants. Local cadres had resented Beijing's "divide and rule" policy in which the national CCP appointed northern Chinese to important Party-state positions on Hainan. Indigenous cadres became subordinate to these outsiders. Over the decades, Beijing sent a large number of demobilized soldiers to settle and colonize the island. These veterans had a hard life and naturally blamed the state for their plight. Peasants had long complained about the army's (composed of northerners) requisitioning of farmland for military use. There had been earlier clashes between the army and peasants over land and, in a few instances, the army had shot and killed protesting peasants. The revolt of July 1979 was precipitated by a public petition protesting Beijing's allotment of a limited quota for Tunchang people in the newly revived nationwide college admission examination. This open demonstration against the state quickly drew a crowd in front of the county government building. Reportedly incited by some veterans passing by, the protestors stormed into and occupied the county radio station and broadcast their grievances, whereupon the veterans ransacked the arsenal of local militia and robbed it of numerous weapons. Some of the peasants were mobilized; others rose spontaneously. They confronted the army to settle old scores. In the end, troops from outside were called in to suppress the revolt and there were casualties. The total number of people involved in the revolt was said to be between seven and 10,000.[65] Apparently, Beijing's use of northerners to control Hainan, designed obviously to counter localism, had backfired; localism was enhanced instead of diminished. I shall have more to say about this in my analysis of Beijing's relationship with ethnic minorities.

1985–1994: Social Revolution

If there ever was a "honeymoon" between the Dengist state and the peasants, it ended sometime in 1985. Ironically, it was due partly to the success of the new household responsibility system in farming in 1983–1984, which ushered in the period of peasant disillusionment. To this day, the state has yet to find a solution. In late 1984 and early 1985 Chinese peasants came face to face with the Dengist state's control of the "choke points" of rural economy. The crisis of the so-called difficulty in selling grains (*maliangnan*) then emerged all over China. Peasants had so few outlets for marketing their grain because the state still maintained a monopoly on grain purchasing and marketing. Now that peasants had a surplus of grain to sell, they found the state purchasing agencies unwilling to buy the grain.

The peasants' heavy dependence on the state to market their goods during the mid- and late 1980s is reflected in a government-conducted survey in 1988. The poll was based on a national sample of 10,938 households and reported that peasants sold the following percentages of their crops to the state: grains, 85.7; cotton, 95.6; oil, 78.1; and sugar, 81.8 percent. Forty-four percent of the peasants interviewed also complained that state-purchasing agencies often arbitrarily downgraded the quality of peasants' goods to justify the agencies' low purchasing prices.[66] Peasants responded to the crisis by withdrawing land from grain production and finding employment in local industry, which was then growing at a high speed. As the Chinese press recounted endlessly, there followed "three years of stalemate in grain production" (*sannian paihui*).[67] By 1988, the phrase "a grim situation in agriculture" was on everybody's lips, from urban residents to high-ranking officials. Minister of Agriculture He Kang told the Chinese parliament (National People's Congress) in January 1988 that the output of grain had been "stagnant . . . in recent years" and that "the nation [faced] a grim agricultural situation."[68]

But the stark reality that peasants confronted after 1985 was not confined to the bottleneck in selling grains. They also suffered from the classic "scissor problem" in socialist systems, that is, low prices for agricultural goods and high prices for industrial goods.[69] Moreover, peasants had to deal with regional and local governments that had acquired a higher degree of autonomy in economic management under Deng's administration. Both provincial and local authorities had been affected by the national state's ethos of marginalizing agriculture. Since agricultural goods commanded considerably less income than industry, provincial governments either refused or grossly reduced its rural investment. Funds originally allocated for agriculture were routinely given to industrial establishments. Bureaucratic departments or offices specializing in agriculture were often the first ones to be closed down in the name of "structural reform."[70] Whereas provincial governments marginalized agriculture, local cadres engaged in the time-honored bureaucratic practice of squeezing the hapless peasants. On the whole, cadres were ill disposed toward the expanding market forces in China and resorted to various rent-collecting measures for self-enrichment.

Emulating the central state, local state agencies established their own choke points. Local monopolies were established here and there; toll stations were set up to prevent peasants from either trading in outside areas or exacting exorbitant fees from them.[71] How much control local authorities exerted on the peasants, even into the 1990s, may be seen in a 1992 poll conducted by the government. Peasants in thirteen provinces were interviewed. The final report said "over one-quarter of the respondents say farmers depend largely on village and township organizations throughout the entire process of production."[72] It is no wonder that the incomes of Chinese peasants decreased precipitously after 1985. A 1991 press report said that "between 1980 and 1984 the per capita net income of farmers increased 15.1 percent each year. But during the Seventh Five-Year Plan period (1986–1990), it only increased 2.4 percent each year. In 1989 it increased by only 1.6 percent over 1988, and in 1990 it only increased by 1.8 percent."[73] The gap in income between peasants and urban residents expanded accordingly. "In 1992, the ratio of per capita rural and urban income widened to 1:2.4 from 1:1.7 in 1985," as reported in a government communiqué.[74] As if all these were not enough, in 1989 the state suddenly reimposed the Maoist system of "state monopoly for purchase and marketing" of grain, cotton, and other major agricultural product—clearly as a deflating measure. At the same time, the state forcibly closed down many rural factories and reassigned some 10 million rural workers back to the farms, hoping to increase grain production.[75] It was Maoism revisited. Now peasants realized that there had been no fundamental change in the state's policy toward them after all. The Dengist state had as strong an urban bias as the Maoist one. The gen-

eral and specific rural public opinion must be understood in the foregoing context.

General Public Opinion

The collective mood of Chinese peasants in the late 1980s can be
summed up in one word: gloom. One Chinese scholar described the
prevailing attitude of peasants as one of "contrariness" *(nixiang xinli)*.
It was manifested in their tendencies toward complaining *(meiyuan)*,
contradicting *(dichu)*, passivity *(xiaoji)*, opposition *(fangan)*, and griev-
ance-telling *(laosao)*. These attitudes in turn caused social deviance, disinterest in productive investment, social alienation in the villages,
cynicism (especially toward any new policy or program from the state),
and the creation of a general negative impression among the people.[76]

Another Chinese scholar reported that the attitude of contrariness
was most pronounced among young peasants. He attributed it to their
loss of faith in socialism and distrust of the CCP. It also seemed that the
"revolution of rising expectations" had affected the young in the countryside. Seeing the urban people enjoying China's new consumer culture,
the rural youth felt increasingly frustrated.[77]

Beneath it all was the peasants' clear recognition that they had been
marginalized and pauperized by the state for a long time. That is evident in
a 1988 survey of peasants in a Sichuan county. For example, they were asked
to rank (from most to least esteemed) seventeen professions in terms of
power and authority. The top five professions were state cadres, tax collec-
tors, security police, village cadres, and electricians (the last were among the
chief extortionists in the countryside, widespread rural electrification being
a post-Mao phenomenon). Peasants apparently did not even think of their
own occupation; all those ranked were nonfarm professions. In terms of
income, the top five identified by the peasants were owners of private shops,
drivers, private transporters, technicians, and state cadres. The lowest five
were peasants, craft workers, soldiers, village cadres, and peddlers. Peasants
were also asked to rank those with a promising future. The top eight were
educated people, technicians, those with connections, those with parents in
high positions, merchants, frugal and diligent people, CCP members, and
village cadres.[78] By implication, Ba County peasants seemed to regard themselves powerless, status deprived, poor, and without a promising future.

Running through these polls and scholarly analyses like a red thread
is the peasants' alienation from and distrust of the state. In the 1988
national survey of 10,938 peasant households mentioned earlier, 57.8 percent of the peasants interviewed said that either they did not believe that
the state's policy on household farming would not change in the future
or they were uncertain about it. In 1993, the state conducted a survey of

1,110 peasant households in fourteen provinces, asking respondents about their perception of the state's promise to control the prices of major farm inputs (chemical fertilizers, fuel, and pesticide). The survey found that 75 percent of the peasants did not think the state's promise was credible, while 74 percent did not believe the state would fulfill its promise to reduce excessive levies on the peasants.[79] After the state announced the new policy of terminating its monopoly on the purchase and marketing of grains and other major farm goods in 1993, a seven-province survey reported that "everyone was still worried and anxious about the permanency of the new policy."[80]

The general distrust that Chinese peasants displayed toward the state encompassed a critical attitude toward cadres. To Chinese peasants, the state and cadres were one and the same. So it should surprise no one that the peasants' evaluation of cadres was, on the whole, negative. The two national surveys mentioned earlier also asked peasants to describe cadres in general. The peasants' responses to the first survey were: 38.1 percent described cadres as "hard-working people leading all the people to be well-off"; 26.5 percent pictured them as caring only for themselves; 9.1 percent said that "all they do is to get subsidies"; 3.3 percent believed cadres did not follow policy in conducting public affairs; 9.7 percent viewed them as using authority to benefit themselves; and 13.4 percent of the peasants refused to respond. If we interpret the refusals to respond to mean a negative appraisal of cadres, then critical responses were given by 62 percent of the respondents.[81] In the second national poll, peasants ranked "making cadres honest and ridding corruption" as the second most important request that they wished to make to the government, the top-ranked being "no change in state policy." Another poll also reported that the peasants' "first request for cadres is serving their communities better 'instead of extorting money' [from the people]." Furthermore, "over half consider cadres' [low] qualifications a weak link at the township and village levels."[82]

These views and moods of the peasants in the late 1980s were ultimately translated into productive conduct. That the production of grain had declined since 1984 has already been mentioned. Underlying that were various concrete actions by the peasants that may be described as "auto-marginalization." As commonly understood among students of agricultural economy, marginalization "implies a decline in the significance of peasant agriculture within the national economy, and the peasantry acts primarily as a source of cheap labor, cheap food, and markets for industrial goods."[83] Thus, by auto-marginalization I mean that the Chinese peasants themselves de-emphasized agriculture. That is another way of saying that peasants felt alienated from their land. For example, peasants' investments on their contracted land steadily went down. In 1983, on an average, Chinese peasants invested 5.7 percent of their annual outlays on their land. In 1984 and 1985, the percentage declined to 4.7 and 3.8, respectively.[84] The year 1985 also saw a sudden rise in peasants' withdrawal of contracted land from farming. In that year, some 15 million *mu* (2.5 million acres) of land were transferred by peasants and rural cadres to nonfarm uses, such as building houses or leasing out acres to become "developmental zones" for industry.[85]

In the early 1990s, auto-marginalization by the peasants continued. A 1994 report vividly illustrated the peasants' alienation from the land and also their continued use of amorphous actions against the state. The report said in part that "Beginning in June last year, it was as if farmers had discussed and agreed on a course of action; suddenly, no one would buy farm machinery any more. It is impossible for so many farmers to have discussed and agreed on it. Yet the fact that 'suddenly nobody would buy' indicates that economic laws are working."[86] In the agricultural provinces of the central region, the phenomenon of peasants' abandoning and wasting land *(tuitian paohuang)* developed. The reasons for this were the minimal or absent (1) interest in farming, (2) farming ability (as the young generation emigrated to cities and only old peasants were left behind to farm the land), (3) human resources (due to increasing outmigration of peasants), and (4) farming support services (facilities were obsolete).[87]

The discussion has so far dealt with the general climate of rural opinion in the late 1980s and early 1990s. But a major change in the Chinese countryside under Deng's administration is the degree of social and economic differentiation among peasants. The degree of differentiation varies significantly across both macro- and micro-regions. The key to differentiation is local industrialization, the main institution of which is the so-called township enterprise *(xiangzhen qiye)*. But these enterprises are distributed unevenly throughout China. They are concentrated especially in the nine cities and provinces of Beijing, Tianjin, Shanghai, Jiangsu, Zhejiang, Shandong, Liaoning, Shanxi, and Guangdong (Shanxi being the only interior and northern province in this group). The rural firms in these nine provinces and localities account for 46 percent of the rural enterprises, 60 percent of all the employed, and 71 percent of the output values in the whole nation.[88]

Rural differentiation is also determined by sub- or micro-regional differences. Table 2.3 presents a portion of the findings of three Chinese scholars who visited thirteen villages across China in 1990–1991.[89] In every village they investigated the proportions of peasants who had changed their main occupations from farm to nonfarm work. They classified the villages into four types according to the degree of differentiation: (I) nondifferentiation, (II) low differentiation, (III) medium differentiation, and (IV) high differentiation. In Table 2.3, I have supplemented these Chinese scholars' data by adding the *general* geographical locations of the villages. The micro-regional differences among the villages are striking. Moreover, proximity to large cities and access to major communication systems, such as rivers or railways, probably facilitated the rise of nonfarm occupations and, hence, high differentiation. But without knowledge of the traditions and cultures of the villages, one cannot analyze fully the reasons for the varying degrees of differentiation. There are anomalies in Table 2.3, such as the two villages in the region of Tangshan City and the two in Anhui Province. The latter case is particularly intriguing as the two villages are located in counties that have similar physical characteristics: part hills and part plains, about thirty kilometers from a major regional city, with access to rivers and railways, and rich in minerals. Behavioral factors must be explored before any plausible explanation can be given about the vast difference in the rise of nonfarm occupations between these two villages.

In propagandizing about rural social differentiation, the Chinese government has often gone to the extreme. For instance, according to the State Council (national government), there are now twelve occupational groups in the countryside. They are traditional farmers, specialized commercial farmers, hired hands, rural intellectuals, migrant workers, self-employed laborers (such as crafts workers), cadres, workers and staff in township enterprises, managers of collective enterprises, self-employed manufacturers and service personnel, owners of private businesses, and owners of family-associated businesses.[90] The reality in most villages—especially those in the central and western provinces—finds approximately 80 percent of the village residents still engaged in traditional farming. About 10 percent have branched out to do part-time work in

Table 2.3   Percentages of Villagers Engaged in Nonfarm Occupations in Selected Rural Areas

Province/County (City)/Village	1978	1989	Type
Hebei/Langfang/Cuori[a]	28.3	96.3	IV
Hebei/Langfang/Xilin	—	62.3	
Hebei/Tangshan/Limayu[b]	4.29	83.81	IV
Hebei/Tangshan/Sashiyu[c]	—	35.0	
Hebei/Tangshan/Xipu[c]	1.97	60.51	III
Henan/Xinxiang/Liuzhuan[a]	59.1	92.2	IV
Henan/Zhengzhou/Zhulin[b]	12.0	100.0	IV
Anhui/Hangshan/Fangwei[b]	29.7	72.5	
Anhui/Fengyang/Xiaogang[b]	0.0	3.0	
Jiangsu/Jiangyin/Huaxi[a]	19.3	98.7	IV
Hubei/Honghu/Honglin[a]	46.5	91.5	IV
Shanxi/Xiyang/Dazhai[c]	—	56.7	III
Jiangxi/Ninggang/Maoping[c]	8.9	10.8	II

[a]Close proximity to modern city or center of communications

[b]Mountain region with good communications to a major city

[c]Mountain region

Source: Lu Xueyi, Zhang Houyi, and Zhang Qizi, "Zhuanxin Shiqi Nongmindi Jiecheng Fenhua" [Differentiation among the peasants during a period of transition], *Nongye Jingji* [Agricultural Economy], no. 8 (1992): 35–49.

nonfarm occupations, and the rest are employed in full-time nonfarm work (about 5 to 6 percent are cadres).[91] Even in Yongjia County, Zhejiang Province, which is under the jurisdiction of Wenzhou Municipality (and famous for its township enterprises), 50 percent of the peasants are preoccupied with traditional farming, another 27 percent have taken on some part-time nonfarm work, and 22 percent have completely switched to nonfarm work.[92]

As far as the opinions of all these groups are concerned, I have yet to come across any systematic record of them. In highly differentiated areas, one generally finds confirmation of Mancur Olson's 1963 thesis that rapid growth left both gainers and losers discontented.[93] For example, one Chinese scholar described the attitudes of various groups in the countryside in the relatively developed areas on the eastern coast as follows:

The privileges and corruptions of some managerial personnel made other groups resentful and angry but the former complained about their low wages. The intellectuals were dissatisfied with the higher wages of manual workers. The latter, however, did not agree with all the talks about improving the living standard of the intellectuals. The self-employed and owners of private businesses enjoyed high incomes, but they complained that "money was all they had." Nonfarm workers claimed that their wages were not equal to their work. Farmers were full of grievances because of the scissor condition of low price for grains and high price of farm inputs.[94]

The new entrepreneurs experienced a high level of anxiety about their status. They were unsure of the Communist Party's attitude toward private business. While visiting a Yunnan village in 1990, Fei Xiaotong met a successful entrepreneur in the business of making popsicles. Fei wrote:

His mind was not at rest; he wanted to expand his business but was afraid of [the state's] policy being not long lasting. . . . In his conversation with me, he said repeatedly that he was very willing to hand his business over to collective ownership and that he would be satisfied with being the manager of the factory. He would rather not be the owner.[95]

In 1988 a state-directed survey of ninety-seven private businesses in the rural areas of eleven provinces found that 60 percent of the owners were pessimistic about their future. The study concluded that their reasons for pessimism were not political. But 22 percent of the owners said that they were worried that their work might be branded by others as "exploitative."[96] A study of the private business owners in rural Guangdong, where commerce and business had developed most in the post-Mao period also found that they were in an anxious mood. The study reported that the private business owners, "without exception, appealed to the state to grant them a secure political status, give them legal protection and assistance, and allow them to have some input in policy-making of concern to them. They also wish that other social groups show some understanding of their professions."[97]

Whether in a highly or lowly differentiated village, one finds corroboration of John Markoff's observation about peasant mobilization in the French Revolution. No other factor was associated as strongly with peasant mobilization as market involvement.[98] In an isolated and peripheral village in Liaoning province, for example, a Chinese scholar found in 1989 that post-Mao reform had little effect on the villagers. Not a single farmer had changed to a nonfarm occupation, but several had begun to branch out to some commercial farming. It was these few who had taken the trouble to go to the nearby town repeatedly to protest to the government about the state purchasing agency's bad faith in honoring contracts.[99]

The foregoing deals mainly with areas having undergone a high degree of socioeconomic differentiation. But the bulk of the Chinese countryside was not so fortunate. Most peasants were still locked into traditional farming, as illustrated by a case study in 1988 of a village in Sichuan. Out of 7,454 peasant households in the village, only seventeen (0.2 percent) had changed to nonfarm occupations. A short-term expedient ethos was said to have prevailed among the villagers. They were willing to exploit whatever opportunity existed for improving the living standards of their families, but refused to contribute to long-term farm construction work such as irrigation and soil improvement. They were reluctant to take any innovative action for fear that the state might change its policy unpredictably.[100]

In China, there are still belts of extreme poverty, which are located, as one Chinese scholar decribed them, in the "old-minority-border" and "three-Westerns" areas. Specifically, these refer to old CCP revolutionary base areas, ethnic minority areas, and border areas. The "three Westerns" refer to two special districts in southern Gansu and one in the southern Ningxia Muslim area.[101] The provinces of Guangxi and Guizhou are also extremely poor. The culture of poverty in Guangxi, according to two scholars, is manifested in a high frequency of internecine fights, low regard for education, disdain for commerce and trade, isolation, dependence on the state for relief, contentment with the status quo, and inbreeding. In Guangxi, illiteracy in the countryside was between 31 and 50 percent. In 1989, 14 percent of the population (six million) lived below the official poverty line, which meant not having enough food to eat. Guangxi political leaders were said to be unwilling to initiate economic development for fear of making their province a "colony" of other provinces and for fear of incurring debts. In certain areas, human beings were still pulling plows in the field.[102] During the Cultural Revolution, internecine fights in Guangxi grew out of control and degenerated into cannibalism.[103]

The culture of poverty was also observed in Guizhou Province and parts of Inner Mongolia. The latter was known to have particularly serious political and factional conflicts.[104] Chinese scholars' discussions of the culture of poverty reminded me of Edward Banfield's study, *The Moral Basis of a Backward Society*. Banfield attributed the predicament of peasants in a southern Italian village to the ethos of "amoral familism" which, in turn, was conducive to an authoritarian state.[105] In contrast, Alessandro Pizzorno suggested an alternative explanation for Banfield's description. According to Pizzorno, the ethos of "amoral familism" is actually a reflection of marginality: The attitudes of passivity, futility, and anomie are responses of a people who have been left out in the capitalist economic transformation.[106] Both theses seem to apply equally well in shedding light on the culture of poverty in contemporary China.

Specific Opinion

Against the background of general gloom and auto-marginalization among Chinese peasants in the late 1980s, specific opinions in the countryside were more dynamic and active. These opinions were prompted by the peasants' desire to resist their twin fate of marginalization and pauperization.

These specific expressions of opinion can now be placed in the broad contexts of Chinese peasants' goals and their means. Figure 2.1 categorizes peasant reactions into four types in terms of forms of reaction (coordinated or uncoordinated actions) and objectives (anti-marginalization or anti-pauperization). In the segment on general public opinion, I discussed mainly anti-marginalization actions. Establishing township enterprises may be regarded as a coordinated action against marginalization. One author, for example, stated that rural enterprises were aimed at "countering urban enterprises' exclusions of surplus rural laborers."[107]

	Anti-marginalization	Anti-pauperization
Coordinated action	Township enterprise	Outmigration Rebellion
Uncoordinated action	Amorphous social action	Deviant social behavior

Figure 2.1 Pattern of peasant reaction in the post-Mao period

Anti-Pauperization Actions

The previous section has analyzed the various amorphous social actions by peasants to resist marginalization by the state. I shall now discuss three forms of anti-pauperization actions by peasants.

Outmigration

Perhaps the most prominent mass movement in the post-Mao period is the migration of peasants to fast-growing coastal provinces, such as Hainan, and major cities, such as Beijing, Tianjin, Shanghai, Guangzhou, and Shenzhen. The Chinese press has described these great movements as "tides of migrant workers" *(mingongchao)*. At first the migrations were concentrated in the winter months when there was a lull in farm work. Now it occurs all year round and involves between 50 and 60 million peasants.[108] They move in large groups and often create bottlenecks in railway traffic. In February 1994 a tragic accident took place at the railway junction in Hengyang (Hunan Province) in which fifty-two migrants were trampled to death.[109] Lack of accurate information about the real employment situation in the cities contributed to the exodus from the countryside. The new migrants were emboldened to head for the urban areas either by word-of-mouth from returning migrants or by letters from fellow villagers working outside.

A Chinese scholar pointed out that, in the 1960s and 1970s, a major transfer of the labor force from rural to urban areas occurred in South Korea, but there were no "tidal waves" of migrants like what happened in China. Korean peasants had accurate information about the employment opportunities in the city and, consequently, their movements became steady but not in a concentrated fashion.[110] However, one must note that Chinese migrants are escaping from the countryside as much as they are rushing to the city. And migrants should perhaps be seen as refugees who typically move in concentrated human waves. They are fleeing from the stark reality of long-term pauperization, which left 270 million peasants underemployed or unemployed in the countryside. Of these, 100 million were eventually absorbed by township enterprises, 30 million became commercial farmers, and 20 million emigrated. This left behind another 120 million surplus labor in the countryside. More could be on the move in the future.[111]

Sociologically speaking, migrants constitute a diffused collectivity: "a large number of people in loose interaction who share some common focus and sense of being part of a larger collectivity."[112] They are either formally or informally organized in their places of origin. The provincial government of Sichuan, for example, established special offices to direct and organize its residents to go out and seek work.[113] But the most common pattern of organization is through friendship and kinship links in the villages. As one account put it: "Few [migrants] set out alone. Most travel in groups organized by themselves or local companies."[114] Although Chinese migration as a social movement does not assume the *form* of a public protest, implicitly it is one. A Chinese journalist described migration as "a spontaneous act to redistribute the social wealth."[115] The chief aim of all the migrants is depauperization.

Migrants are part of the general phenomenon of peasants' alienation from their land. Thus, the first upsurge of rural-to-urban migration occurred simultaneously with the rise of auto-marginalization in the countryside from 1984 to 1988.[116] Most of the migrants came from the agricultural provinces of China that had been most affected by Mao's long-term policy of marginalizing agriculture. These provinces in central China—Sichuan, Henan, Anhui, Hunan, Guangxi, and Hebei—were the same places in which decollectivization was carried out rapidly and thoroughly during the first phase of Deng's reform. In the early 1990s, new provinces joined in the tide of migration, such as those in the northeast, which in Mao's time used to receive migrants sent by the state.[117] Even the peasants of Guizhou, a hitherto poor and peripheral area, are now on the move.[118] Map 2.1 shows the provinces from which most migrants originated, along with their destinations.

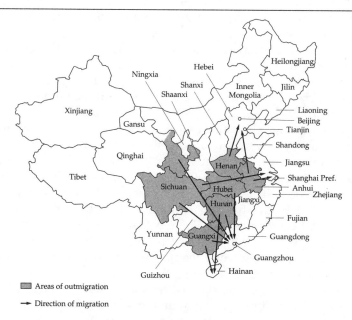

Areas of outmigration

→ Direction of migration

Map 2.1 Areas and Direction of Peasant Migration

By all accounts, rural migrants are young and represent the better-educated people in the countryside. They are mostly in the age bracket of fifteen to thirty-four years old. More and more young women have joined the migration since their skills as domestic servants are much in demand in the cities.[119] The average migrant has a junior high school level education—the highest level most rural youths ever reach.[120] Their exodus from the countryside contributes further to the phenomenon of auto-marginalization. Now farming is done increasingly by old and less-educated peasants. And as long as a gross disparity in economic development between the eastern and other regions of China remains, emigration in rural China will continue. A press report showed that in 1991 "the disparity of annual per capita rural output value between Central and East China was 1,858 *yuan* ($320), compared with 452 *yuan* ($78) in 1985."[121] Like the overall disparity in economic growth between the developed and less developed countries in the world, regional gaps in China keep widening over the years.

All indications point to the worsening of the migrant problem in the foreseeable future. In the western region of China, for example, peasants are already taking the first step toward migration. They are rapidly getting into nonfarm occupations. A government report stated: "In 1993, more farm labor transferred to nonfarm jobs in west China at a markedly accelerated pace." Nationwide, of those who shifted to nonfarm jobs, about 19.4 percent eventually moved outside of their provinces.[122] At one time the state hoped that township enterprises would absorb most of the surplus labor force in the countryside. But the recent trend indicates that these rural enterprises have reached a limit in employing the surplus people. According to a Chinese Ministry of Labor and Personnel report in 1994, "various township enterprises recruited an average of 12.6 million [surplus] workers each year from 1984 to 1988, but the numbers dropped sharply from 1989 to 1992, to an average of 2.6 million each year."[123]

In the meantime, cities already have 10 to 15 million underemployed workers who are likely to be dismissed if the state pushes forward its policy of streamlining Chinese industry. In 1993 there were 3 million unemployed in the urban areas.[124] In the coming century, a 1993 government document warned, the number of rural surplus laborers is likely to reach 230 million.[125] The state has apparently done little to deal with the problem. In a 1990 conference, the Chinese Association of Township Enterprises announced that the state had a policy for urban, but not rural, employment and that presently the state had no plan whatsoever to deal with the migrants—such as assisting them to find work or training them to acquire modern industrial skills before they left their villages.[126]

Socially, in the short-term, migration intensifies pauperization of the peasants. However, major cities along the coast have adopted various measures to stem the tide of migrants. Shanghai has issued "labor certificates" to a number of migrants; those without it are not entitled to work and reside in the city.[127] Jiangsu Province has enacted a law on transient population with provisions punishing employers who hire illegal rural migrants.[128] The special economic zone of Zhuhai in Guangdong set up a wire fence around the area to keep out migrants.[129] The local government of Hainan punishes any firm employing migrants without first getting permission from the government.[130] Most telling of all is the Shenzhen (the most successful special economic zone in Guangdong Province) government's 1994 campaign to rid the zone of illegal migrants. The action was referred to as a "clean-up" campaign and the migrants were called "the three without's": those without legal identity certificates, residency, or legitimate occupations.[131] Under Mao's rule, Chinese peasants were, according to some scholars, treated like serfs.[132] Under Deng's rule, peasants were treated by their fellow Chinese as pariahs. In Beijing they lived in segregated areas.[133] "We are looked down upon everywhere we go," said a migrant to a reporter from Hong Kong.[134]

Peasant Riots

As a form of collective action, migration is nonpolitical and carries no threat of group violence. In the late 1980s and early 1990s, however, Chinese peasants expressed their feelings in violent or confrontational collective actions. These actions may be classified into two types in terms of their cause. The first type is made up of what Tilly calls reactive movements. "They consist of group efforts to reassert established claims, when someone else challenges or violates them."[135] The second type consists of "proactive" movements. These are collective actions that assert group claims, which have not previously been exercised.[136]

Reactive actions by the peasants can be further classified into three kinds in terms of the cause of the action and the target of peasants' attack. The first kind usually occurred in areas of rapid market and commercial development such as in Guangdong. Peasants rebelled against fraudulent deals affecting their land. One such case occurred in Huiyang County, Guangdong, in April 1994. The county is close to the special zone of Shenzhen and its land is highly valued for its development possibilities. Peasants rioted because they were not adequately compensated for the land that was taken from them for industrial development.[137] In May 1993 the peasants in the Luoyang area of Henan rioted for similar reasons.[138]

The second type of reactive revolt is against cadre oppression, particularly excessive levies. Cases of this type invariably took place in the interior areas, away from post-Mao economic development. The internationally known case of the riot in Renshou County, Sichuan, in May 1993 belongs to this category. Renshou is located in a hilly region in central Sichuan. Although it is a traditional farming community, it has developed substantial commercial farming, especially in sugar. The revolt, which lasted from May to June, was provoked by the peasants' resentment of local government's repeated and excessive levies in the name of highway construction. Unrest and agitation by local peasants started as early as January 1993. The strain on the peasants was made worse by a persistent drought in the area. At the height of the demonstration, some 15,000 peasants participated. Apparently, natural leaders emerged quickly among the peasants. These were literate and knowledgeable people who spoke to large crowds and used copy machines to duplicate propaganda pamphlets. That there happened to be a rural fair going on at the time greatly contributed to the assembling of a large following. Crowds gathered whenever the police tried to arrest the leaders. The peasants obtained moral support from students in nearby cities. But the peasants who started the revolt were not ordinary peasants; they were commercial farmers and, as one report put it, they "drove their trucks and tractors" to destroy government properties.[139] Anti-cadres' exaction riots occurred elsewhere in China in traditional farming areas such as in the old Communist guerrilla base areas in Anhui and Shandong.[140]

The degree to which peasant riots were provoked by excessive state levies was reflected in the absence of such conflicts in areas with prosperous township enterprises. Some Chinese scholars found an inverse relationship between the number of local enterprises and cadre-peasant tensions. Villages with numerous township enterprises had fewer incidents of peasant-cadre conflicts. The profits from these local firms enabled the cadres to pay all the taxes and apportionments for individual peasants.[141] A Guangdong agricultural official maintained that the peasants in his province did not complain about the levies that were paid by the township enterprises.[142]

The third kind of reactive revolt in the 1990s is directed against the national government. In these cases the state unwittingly infringed upon the peasants' right to subsistence. In August 1993, for example, state agents went to the village of Zhouchen in eastern Jiangsu to shut down illegal salt mining by the peasants. As the agents arrived, the local radio station began calling villagers to arms to defend their lucrative sideline business. It was reported that within ten minutes, four hundred peasants, wielding sickles and spades, confronted the state agents.[143] In March 1994, some five thousand peasants in Yichang protested against the government's bad faith. Farmers were dislocated from their villages when the government requisitioned their land to build the massive Three Gorges Dam project. (Premier Li Peng was personally involved in this project.) Peasants were promised new housing before the onset of winter, but the government failed to deliver on its promise.[144]

These incidents represent the most serious collective actions by peasants against the state. In 1993 there was also a surge of peasant attacks on local post offices and demonstrations in front of township or county government buildings. These were mostly provoked by the refusal of postal officials to cash in the IOUs that government purchasing agencies had given the peasants in lieu of cash at the time of grain collection. This practice was common, especially in major grain-producing provinces such as Sichuan, Hunan, Hubei, and Jiangxi. But it also existed in other provinces.[145] A Chinese scholar had called these IOUs a form of state robbery of the peasants. He said, "With signing 'bills' of debt to farmers, towns and grain purchasing departments just temporarily grasp farmers' products."[146]

The most immediate reason for these clashes between the peasants and local state agencies in 1993 was Deng Xiaoping's inspection tour of the fast-growing towns in Guangdong in 1992. Deng was impressed by the economic development there and called on the whole nation to emulate these special cities. In response, Party cadres elsewhere in the nation increased the pressure on peasants to raise funds for local developmental projects.

There were other conditions conducive to the riots in the countryside in the early 1990s. The first one was the incoherence of Party control at the lowest level of rural administration. On the one hand, there was a significant reduction of the Party presence at the administrative village level. In 1991, one report stated that 65 to 75 percent of Party organizations in the administrative villages were "not functioning normally."[147] A CCP investigation in 1992 determined that Party strength in the villages had been grossly reduced by a resurgence of clans, clan alliances, and religious societies.[148] The last made it possible for villagers to recover local solidarity. On the other hand, the local government at the county and township levels is now much more powerful because the Deng administration granted a higher degree of regional autonomy than ever before. Encouraged by the national government, and Deng in particular, county and township governments all over China conceived ambitious projects for local economic development. To finance these projects, they imposed all kinds of levy or apportionment on the peasants. These two conditions—exactions by the cadres and local solidarity—were bound to clash with each other sooner or later. The third conducive condition was the segmentation of the state, which provided peasants with political space in which to maneuver. For example, the riot at Renshou was triggered by several literate peasants who discovered by reading the national press that local cadres had exceeded the limit of legitimate levies that were sanctioned by the national government. One peasant leader was reported to have said: "The central newspaper is now supporting us. If we do not take action now, when should we?"[149]

These riots reflect the changing times and the peasants' adaptation to the political reality, especially the overwhelmingly repressive power of the state. Compared with peasant rebellions during the collectivization campaigns of the 1950s, rebellions in the 1990s usually involve entire villages, instead of the separate small bands seen in the fifties. This is due to the withdrawal of the national government in the post-Mao period. Village solidarity is recovering in many areas of China. Rebellions now occur not only in peripheral areas but also in key areas where market economy has gone the furthest, such as in Guangdong. Moreover, despite reports of revival of secret and religious sects in the countryside, they play no significant role in the peasant revolts of the 1990s. Over the years, peasants have learned that a traditional type of rebellion is out of the question, given the gross disparity in coercive power between the state and the peasant. But there is one basic similarity between the riots in the 1950s and those in the 1990s, and that is the provocative role played by local cadres. Cadres always seem to provide the last straw, the straw that breaks the peasants' backs and drive them to revolt.

The conditions that contributed to reactive peasant actions also facilitated proactive peasant actions. This second type of peasant movements consisted of group raids on public (state) property. Sometimes, during the process of these actions, peasants of one village came into violent conflict with those of another village because they had staked out a claim on the same public property. In these cases, proactive collective action changed itself into "competitive action."[150]

Beginning in the late 1980s, the Chinese press frequently reported on groups of peasants, sometimes an entire village, that acted as one unit to raid state forests, industrial and communication installations (such as irrigation works, power lines, and oil pipelines), trains, and factories.[151] To defend its property, the Wuhan Iron and Steel Works built a high wall surrounding the factory that extended to forty-two kilometers and assigned a one-hundred-member patrol to maintain security. Even with that, peasant raids did not stop.[152] The official *China Daily* reported in April 1994 that the police had arrested over 1,000 peasants the year before for stealing power supply property and damaging facilities. The report stated: "Farmers in poor areas stole power and phone lines, transformers, and poles and sold them as scrap metal to waste recycling stations."[153]

These raids on state property are yet another form of the Chinese peasants' active resistance to their twin fate of marginalization and pauperization. The raiders are also prompted by their position in the periphery of the nation (especially those who robbed the state forests) and their proximity to highly valued property. On the surface, the peasants are simply trying to capture their share in the rising consummerism of the cities. But deep down the raids express rural alienation from the state and urban society. The withdrawal of the national state from the villages after Mao's death exposed in a bold way the Communist Party's total failure to establish a national identity and collective norms for the entire Chinese population.

Deviant Social Behavior

The various forms of peasants' specific public opinions that we have been describing are both symptoms and contributory causes of a general social disorganization in the Chinese countryside. In the 1990s, disorder in rural China has become a national and even international concern.[154] In a 1992 national poll, peasants distinguished themselves by naming "bad mainte-nance of social order" their first and foremost concern. Other social groups such as workers and employees ranked social disorder much lower among their concerns. The pollsters reported that "the peasants do not have a firm sense of safety."[155] In May 1994, the chief publication on Chinese legal affairs, *Fazhi Ribao* [Legal Daily], reported that a chaotic sit-uation existed in the countryside. It said:

> In a few places, serious cases of violence—including murders, explosions, injuries, and other incidents—have increased by a larger margin than in cities. . . . Various kinds of evil forces—including "village tyrants," "land tyrants," "water tyrants," "grain tyrants," and so-on—have emerged in a small number of rural areas and become a ferocious force that has jeopar-dized social security.[156]

Another report by the same newspaper said that in some rural areas, members of the traditional secret society, the Triads, have reemerged. "In some places clans and triads are now more powerful than the Communist Party."[157]

These reports named rural migrants as among some of the major cul-prits of the crimes. One account has it that "in the river valley areas of northern and southern Jiangsu, the alien population accounted for more than 60 percent of the crimes committed, and for more than 80 percent in some areas." The same report said that, in Guangdong, 70 to 95 percent of the crimes were committed by migrants and escaped prison inmates.[158] Aside from these statistics, the authorities have yet to come up with any specific cases to prove that migrants are responsible for many of the crimes. At times, the national government threatens migrants with possi-ble forcible return to the countryside. A government spokesperson declared that the state might "impose tough administrative measures to make migrants choose between giving up their contracted land and returning home to keep it."[159] However, a visiting U.S. scholar warned the Chinese government that "stability may be threatened more by trying to reverse the migration trend."[160] The Chinese government should have known better. In 1989, the state did send millions of migrants back to the countryside. The result was increasing cases of crimes in rural areas.[161]

However, blaming the rising rate of deviant social behavior in the countryside on the migrants is to mistake the symptom for the cause. It is the state's forty-odd years of urban bias that is the real cause of rural deviance. It may be a sign of the Dengist state's desperation that the national press now talks about establishing a system of collective security in the countryside, which seems to be similar to the notorious *baojia* system of the past. Under the Nationalist government, ten peasant households were organized into a *jia*; each *bao* contained ten *jias*. Members of this collective security system were held accountable for each other's social and political conduct. In the past the CCP always denounced the *baojia* as "fascist." Nevertheless, in 1994, the main journal of the CCP Central Committee advocated a system of "joint defense among ten households."[162] Whether the CCP will retrieve the *baojia* system from history is a moot point at the time of this writing. But Beijing should know that the *baojia* did not arrest social disorganization in the countryside before 1949. After all, the Nationalists lost the civil war to the Communists. No externally imposed system of collective security is likely to work in the Chinese countryside since the causes of the present disorder lie in the state's long-term marginalization and pauperization of the peasantry.

Institutional Fluidity: The Rise of *Gemeinschaft*

Whether there will ever be institutionalized public opinion in the Chinese countryside in the future depends on the types of institutions that interest the peasants or their capability in establishing them among themselves. This stress on the prospects for institutionalized public opinion is because it insures timely feedback and signifies a fundamental change in the status of the peasants.

The major rural *intermediary* institutions in post-Mao China may be classified into three types in terms of the social relation that they embody: *gemeinschaft, gesellschaft,* and mixed (as shown in Table 2.4). I did not include the Party organization—the Party branches—in the table since it is not an intermediary organization.

By all accounts, the *gesellschaft* institutions to which the state attached great significance are the weak ones in the sense that peasants do not use them as frequently as they do the other institutions. The strong ones are the *gemeinschaft* and the mixed types: clan, affinal group, and rural enter-

Table 2.4   Rural Intermediary Organizations

Gemeinschaft	Mixed	Gesellschaft
Clan	Affinal group	Village committee
		Economic cooperatives
	Township	Technical-aid association
	enterprises	Trade association

prise. In this, as in other matters dealing with rural society, the Chinese state persistently misjudged the peasants.

Gesellschaft Institutions

Officially, the Dengist state seemed to have put considerable stock in the newly established village committees. The state's declared intention was for peasants to govern themselves through these committees. The state structure stopped at the townships, which oversaw the villages in China, leaving the latter to practice self-rule. The committees were supposed to represent genuine local democracy; its members were elected by the peasants. In theory, village committees were held accountable to the "village assemblies," which included all village residents aged eighteen or older.[163] According to the Dengist state, villages were presumed to own some economic cooperatives. In 1990 it was reported that 70 percent of the villages had created these.[164] The state also envisioned dynamic rural development led by the village committees and economic cooperatives.

In reality, as many studies by Chinese scholars have reported, village committees are primarily agents of the township governments. Their main tasks are collecting taxes, carrying out state-assigned birth control measures, assigning the state's grain-requisitioning quotas, and managing land and public facilities. The only major function of village committees that may be considered social is the mediation of disputes among villages.[165] Chinese scholar Zhou Wei compared the functions of village committees with affinal groups and families in forty Shandong villages (as presented in Table 2.5). He found that village committees carried out state functions, such as the clarification of rules and regulations and the assignment of mandatory farm tasks (amount of grain to be planted, for example). Zhou asked peasants the following question: "In general, when you encounter problems (such as lack of cooperation in production and need for mediation in disputes) in daily life, which you cannot solve within your family, to whom do you turn for help?" Only one-third of the respondents said they would ask cadres in the village committee for help. More would go to their relatives (39 percent) or neighbors (19 percent). Zhou reported that, in one village, peasants derided the head of the village committee whose standard reply to the peasants was: "The higher-ups said so."

Like the collectives under Mao's rule, these village committees were conceived by the state and the so-called legislators in the city. As far as one can determine, peasants were never consulted as to the need for or acceptability of the committees. At the time of deliberation by the "legislators", there were some doubts about the viability of the committees. Some had suggested that these committees were but new names for the old communal units of the "production brigades".[166] Today, the commune has recovered its old, pre–1949 title of township. It is not surprising that

Table 2.5 Rural Organizations and Their Functions in Forty
             Administrative Villages in Southwest Shandong

Function	Village committee	Affinal group	Family	Others
Rules and regulations	77.90	1.40	17.90	2.80
Assigning farm task	92.90	2.10	5.00	0
Purchasing farm input	7.14	66.43	20.00	6.43
Sale of produce	5.00	75.00	15.00	5.00
Obtaining technical know-how	19.29	15.00	64.29	1.42

Source: Zhou Wei, "Xiangcun Shehui Zuzhi Xinshidi Xianshi Zhuangkuang Yu Fazhan
Qushi," [The present condition and trend of village social organizations], *Shehuixue*
[Sociology], no. 5 (1991): 110.

these urban-conceived entities did not become "self-governing" institutions of the peasants. Data from village studies and polls show that peasants generally paid little attention to the public affairs of their villages. For example, the survey of a Sichuan county that was mentioned earlier found that peasants discussed the rate of the state's withholding their incomes (70 percent of the respondents) more frequently than they did the production planning of their villages (21 percent).[167] Other polls found that, in some villages, peasants could not even name the heads of their village committees.[168]

The existence of economic cooperatives varied widely among the regions. The survival of these cooperatives is closely connected with the decollectivization process discussed earlier. It was shown that decollectivization went much further in the central and western regions of China than it did in the eastern region. The number of economic cooperatives in a locality is inversely related to the decollectivization process. Table 2.6 illustrates my point. It is in the eastern provinces that one sees the significant, albeit declining, collective-farming support services that are provided by the cooperatives.

A number of Chinese scholars expressed hope that the cooperative service organizations in the countryside would foster a strong associational sentiment among peasants. They thought that a kind of civic culture would emerge from these collective economic actions. But by the 1990s, they were disillusioned by the fact that farming support services remained the "weak link" in village lives. Where these farming support services did exist, they were controlled by cadres and were not the result of peasant cooperation.[169]

Table 2.6 Percentages of Villages with Collective-Farming Support Services

	East Region		Central Region		West Region	
	1984	1987	1984	1987	1984	1987
Mechanized farming	80	76	40	34	27	20
Irrigation	87	85	43	36	25	16
Seed improvement	55	46	34	17	28	15
Chemical fertilizer	56	50	38	30	27	21
Pesticide	57	51	39	26	26	23
Diesel oil	76	65	48	29	35	20
Plastic sheet	57	45	58	37	54	36

Source: Wang Haiquan, Qu Linfeng, and Wu Dage, "Jiaqiang Woguo Nongcun Cunjizuzhi Jianshe Wenti Qianlun," [A preliminary discussion on strengthening the village organization construction of our country], *Nongye Jingji* [Agricultural Economy], no. 10 (1990): 54.

A few Chinese writers were bold enough to suggest the organization of peasant associations for the representation and protection of peasant interest. One even used the peasant associations in Taiwan as an example for the mainland Chinese to emulate.[170] But the talks on organizing peasant associations touched sensitive nerves. There were fears that the associations might turn into opposition groups, pressure groups, or yet another bureaucratic establishment providing sinecure for cadres.[171]

The early 1990s saw the state advocating associations of an economic and technical-aid nature, instead of peasant associations. A 1993 report stated that there were some 130,000 technical-aid societies in the rural areas, which were organized by commercial farmers or local governments. But these associations were concentrated in the eastern region, especially in suburban areas.[172] It should be noted that the proportion of commercial farmers in China was 1.7 percent of all peasant households in 1988.[173] In 1994 a campaign was launched by provincial governments to foster associations among the peasants for marketing purposes. These are known as "peasant trade associations." Like the village committees, these so-called associations are primarily state-sponsored.[174] The campaign obviously is part of the state's response to the general depression in the countryside. In advocating peasant associations of a trade or a technical-aid nature, the state once more refuses to deal with the crux of the numerous problems in the countryside. A Guangdong agricultural official described the peasant predicament well: "The peasants are scattered. Their interest is easily violated. Whenever there is any [national difficulty] the interests of other groups cannot be infringed upon and so [the state] reaches its arms to take things from the peasants with impunity."[175]

Mixed Institutions

In contrast to the feebleness of all the *gesellschaft* institutions, the two mixed organizations—the affinal groups (based on interfamily coopera-tion) and the rural enterprises—are growing fast, especially the latter. These institutions possess qualities of both *gemeinschaft* and *gesellschaft*. Affinal groups or enterprises are based on kinship through marriage. Township enterprises are primarily based on common habitat. At the same time, the main purpose of these two institutions is for business. Their organizations are amorphous with respect to membership and ownership. Moreover, the title "township enterprises" is misleading, since most of the firms are not owned by the township but by villages and families. There are five types of "township enterprises," commonly referred to as the "five wheels" of the countryside. They are firms owned by townships, villages, community groups (primarily neigh-bors), affinal groups, and single families. In 1991, 26 percent of all rural enterprises were owned by townships; the rest were owned by villages and other groups.[176]

The strength of the affinal institutions varies widely from area to area. In Jiangsu, for example, rural enterprises are primarily owned by the township or even the county. The proportion of income earned by the affi-nal enterprises was a mere 0.88 percent of the total in 1988. But in the famous Wenzhou Municipality in Zhejiang, where the primary form of rural firms is family-owned, the proportion of income earned by affinal institutions constituted 68 percent of the total in 1988.[177]

"Township enterprises" are the most spectacular kind of rural institu-tions. Their growth in the post-Mao period has been phenomenal. By 1993, the total number of rural workers in these enterprises amounted to 112 mil-lion.[178] The year before that, more than half of China's net increase in gross domestic product and 68 percent of the net increase in tax revenue came from township enterprises.[179] In 1994 the output of these rural firms accounted for 45 percent of China's total export value.[180] Finally, these enter-prises accomplished the ultimate goal of auto-marginalization. In 1993 the state announced that, for the first time in Chinese history, the income from nonfarm occupations in rural areas exceeded that from farm work. The non-farm revenue constituted 64.7 percent of total rural income in 1992.[181]

These rural firms, however, are still amorphous in nature. There is ambiguity in the ownership status of the enterprises. One recent account described the situation as follows: "Ownership is shared by everybody, while none is responsible for the enterprise; responsibilities for property rights are unclear, and so are the respective responsibilities for adminis-trative duties and enterprise management; rural administrative leaders frequently interfere arbitrarily with enterprises."[182] The state is now pushing for the "third reform wave" of these enterprises—turning them into shareholding institutions. In the meantime, the firms are facing new challenges. Under the new tax law of 1994, the rural firms lost their tax-exemption status. They are also subject to new regulations, especially on pollution, and to increased competition from large state firms that are rapidly entering the market. The latter have more revenues and advanced technology. Township enterprises already seem to be reeling from the competition. The proportion of firms running a deficit increased from 9 percent in 1993 to 16 percent in the first quarter of 1994.[183]

As befitting their amorphous nature, township enterprises are multifunctional institutions, like traditional shops. They provide jobs for surplus rural labor, income for cadres, revenues for rural governments, taxes for the state, and welfare services to the poor in the villages. Most significant of all, township enterprises have become the raison d'être of the township administration and the village committees. In today's China, whether or not a local state administration is efficient depends on the number of township enterprises in the area.[184] Chinese sociologist Fei Xiaotong, an ardent supporter of township enterprises, attributes to these undertakings some crucial national functions: the reduction or eventual termination of the urban-rural gap, the diminution in number of rural migrants in the cities, and a contribution to urbanization in rural China.[185]

If township enterprises survive the new challenges in the 1990s, they will have the potential for fostering a "civil society." These firms create a culture of pragmatism and *gesellschaft*. Earlier, I mentioned that the new rural entrepreneurs are in an anxious mood. But, at the same time, they are also the ones who are more politically aware and make active demands upon the state for the right to participate in policymaking. Politically oriented cadres may yet be resocialized into accepting a business ethos, somewhat like the transformation of the former samurais into business managers in nineteenth-century Japan.

Gemeinschaft Institutions

While township enterprises have received wide acclaim from the state and the Chinese public, the reverse is true for clans. The resurgence of clans is one of the most striking developments in rural China following the death of Mao. It aroused anxiety and provoked severe criticism from the state. For peasants, however, clans represent their traditional autonomy and a time-tested mode of survival that is superior to anything the Chinese state had ever offered them. "If the peasants were given a chance to choose one organization for their self-rule," wrote Chinese scholar Qian Hang, "many would pick the organization that they are most familiar with—the clan. In reality, this is no longer a hypothetical statement; it has already come about."[186] Clan revival is of crucial importance to the study of peasant public opinion, especially regarding the peasants' capability for collective action.

Reports from China have indicated that clans were able to gather a large following—sometimes in the thousands—for some collective undertakings. Of considerable interest were the rural cadres who were ineffective in mobilizing peasants for collective production in Mao's time but became highly efficacious in organizing the villagers once they assumed positions in the clans.

Like any cultural activity in China, clan revival varies according to region. That it is, on the whole, a nationwide phenomenon is without question, as the fifteen-village survey by Wang Huning and his associates has shown.[187] Everywhere the symbols, rituals, and authoritative relationships of clans have been restored. Clan books or genealogies *(jiapu)* have been reissued and clan temples *(zongci)* rebuilt. Clan elders *(zulao)* have been reappointed and clan rules *(zugui)* imposed on the members, especially those pertaining to marriages and funerals. Ceremonial and recreational activities organized by clans have been revived and many Communist cadres have taken the lead in participating.[188] The resumption of clan activities seems to be most vigorous in southern China, especially in Hunan, Jiangxi, Fujian, and Guangdong.[189] These areas were strong in clan organizations before 1949. That they have now staged a strong comeback is yet another piece of clear evidence demonstrating the CCP's failure to offer Chinese peasants a superior way of survival.

There are two major reasons for the resurgence of clans: spiritual and practical. Clans, as Qian Hang pointed out, provide peasants with both the means and the cultural framework for connecting themselves with history and the universe. Identification with the clan is the peasant's way of self-actualization.[190] The CCP's efforts to supplant this traditional identity of the peasants with Marxism and socialism were in vain. Practically speaking, with the decollectivization and marketization of the Chinese economy, peasants need clans for cooperative economic undertakings. The return of clans bespeaks of the underdeveloped nature of rural economic infrastructure.[191] The Party-state's strategy of marginalizing and pauperizing the peasantry must be one of the most important reasons for the revival of clans.

But Chinese scholars also point out that the present clans are but shadows of their counterparts before 1949. Nowadays, their organizations are not as elaborate and the authority of clan elders is not as extensive or powerful as in the past.[192] In areas where commercialization is advanced, clans are rivaled by affinal groups. The latter are more *gesellschaft* than *gemeinschaft* and, hence, more adaptive to the market than the clans.[193] These days, the functions of clan elders are primarily internal, maintaining some basic norms of the clans. Adaptation to the external environment, such as politics and commerce, is now the job of younger and better-educated members of the clans.[194] This metamorphosis of the post-Mao clans seems to be in tune with the universal trend. While commenting on the role of aged political leaders across the cultures, David Gutmann observed: "Older persons are less (rather than more) apt to control resources that have to do with pragmatic, economic production, but, by the same token, their grip over the ritual sources of sacred powers increases with age."[195] Undoubtedly, aside from the growing complexity of external socioeconomic conditions, repression by the Communist Party-state for thirty years also must have contributed to the weakening of clans. This does not contradict my earlier observation that the Party-state's urban bias contributed to the strong revival of clans. Like the effect of colonial rule on traditional authority in the former colonies, the Communist rule undermined, but did not destroy, clan authorities.

Clans both reflect and reinforce rural social segmentation. They are the results of geographical and cultural divisions within China. Thus, from the national perspective that Chinese commentators on clans always take, clans are a divisive force. Clans are blamed for increasing disunity among villagers, usurping the Party-state authority in the countryside, and inciting clan warfare among peasants.[196] More specifically, clans are said to have caused the following: (1) hindered village economic development by practicing nepotism, (2) prevented the establishment of the rule of law in the countryside, (3) interfered with the government's new marriage law, (4) obstructed the state's birth control program among the peasants, and (5) constrained individual liberty and personal fulfillment.[197] But in reality, the roles of clans vary widely from place to place. Qian Hang, for example, found that, in the central region of Jiangxi Province, clans cooperated with the local administration to maintain social order. Peasants there did not regard clans as a rival to state authority.[198]

From the peasants' or clans' perspective, they operate within a limited social milieu in which they are able to mobilize resources for the collective good. For valuable insights on the interaction between clans and their milieu, I used the field data gathered from fifteen villages across China by Wang Huning and his associates in 1988–1989.[199] Each village's history, social structure, and economic conditions were recorded. The most pertinent data for my purpose were the distribution of families with the same surnames in each village. Those with the same surname belong to a single clan and, more often than not, share a common habitat, which is referred to as a "natural village" *(zirancun)*. My purpose was to see if there was any connection between the clan composition of a village and the propensity of the village to take collective action. I found seven patterns of clan distribution in the fifteen villages as presented in Table 2.7.

The first pattern—unipolarity—is the simplest: the single-clan village. Members of the village share the same surname and identify one another as relatives. The Sanjiang Village in Jiangxi has this type of unipolar-clan presence. The village has a history of taking collective action. Its village committee is entirely absorbed in the clan organization and is one of the few that is efficient in managing public (clan) affairs. Sanjiang is powerful enough to have incorporated some outlying villages as its protectorates. Significantly, Sanjiang is also well known for the social mobility of some of its members who, in both pre-and post-Communist eras, had illustrious careers in the

Table 2.7   Pattern of Clan Structure in Fourteen Villages

Pattern	Distribution of families with same surnames
Unipolar[a]	Single surname for entire village
Hegemonic[b]	Members of one clan constituting over 70 percent of the village population
Semi-hegemonic[c]	One big clan and several small families
Bipolar[d]	Two big clans constituting 80 percent of the village population
Multipolar(A)[e]	Near-equal distribution of population among all the clans
Multipolar(B)[f]	One medium-sized clan (for example, with 17 percent of the population) and a number of small clans
Nonpolar[g]	An entire village consisting of small families

[a] Jiangxi, Sanjiang cun.

[b] Guangxi, Lu cun; Sichuan, Yiwanshui cun; Gansu, Suiquan cun; Hebei, Guojiahe cun.

[c] Gansu, Dongjiazhuang; Shaanxi, Shanglubai cun; Zhejiang, Sanchaojienan cun; Guangdong, Chandang cun.

[d] Anhui, Lingang cun.

[e] Fujian, Hongjiang cun (Jiangtou area); Jiangsu, Guanzhuang cun.

[f] Jiangsu, Longtan cun; Zhejiang, Xiaoyi cun.

[g] Fujian, Hongjiang cun (Xiqiao area); and Lianoning, Hongliang cun

Source: Wang Huning, *Dangdai Zhongguo Cunluo Jiazu Wenhua* [The village and clan culture of contemporary China] (Shanghai: Renmin Chubanshe, 1991).

Chinese bureaucracy. One of the functions of the traditional Chinese clan was to provide scholarships for bright and promising clan youngsters. They were able to leave the countryside and make a career for themselves in the bureaucracy, thereby bringing honor and glory to the clan.

The second pattern, the hegemonic clan village, is dominated by a powerful "big family" *(dahu)*. One example is the Lu Village in Guangxi where the Jiang clan constitutes 90.47 percent of the population. It is also effective in undertaking collective action. For twenty or thirty years during Mao's time, cadres in the village were not able to renovate the village school and it deteriorated so badly that it endangered the lives of the pupils. In 1986 the Jiang clan took responsibility for repairing the school by apportioning to each household a percentage of the expenses. Even clan members who had moved to the city sent their contributions to the village. Within a year, a new school building was completed. But in Mao's time, villages with a hegemonic clan risked state repression. For one reason or another, the Lu Village escaped that fate. The other three villages in this category all experienced state repression and were therefore not particularly effective in collective actions. Instead, the clans in these villages staged a strong comeback. However, the villages generally remained divisive, in part due to the class struggles that the Maoist state had carried out.

All other patterns of clan distribution, from the semi-hegemonic to the nonpolar, vary in degrees of social fragmentation and lack any record of effective collective action. The only distinction is that those with semi-hegemonic, bipolar, and multipolar (A-type) patterns tend to have instances of internecine fights. The multipolar (B-type) and the nonpolar villages tend to be close to commercially and industrially developed areas; peasants in those villages are preoccupied with entrepreneurial and commercial activities, instead of internecine fights. This is especially true in Jiangsu, Zhejiang, and Fujian, all located in the fast-growing eastern coastal region. In summary, one is reminded of Fei Xiaotong's caveat: "In China, the term 'village' encompasses many different groups and ways of life. So if one wishes to study Chinese villages, he or she must first recognize that the villages in various areas of China are not identical."[200] In his study of rural society, Fei treated Chinese villages as if they were different ethnic tribes.

An important implication in conceptualizing Chinese villages as tribes is that tribal people are almost always involved in tribal warfare. Thus, with revival of clans in the post-Mao period, clan warfare also returned to the Chinese countryside. Violent village or clan fights may be thought of as perversions of the clan's capability to obtain collective goods. The usual causes of such violent conflicts are disputes over ownership of hills, water sources, fields, forests, roads, and houses.[201] In other words, the zero-sum conflicts between the state and the peasants in Mao's time changed to inter-clan or village conflicts in the post-Mao period. Occurring chiefly in central-southern Chinese provinces such as Jiangxi, Hunan, and Guangdong, clan fights began in the early 1980s and continues today. In 1982 alone, one prefecture in Hunan experienced 331 clan-organized fights, involving thousands of peasants.[202] In the county of Jian in Jiangxi Province, there were 73 incidents of clan wars from 1989 to 1991. These clashes involved from a few hundred to several thousand people. Many of them were killed or wounded. In one incident, when the police intervened, the participants laid siege to the township government's building and declared: "The students in Beijing demonstrated at Tian'anmen Square. We will attack the township government."[203] In May 1993, the municipal government of Guangzhou mobilized special teams of cadres to go to the countryside and stop clan fights. The Guangdong clans were then warring with each other, using guns and explosives. Their main dispute was over prime property.[204]

There is an interesting parallel between clan warfare in post-Mao China and ethnic violence in the former Yugoslavia and elsewhere in the former Soviet Union. In all these violent incidents, former Communist officials played a significant role in inciting the masses.[205] Clan warfare in southern China shows not only that the Party cadres are deeply involved in the fights, but also that the clans' attempts to obtain collective good may be easily perverted into collective bad. According to a report by two Chinese scholars, a typical scenario of clan or inter-village warfare starts with the cadres' organizing local enterprises. They hire exclusively members of their own clans. Other clans soon follow suit. Conflicts and fights between these exclusive clan groups become almost inevitable, given the limited land and other resources in the countryside. Reportedly, whenever the cadres are involved in the fights, the conflicts are on a larger scale than usual and are particularly violent.[206] Whether in the cases of ethnic wars in Eastern Europe or clan wars in China, the same factors seem to operate. These former Communist officials have political skills (organization and propaganda) and command national or local resources. The self-selective mechanism in occupation also means that Communist cadres are usually of certain personality types. The Chinese refer to these cadres as "specialists in struggle" (douzheng zhuanjia). The Maoist system, wrote Friedman, Pickowicz, and Selden, "penalized idealistic and democratic people and rewarded vengeful ones."[207] Now that these cadres' larger identity (either Communism or nationalism) has collapsed, the cadres displace their power motives and skills in political combat with fights over parochial identity.

The brief institutional survey of the countryside that I have done shows unmistakably that after the political culture of the Party-state was withdrawn, there arose not a civic culture but what Chinese scholars called "the village-clan culture" (cunluo jiazu wenhua).[208] Like what has happened in the former Communist states in Eastern Europe, in the Chinese countryside gemeinschaft rose after the collapse of the Communist universal order. But gemeinschaft institutions are not likely to deliver the peasants from their twin fate of marginalization and pauperization. Strengthening the clans may restore the peasants' sense of identity and dignity, but they still have to adapt to the increasingly complex socioeconomic conditions in the "national society" of China. The key seems to lie in intermediary gesellschaft institutions, which are woefully lacking in the Chinese countryside. Only these intermediary institutions, such as peasant associations elsewhere in East Asia, can connect the peasants with the relatively marketized urban society and safeguard the peasants' political rights as well.

Conclusion

Four generalizations may be made concerning the state-peasant relationship in China since the founding of the PRC in 1949. First, V. O. Key's observation about a basic division in U.S. public opinion applies to the Chinese situation as well. He wrote: "A major finding from all the analyses is that opinions among those occupational groups from which most political leaders, political activists, and political influentials come differ from those of groups lower in the occupational and class hierarchies."[209] In the U.S. context, Key said that these differences in opinion are not black or white, but vary in degree. In the segmented social context of China, however, the differences of opinion between the state builders, such as Mao, and the peasants, are that of kind, not of degree. A revolutionary state is particularly prone to alienation from popular mores, habits, customs, and values. This is even more true for revolutionists such as the Chinese Communists whose revolution was highly protracted. In this case, a distinct political culture emerged among the revolutionists. Their conflicts with various social groups such as the peasants were more dissensual than consensual. The former type of conflict stems from cultural incompatibility.[210] Such a revolutionary state is better described as a "hard," not a "strong," state in the sense that the state is disinclined to receive any goal-change feedback from society. Friedman, Pickowicz, and Selden pointed out that if the CCP cared to do so, there were plenty of lessons to learn from the peasants *before* 1949 concerning their opposition to collectivization.[211]

The second generalization concerns the power of opinion that stems from the elemental need of the masses. "Political art cannot undo what is elemental," wrote J. R. Vincent. "It cannot make a majority of those enjoying authority vote for its diminution, nor a majority of those without it habitually vote for their continued exclusion."[212] In the Chinese case, one may go further to say that the so-called political art of the CCP actively, but unwittingly, mobilizes the peasants and makes them into a diffused and loose public. The extremely exploitative actions of the Chinese state sharpen the boundary between the state and the peasants who, without conscious coordination, act as a class.

Third, the Chinese peasants' reactions to the Party-state over the decades also point to the problematic aspects of the state's gauging or exploiting latent opinion. In the U.S. context, Key wrote that latent opinion causes anxiety among politicians because they are not certain how the "silent majority" might react to a particular issue.[213] Politicians might anticipate the public's latent opinion by speculating on the ideas in people's heads and then adjusting their strategy accordingly. However, latent opinion might also be exploited by ambitious politicians and thus test political leaders' self-restraint.[214] The Chinese case illustrates how latent opinion lends itself to leaders' imagining mass support. In the early 1950s, Mao and the CCP believed that they alone among the Chinese truly "knew" the peasants. In a pugnacious speech directed at scholar Liang Shuming, Mao said: "Mr. Liang says that he is wiser than the Communist Party on the peasant question—will anybody believe that? . . . He asserts that he is better qualified than the Communist Party to represent the peasants, isn't that ridiculous?"[215] Socialist economic planner

Chen Yun said in 1953: "We Communists have cultivated a close relationship with the peasants through our long revolutionary struggle."[216] After the death of Mao, the peasants' opinions became explicit, no longer latent. But Deng and his associates are constrained by Mao's previous commitments to the urban population—promises made possible by exploiting the peasants. Even if Deng wished to change the state's long-standing urban bias (and there is no evidence that he does), he could not do so for fear of creating urban unrest.

Finally, the state and peasant interaction in China provides yet another piece of evidence of the power held by the seemingly powerless. Chinese peasants, as this chapter shows, have been denied even symbolic representation in the Chinese political system, since they do not have their own professional organization as the workers' do in their trade unions. But through their amorphous mass actions, Chinese peasants, more than any other group in Chinese society, have brought about the dissolution of the top leadership. Mao's break with his erstwhile colleagues (such as Liu Shaoqi and Marshal Peng Dehuai) and his decision to launch the disastrous Cultural Revolution were primarily caused by disputes over the peasant question. Today, peasants' actions to escape marginalization and pauperization have once more brought the stability of the state into question, this time the state led by Deng Xiaoping.

Notes

1. Taken from a speech entitled "What *Are* the Agricultural and Rural Problems?" (emphasis added), given at a 1994 conference on Chinese agriculture. See *Liaowang* [Looking farther], no. 18 (May 2, 1994), in Foreign Broadcast Information Service, *China Daily Report*, [hereafter cited as FBIS, *CHI/DR*], June 3, 1994, p. 36.

2. Louis Kriesberg, *Social Conflicts*, 2d ed. (Englewood Cliffs, N. J.: Prentice-Hall, 1982) p. 17.

3. For studies on the Chinese agricultural economy, see Nicholas R. Lardy, *Agriculture in China's Modern Economic Development* (Cambridge, England: Cambridge University Press, 1983); and Dwight Perkins and Shahid Yusuf, *Rural Development in China* (Baltimore and London: Johns Hopkins University Press, 1984).

4. Theda Skocpol, "France, Russia, China: A Structural Analysis of Social Revolutions," in *Revolutions*, ed. Jack A. Goldstone (Fort Worth, Tx.: Harcourt Brace College Publishers, 1994), p. 4. It is no wonder that Skocpol, who is not a Chinese specialist, believes that the CCP has achieved a genuine social revolution in the countryside even when evidence to back that idea is not clear. See her *States and Social Revolutions* (Cambridge, England: Cambridge University Press, 1979). For a similar view, see also the chapter on China in Eric R. Wolf, *Peasant Wars of the Twentieth Century* (New York: Harper and Row, 1969).

5. For Pool's discussion on mass media and rapid social change, see Ithiel de Sola Pool, "The Role of Communication in the Process of Modernization and

Technological Change," in *Industrialization and Society*, ed. Bert F. Hoselitz and Wilbert E. Moore (Mouton, The Netherlands: UNESCO, 1966), pp. 279–295.

6. Daniel Bell, *The End of Ideology* (Glencoe, Ill.: Free Press, 1960), p. 328.

7. Joel S. Migdal, *Strong Societies and Weak States* (Princeton: Princeton University Press, 1988), p. 4.

8. T. Shanin, "Defining Peasants: Conceptualizations and Deconceptualizations, Old and New in a Marxist Debate," in *Social Anthropology of Peasantry*, ed. Joan P. Mencher (Bombay: Somaiya Publications, 1983), p. 70, cited in Grant Evans, "The Accursed Problem: Communists and Peasants," *Peasant Studies* 15, no. 2 (Winter 1988): 86.

9. Kriesberg, *Social Conflicts*, chapter 5.

10. Feng Xianzhi, "Mao Zedong He Tade Mishu Tian Jiayin" [Mao Zedong and his secretary Tian Jiayin], part 2, *Qiushi*, no. 23 (1989): 37.

11. The interested reader might consult *Mao Tsetung Ssu-hsiang Wan-sui* [hereafter cited as *Wan-sui*], no. 2 (Beijing, 1969, reprint, Washington, D.C.: Center for Chinese Research Materials, 1969), p. 17, 29, 73, and 200.

12. The best account of the peasants' latent attitudes toward the CCP is Yuan-tsung Chen, *The Dragon's Village* (New York: Penguin Books, 1980).

13. Morton H. Fried, *Fabric of Chinese Society* (New York: Octagon Books, 1969), p. 225.

14. Shang Gedong, "Tugaihou Xiaonongjingjidi Fenghua Wenti" [The problem of polarization of the small farm economy after land reform], *Hsueh Hsi* 2, no. 9 (1950): 10.

15. *Renmin Ribao* [People's Daily] (hereafter cited as *RMRB*), April 20, 1953, in U.S. Consulate General in Hong Kong, *Survey of China Mainland Press (SCMP)*, no. 555, pp. 23–24; *RMRB*, April 17, 1953, in *SCMP*, no. 557, pp. 15–16.

16. These cases were taken from English translations of Chinese press accounts as published in *SCMP*, nos. 1087, 1092, 1096, 1098, 1133, 1602, 1638, 1649, 1652, 1656, 1663, 1675, 1698, 1723, 1746, 1757, 1775, and 1869; and U.S. Consulate General in Hong Kong, *Extracts from China Mainland Magazines* (hereafter cited as *ECMM*), no. 177.

17. See reports on peasant uprisings in *SCMP*, nos. 1087, 1092, 1096, 1098, 1133, 1602, 1638, 1649, 1652, 1656, 1663, 1675, 1698, 1723, 1746, 1757, 1775, and 1869; and *ECMM* no. 177.

18. Eric R. Wolf, "Peasants and Revolutions," in *Revolutions*, ed. Jack A. Goldstone (Fort Worth, Tex.: Harcourt Brace, 1994), pp. 55–63.

19. See also analysis by Elizabeth Perry, "Rural Violence in Socialist China," *China Quarterly*, no. 103 (September 1985): 414–440.

20. Evans, "The Accursed Problem," p. 76.

21. Liu Lantao, "Implement Correctly the Party's Rural Class Policy," *RMRB*, in *SCMP*, no. 1181, pp. 20–26.

22. *Hsin-hua Pan-yueh-kan*, no. 21 (1957): 89–90; no. 1 (1958): 64–66; no. 22 (1958): 30–31.

23. *Wan-sui*, no. 2, p. 281.

24. *Wan-sui*, no. 1, p. 49.

25. For examples from the field, see Anita Chan, Richard Madsen, and Jonathan Unger, *Chen Village* (Berkeley: University of California Press, 1984); Richard Madsen, *Morality and Power in a Chinese Village* (Berkeley: University of

California Press, 1984); and Huang Shu-min, *The Spiral Road* (Boulder: Westview Press, 1989).

26. For an eyewitness account of this campaign, see Liang Heng and Judith Shapiro, *Son of the Revolution* (New York: Random House, 1984), chapter 15.

27. Doug McAdam, "Micromobilization Contexts and Recruitment to Activism," in *From Structure to Action: Comparing Social Movement Research Across Cultures*, vol. 1, ed. Bert Klandermans, Hanspeter Kriesi, and Sidney Tarrow (Greenwich, Conn.: JAI Press, 1988), p. 132.

28. C. S. Chen, ed., *Rural People's Communes in Lien-Chiang*, trans. Charles Price Ridley (Stanford, Calif.: Hoover Institution Press, 1969), pp. 112–114.

29. For such a view, see Migdal, *Strong Societies.*

30. See the collection of Chinese press reports in U.S. Consulate General in Hong Kong, *Current Background,* no. 818 (1967): 11–78.

31. Lois Dougan Tretiak, "Feeding Revolution," *Far Eastern Economic Review,* October 26, 1967, p. 169.

32. Tian Fang and Lin Fashang, *Zhongguo Renkou Qianyi* [Population migration in China] (Beijing: Zhishi Chubanshe, 1987), p. 288.

33. "National Revolutionary Rebel Committee of Finance and Trade Organizations and Other Revolutionary Rebel Organizations Issue Urgent Announcement on Exercise of Stronger Market Control During the Spring Festival," *RMRB,* February 6, 1967, in *Current Background,* no. 818, p. 28.

34. "Jianjue Daji Fanggemin Jingjizhuyi Yaofeng" [Resolutely strike at the ill wind of counterrevolutionary economism], *Radio Nei Menggu,* CNA-PBS, January 12, 1968; "Qunzhong Zhuanzheng Weijian Diren" [Dictatorship of the masses attacking enemy], *Radio Nei Menggu,* China News Analysis-Provincial Broadcasting Stations (CNA-PBS), February 8, 1968.

35. The references to these were quite frequent in the official *RMRB* from 1979 to 1981. For example, see *RMRB,* May 2, 1980, p. 2; May 21, 1980, p. 3; and March 6, 1981, p. 2.

36. "Jiaqiang Lingdao, Gaohao Shuangqiang" [Strengthen leadership, manage well two rushes], *Radio Hunan,* CNA-PBS, July 9, 1972.

37. Liu Binyan, *Liu Binyan Baogao Wenxue Xuan* [Selections from Liu Binyan's reports] (Beijing: Beijing Chubanshe, 1981), p. 316.

38. *RMRB,* December 21, 1976, p. 3.

39. Lin Bai, Jing Guowen, Zhou Yilin, and Hu Fangsong, eds., *Wenzhou Moshi De Lilun Tansuo* [An exploration of the theoretical implications of the Wenzhou model] (Nanning: Guangxi Renmin Chubanshe, 1987).

40. Wu Xiang, "Yangguandao Yu Dumuqiao" [Broad road and the log bridge], *RMRB,* November 5, 1980, p. 2.

41. John H. Hamer, "Can the Collectivization of Agriculture Be Made Palatable Through Organization and Incentives?" *Peasant Studies* 15, no. 4 (Summer 1988): 233–251.

42. Victor Nee, "Peasant Household Individualism," in *Chinese Rural Development: The Great Transformation,* ed. William Parish, (Armonk, N. Y.: M. E. Sharp, 1985), pp. 164–190; see also Shulamith H. Potter and Jack M. Potter, *China's Peasants: The Anthropology of a Revolution* (Cambridge: Cambridge University Press, 1990), p. 210.

43. Edward Friedman, "Deng Versus the Peasantry: Recollectivization in the Countryside," *Problems of Communism* 39, no. 5 (September–October 1990): 32.

44. Edward Friedman, Paul G. Pickowicz, and Mark Seldan, *Chinese Village, Socialist State* (New Haven: Yale University Press, 1991), p. xxiii.

45. Paul Wehr, *Conflict Regulation* (Boulder: Westview Press, 1979); Kriesberg, *Social Conflicts*, pp. 155–156.

46. Jeffery M. Paige, *Agrarian Revolution* (New York: Free Press, 1975), p. 20.

47. *Liaowang*, no. 18 (May 2, 1994), in FBIS, *CHI/DR*, June 3, 1994, p. 33.

48. David Zweig, "Opposition to Change in Rural China: The System of Responsibility and People's Communes," *Asian Survey* 23, no. 7 (July 1983): 879–900; Chan, Madsen, and Unger, *Chen Village;* Jonathan Unger, "Remuneration, Ideology, and Personal Interests in a Chinese Village, 1960–1980," in *Chinese Rural Development*, ed. Parish, pp. 117–140; David Zweig, "Peasants, Ideology, and New Incentive System: Jiangsu Province, 1978–1981," in *Chinese Rural Development*, ed. Parish, pp. 141–163; Jonathan Unger, "The Decollectivization of the Chinese Countryside: A Survey of Twenty-eight Villages, *Pacific Affairs* 58, no. 4 (Winter 1985–1986); and Jean C. Oi, *State and Peasant in Contemporary China* (Berkeley: University of California Press, 1989).

49. For an official view of that, see *Beijing Review* 29, no. 49 (December 8, 1986). For scholarly analysis, see G.J.R. Linge and D. K. Forbes eds., *China's Spatial Economy* (Hong Kong: Oxford University Press, 1990); Dali Yang, "Patterns of China's Regional Development Strategy," *China Quarterly*, no. 122 (June 1990); and Fuh-Wen Tzeng, "The Political Economy of China's Coastal Development Strategy: A Preliminary Analysis," *Asian Survey* 31, no. 3 (March 1991).

50. Du Rensheng, "Nongye Shengchan Zerenzhi Yu Nongcun Jingji Tizhigaige" [The agricultural responsibility system and the reform of the agricultural economic system], *Hongqi* [Red Flag], no. 19 (1981): 20.

51. Guo Jiaoyang, "Gansu: Dongjiazhuan" [Gansu: The village of Dongjia], in Wang Huning, *Dangdai Zhongguo Cunluo Jiazu Wenhua* [The village and clan culture in contemporary China] (Shanghai: Renmin Chubanshe, 1991), p. 496.

52. Fei Xiaotong, "Chongfang Yunnan Sancun" [Revisit three villages in Yunnan], *Shehuixue*, no. 1 (1991): 145.

53. Aiguo Lu and Mark Selden, "The Reform of Land Ownership and the Political Economy of Contemporary China," *Peasant Studies* 14, no. 4 (Summer 1987): 232.

54. *RMRB*, January 11, 1979, p. 2; June 17, 1979, p. 2.

55. *RMRB*, November 24, 1981, p. 2.

56. Thomas Bernstein, "Ideology and Rural Reform: The Paradox of Contingent Stability," in *State and Society in China*, ed. Arthur Lewis Rosenbaum (Boulder: Westview Press, 1992), pp. 143–44.

57. Kuang Di, "Village and Peasant: The Dynamics and Transformation of China's Rural Reform" [in Chinese], in *Papers of the Center for Modern China* 4, no. 4 (April 1993): 4.

58. *RMRB*, October 26, 1986, p. 4.

59. *Chung-kuo Shih-pao* [China Times], June 21, 1992, p. 10.

60. For more descriptions of these conflicts, see David Zweig, "Prosperity and Conflict in Post-Mao Rural China," *China Quarterly*, no. 105 (March, 1986).

61. See Elizabeth J. Perry, "Rural Collective Violence: The Fruits of Recent Reforms," in *The Political Economy of Reform in Post-Mao China*, ed. Elizabeth J. Perry and Christine Wong (Cambridge, Mass.: Council on East Asian Studies, Harvard University, 1985), pp. 175–194.

62. See, for example, the description of Guangxi Province in Zhang Zhenggui and Lu Jiaxiang, "Chujijieduan Yinchongfengrenshi Guangxi Yumeixin Pinkun" [We must understand fully Guangxi province's poverty due to ignorance during the primary stage of socialism], *Shehuixue* [Sociology], no. 3 (1989): 101–108.

63. See the reports on Baoding in *RMRB*, January 21, 1983; May 3, 1983; November 14, 1983; and November 19, 1983. The national press reports about the social breakdowns in northern Jiangsu and Anhui also suggested this type of dynamics; see *RMRB*, August 3, 1981, p. 4; and August 9, 1981, p. 5.

64. Liang Shu-ming, *Hsiang-ts'un chien-she li-lun* [Theory of rural construction] (Tsou-p'ing: Hsiang-ts'un shu-tien, 1937).

65. *Ming Pao*, August 18 and 23, and October 17, 1979; also reported in a dissident journal, *Zhanwang*, September 1, 1979, in Case Team of the Collection of the Mainland Underground Publications, *Ta-lu Ti-hsia K'an-wu H'ui-pien*, book 4 (Taipei: Institute for the Study of Chinese Communist Problems, 1980), p. 29.

66. *RMRB*, April 12, 1988.

67. Du Rensheng, "Guanyu Xibei Diqu Nongye Wenti" [Concerning the agricultural problems in the Northwest], *Nongye Jingji* [Agricultural Economy], no. 12 (1993): 22–27.

68. "He Kang on Shortages," *Xinhua* [New China News Agency], January 16, 1988, in FBIS, *CHI/DR*, January 20, 1988, p. 13.

69. For an expert and more comprehensive analysis of these problems of the peasants, see Robert F. Ash, "The Peasant and the State," *China Quarterly*, no. 127 (September 1991): 493–520.

70. Jiang Li, "Shehuizhuyi Shichang Jingji Tiaojianxia Nongye Mianlindi Wenti" [Problems that agriculture faces in a socialist economy], *Nongye Jingji* [Agricultural Economy], no. 12 (1993): 28–31; Zhang Yuanhong, "Gaijing Nongye Zhengce Jiaqian Hongguan Tiaokun" [Improve agricultural policy, strengthen macro-controls], *Nongye Jingji*, no. 12 (1993): 38–40.

71. Chen Yanxin, "Lun Zhengfu Yu Nongmin Guanxide Gaige" [On reform of the relationship between the state and the peasant], *Nongye Jingji* [Agricultural Economy], no. 3 (1988): 11–14.

72. *China Daily*, September 29, 1992, p. 4. The most detailed account of the local government's control over peasants is Oi, *State and Peasant*.

73. "Low Income of Farmers Affects Growth," *China Daily*, November 25, 1991, p. 4.

74. *China Daily*, February 2, 1994.

75. "Nongcun Jiujing Fashengle Shenme Wenti?" [Just what sort of problems have taken place in the countryside?], *Nongye Jingji* [Agricultural Economy], no. 12 (1993): 14–17.

76. Wang Changyi, "Xiandai Nongcun Nixiang Xinli Qianlun" [A general discussion on the spirit of contrariness in contemporary villages], *Shehuixue* [Sociology], no. 5 (1989): 111–114.

77. Fan Hensheng, "Dongqian Nongmin Taiduqinxiang Chutan" [A preliminary study of the attitudes of contemporary peasants], *Nongye Jingji* [Agricultural Economy], no. 10 (1989): 19–22.

78. Li Sheng, Jian Shiming, and Li Xueming, "Chongqing Baxian 450 Nonghu Shenghuozhiliangdi Diaocha" [A survey of the quality of life of 450 families in Ba county of Chongqing], *Shehuixue* [Sociology], no. 5 (1990): 101–108.

79. "Nongmindui Xinchutaidi Jixiang Nongcunzhengcedi Fangyang" [The peasants' reactions to several new state policies], *Nongye Jingji* [Agricultural Economy], no. 9 (1993): 20–23.

80. "Lianggai" [Reform in grains], *Nongye Jingji* [Agricultural Economy], no. 4 (1993): 155–162.

81. *RMRB*, April 12, 1988.

82. *Shijie Ribao* [World Press Journal] (Los Angeles), May 3, 1992.

83. Evans, "The Accursed Problem," p. 86.

84. Chen Yanxin, "Lun Zhengfu Yu Nongmin," p. 12; see also, Wang Changyi, "Lun Tigao Woguo Nongmin Zuzhihua Chengdu" [On enhancing the organization of the peasants of our country], *Nongye Jingji* [Agricultural Economy], no. 7 (1990): 36–39.

85. Zhang Yuanhong, "Gaijing Nongye Zhengce," p. 39.

86. *Liaowang*, no. 18 (May 2, 1994), in FBIS, *CHI/DR*, June 3, 1994, p. 37.

87. Li Wangsheng, "Nongmin Tuitian Paohuang Xianxiangdi Yuanyin Yu Duice" [The causes of and policy toward the peasants' abandoning and wasting the land], *Nongye Jingji* [Agricultural Economy], no. 1 (1993): 154–155.

88. Chen Jiyuan and Xia Defang, eds., *Xiangzhen Qiye Moshi Yanjiu* [A study of models of rural enterprises] (Beijing: Zhongguo Shehuikexue Chubanshe, 1988), pp. 355–356.

89. Lu Xueyi, Zhang Houyi, and Zhang Qizi, "Zhuanxin Shiqi Nongmindi Jiecheng Fenhua" [Differentiation among the peasants during a period of transition], *Nongye Jingji* [Agricultural Economy], no. 8 (1992): 35–49.

90. Yin Jitang and Wen Tianfei, "Nongminxinwei Moxin Yunongmin Shengchanjijixin" [Patterns of peasant behavior and productive initiativeness], *Nongye Jingji* [Agricultural Economy], no. 5 (1991): 9.

91. See, for example, the conditions in Gansu in Duan Huamin, "Zhongguo Bufada Diqu Nongcunshehuidi Jiecheng Jiegou" [Rural status structure in China's underdeveloped areas], *Shehuixue* [Sociology], no. 6 (1990): 121–125.

92. Li Wenzhao, "Yongjiaxian Nongmin Jiechengdi Bianhua He Fazhan Qushi" [Changes and prospects of peasant status in Yongjia County], *Nongye Jingji* [Agricultural Economy], no. 3 (1992): 60–63.

93. Mancur Olson Jr., "Rapid Growth as a Destablizing Force," *Journal of Economic History*, no. 23 (1963): 529–552.

94. Xiao Wentao, "Dui Yanhai Kaifangdiqu Nongcun Shehui Jiecheng Fenhua Zuhe Zhuangkuangdi Jiban Fenxi" [A basic analysis of differentiation and combination of rural social strata in the open and coastal areas], *Nongye Jingji* [Agricultural Economy], no. 8 (1992): 54.

95. Fei Xiaotong, "Chongfang Yunnan Sancun," p. 144.

96. "Dui Baijia Nongcun Siyin Qiye Diaochadechubu Fenxi" [A preliminary analysis of a survey of a hundred private businesses in rural areas], *Nongye Jingji* [Agricultural Economy], no. 7 (1989): 75–80.

97. "Guangzhoushi Fanyuxiangertihu Siyinqiyezhu Jiecheng Zhuankuangde Fenxi" [An analysis of the condition of owners of private businesses and the self-employed in Fanyu County of Guangzhou], *Nongye Jingji* [Agricultural Economy], no. 5 (1990): 53.

98. John Markoff, "Contexts and Forms of Rural Revolt: France in 1789," *Journal of Conflict Resolution*, 30, no. 2 (June 1986): 285.

99. Song Dianliang, "Liaoning: Hongliang Cun" [Liaoning: Hongliang Village], in Wang Huning, *Dangdai Zhongguo Cunluo,* p. 564.

100. Lai Songmin, Lu Chaojun, and Zheng Changjing, "Xian Jieduan Nongminde Xianzhuan, Xinli Tezheng Yu Nongcun Zhengce," [The present condition of the peasants, their psychology, and policy toward the villages], *Nongye Jingji* [Agricultural Economy], no. 3 (1990): 164–166.

101. Chen Weiqun, "Woguo Nongcun Luohoutiqudi Xianzhuan Jiqijingjifazhan" [The present condition of the agriculturally underdeveloped areas and their economic development], *Nongye Jingji* [Agricultural Economy], no. 11 (1988): 27–36.

102. Zhang Zhenggui and Lu Jiaxiang, "Chuji Jieduan Yinchongfeng Renshi Guangxi Yumeixin Pinkun" [We must understand fully the ignorance and backwardness of Guangxi during the primary stage of socialism], *Shehuixue* [Sociology], no. 3 (1989): 101–108.

103. Nicholas D. Kristof and Sheryl WuDunn, *China Wakes* (New York: Random House, 1994), chapter 3.

104. Li Qiang, "Lun Pinkundi Wenhua" [On the culture of poverty], *Shehuixue* [Sociology], no. 1 (1990): 158–169; and Song Fuquan, "Pinkunxianxiade Jingjiwenhua Tezheng" [The economic cultural characteristics of poverty], *Shehuixue* [Sociology], no. 2 (1989): 141–144.

105. Edward C. Banfield, *The Moral Basis of a Backward Society* (Chicago: Research Center in Economic Development and Cultural Change, University of Chicago in association with the Free Press, 1958).

106. Alessandro Pizzorno, "Amoral Familism and Historical Marginality," *International Review of Community Development,* no. 15 (1966): 55–66.

107. Liu Ping, "Woguo Dangqian Liuminde Teshuxin" [The characteristics of the current migrants of our country], *Renkouxue* [Demography], no. 5 (1989): 67.

108. Yang Yiyung, "Mingongchao Yu Nongcun Laodongli Zhuanyi" [Tides of migrant workers and transfer of rural labor force], *Nongye Jingji* [Agricultural Economy], no. 9 (1993): 95.

109. *Ming Pao* (Hong Kong), February 22, 1994, in FBIS, *CHI/DR,* February 22, 1994, pp. 26–27.

110. Yang Yiyung, "Minggongchao Yu Nongcun."

111. "Guanyu Nongcun Laodongli Liudongde Yanjiu" [A study on the movement of rural labor force], *Nongye Jingji* [Agricultural Economy], no. 8 (1993): 150–156.

112. Pamela E. Oliver, "Bringing the Crowd Back In: The Nonorganizational Elements of Social Movements," in *Research in Social Movements, Conflicts and Change,* vol. 11, ed. Louis Kriesberg (Greenwich, Conn.: JAI Press, 1989), p.24.

113. "Guanyu Nongcun Laodongli Liudongde Yanjiu" [A study on the movement of rural labor force], *Nongye Jingji* [Agricultural Economy], no. 8 (1993): 152.

114. *China Daily,* May 21, 1994, p. 4; I have also described this aspect in some detail in "Economic Reform, Mobility Strategies, and National Integration in China," *Asian Survey* 31, no. 5 (May 1991): 393–408.

115. Xi Mi, "Farmers Flock Like Birds to Seek Nest Eggs," *China Daily,* March 11, 1993, p. 4.

116.   Zhang Qingwu, "Woguo Liudong Renkou Fazhandi Licheng Yu Duice" [A history of the migrants of our country and countermeasures], *Renkouxue* [Demography], no. 1 (1992): 71–78.

117.   *China Daily,* January 10, 1994.

118.   *Radio Guiyang,* May 21, 1994, in FBIS, *CHI/DR,* May 26, 1994, p. 58.

119.   Wu Huailian, "Bashiniandai Nongmin Litu Langchao" [The tide of peasants' leaving farms in the 1980s], *Renkouxue* [Demography], no. 6 (1989): 71–79.

120.   Zhou Shaoshan and Wang Jianmin, "Zhongshi Qingnian Nongmindi Liushi Wenti" [We must pay attention to the problem of loss of young peasants], *Nongye Jingji* [Agricultural Economy], no. 3 (1990): 180–182.

121.   *China Daily,* March 11, 1993.

122.   *Xinhua,* June 27, 1994, in FBIS, *CHI/DR,* June 28, 1994, p. 56.

123.   Li Tan, "Population Flows into Big Cities," *Beijing Review,* no. 29 (July 1994), in FBIS, *CHI/DR,* July 20, 1994, p. 20.

124.   *China Daily,* June 28, 1993.

125.   *China Daily,* May 26, 1993, in FBIS, *CHI/DR,* May 28, 1993, p. 33.

126.   *Jingji Ribao* [Economic Daily], Beijing, October 9, 1990.

127.   FBIS, *CHI/DR,* March 29, 1994, p. 47.

128.   *Xinhua Ribao* [New China Daily] (Nanjing), March 5, 1994, in FBIS, *CHI/DR,* April 11, 1994, pp. 60–63.

129.   *South China Morning Post,* February 23, 1994, in FBIS, *CHI/DR,* February 23, 1994, p. 44.

130.   *Radio Haikou,* February 21, 1994, in FBIS, *CHI/DR,* February 23, 1994, p. 45.

131.   *Zhongguo Xinwenshe,* April 24, 1994, in FBIS, *CHI/DR,* April 25, 1994, p. 58.

132.   Potter and Potter, *China's Peasants,* chapters 5 and 15.

133.   *China Daily,* June 7, 1994.

134.   *Cheng Ming* (Hong Kong), May, 1993, p. 33.

135.   Charles Tilly, *From Mobilization to Revolution* (Reading, Mass.: Addison-Wesley Publishing, 1978), p. 145.

136.   Ibid., p. 147.

137.   See a few reports on this case in FBIS, *CHI/DR,* April 4, 1994, pp. 60–62. Other cases were reported in FBIS, *CHI/DR,* June 3, 1993 and April 19, 1994.

138.   *Zhongguo Qingnian Bao* [China Youth Paper], May 25, 1993, in FBIS, *CHI/DR,* June 2, 1993, p. 55.

139.   *Hsin Pao,* (Hong Kong), June 10, 1993, in FBIS, *CHI/DR,* June 10, 1993, pp. 10–15; *South China Morning Post,* June 13, 1993, in *FBIS, CHI/DR,* June 14, 1993, pp. 27–28; *Zhongguo Xinwen She,* June 12, 1993, FBIS, *CHI/DR,* June 14, 1993, pp. 28–29.

140.   See the Anhui case in *Cheng Ming,* September, 1993, p. 93; and the Shandong case in Wang Zhaojun, "Dalu Nongcun Xianzhuan Hechulu" [The present condition and prospects of the villages in mainland China], *Dangdai Zhongguo Yanjiu* [Modern China Studies] 1, no. 1 (January 1994): 69–81.

141.   Lu Xueyi, Zhang Houyi, and Zhang Qizi, "Zhuanxin Shiqi Nongmindi."

142.   *RMRB,* January 22, 1993.

143.   FBIS, *CHI/DR,* August 26, 1993, p. 24.

144.   *Eastern Express* (Hong Kong), March 4, 1994, in FBIS, *CHI/DR,* March 9, 1994.

145. Xie Liangjun, "Plan Is Devised to Cash Farmers' Overdue IOUs," *China Daily*, July 1, 1993, p. 3.

146. "IOUs Not Worth a Scrap of Paper," *China Daily*, May 26, 1993, p. 4.

147. Zhou Wei, "Xiangcun Shehui Zuzhi Xinshidi Xianshi Zhuangkuang Yu Fazhan Qushi" [The present condition and trends of social organizations in the villages], *Shehuixue* [Sociology], no. 5 (1991): 109–113.

148. Wang Shulin, "Dangqian Nongcun Shehui Liliangdi Bianhua Yu Wodangde Nongcun Zhengzhi Celue" [The current changes in rural social forces and our Party's political strategy in the villages], *Nongye Jingji* [Agricultural Economy], no. 12 (1992): 39–42.

149. FBIS, *CHI/DR*, June 10, 1993, p. 11.

150. Tilly, *From Mobilization to Revolution*, p. 144.

151. On raids to forests, see *RMRB*, August 8, 1987 and August 29, 1987; on raids to various industrial installations, see *RMRB*, October 23, 1990; on raids of trains passing by, see *RMRB*, August 7, 1990, and April 2, 1991; on raiding factories, see *RMRB*, June 15, 1991.

152. *RMRB*, June 15, 1991, p. 5.

153. FBIS, *CHI/DR*, May 3, 1994, p. 24.

154. Patrick E. Tyler, "Top Chinese Judge Warns of Serious Crime Problem in Rural Areas," *New York Times*, May 23, 1994.

155. Lu Jianhua, "Yijiujiuernian Shehui Gejieceng Dui Shehuixinshide Jiben Kanfa" [Various social strata's basic views toward social trends in 1992], *Shehuixue* [Sociology], no. 4 (1993): 80.

156. FBIS, *CHI/DR*, May 6, 1994, pp. 19–20.

157. FBIS, *CHI/DR*, May 3, 1994, p. 21.

158. FBIS, *CHI/DR*, May 6, 1994, p. 20.

159. *Window* (Hong Kong), August 12, 1994, in FBIS, *CHI/DR*, August 12, 1994, p. 24.

160. *China Daily*, June 20, 1994, p. 4.

161. Xu Keren, "Nongcun Shengyu Laoli Niliu Xiangxiangde Sidazhengyin" [Four reasons for the reverse flow of surplus labor force in the countryside], *Renkouxue* [Demography], no. 1 (1990): 48–50.

162. *Liaowang*, June 6, 1994, in FBIS, *CHI/DR*, June 17, 1994, p. 20.

163. *RMRB*, November 25, 1987, p. 3.

164. Wang Haiquan, Qu Linfeng, and Wu Dage, "Jiaqiang Woguo Nongcun Cunjizuzhi Jianshe Wenti Qianlun" [A preliminary discussion on strengthening the formation of village organizations in our country], *Nongye Jingji* [Agricultural Economy], no. 10 (1990): 51–59.

165. The best evidence for the ineffective condition of village committees is the fifteen-village survey by the team of Chinese scholars led by Wang Huning (*Dangdai Zhongguo Cunluo*). See also Ding Guohua, "Lun Nongcun Jiceng Zuzhi Jianshe" [On the construction of primary organizations in the villages], *Nongye Jingji* [Agricultural Economy], no. 1 (1990): 79–84; and Zhou Wei, "Xiangcun Shehui Zuzhi."

166. *RMRB*, November 28, 1987.

167. Li Sheng, Jian Shiming, and Li Xueming, "Chongqing Baxian 450 Nonghu."

168. *RMRB*, May 28, 1988.

169. Wang Xiaohua, "Fazhan Nongcun Shehuihua Fuwutixi Yinzhuyi Kefu 'Zhengfuhua' Qingxiang," [Pay attention to the tendency toward "governmentalization" in the process of developing farming support services], *Nongye Jingji* [Agricultural Economy], no. 8 (1992): 97–98; and Chen Tianmin, "Yao Zhua Boruo Huanjie" [Must grasp at the weak links], *Nongye Jingji,* no. 9 (1992): 75–76.

170. Qiang Ya and Li Xuekui, "Zhuanmian Gaige Woguo Xianxin Nongye Jingjitizhide Xinshilu" [A new thought on a comprehensive reform of our current agricultural economy] *Nongye Jingji* [Agricultural Economy], no. 12 (1988): 27–31.

171. Li Xiuyi, "Guanyu Shiban 'Nongmin Xiehui' De Ruoganwenti" [On some problems concerning a trial establishment of peasant associations], *Nongye Jingji* [Agricultural Economy], no. 8 (1992): 31–34.

172. "Zhongguo Nongcun Tudi Zhengbao Jingyinzhidu Ji Hezuozuzhi Yunxinkaocha" [An investigation into the management and contracting of rural land and the operation of cooperative organizations], *Nongye Jingji* [Agricultural Economy], no. 12 (1993): 117.

173. Chen Yanxin, "Lun Zhengfu Yu Nongmin," p. 12.

174. *Xinhua,* February 23, 1994, in FBIS, *CHI/DR,* March 10, 1994, pp. 76–77; *Xinhua,* July 3, 1994, in FBIS, *CHI/DR,* July 5, 1994, p. 76.

175. *RMRB,* January 22, 1993, p. 2.

176. *Yijiujiuer Zhongguo Jingji Nianjian* [Almanac of China's Economy, 1992] (Beijing: Jingji Guanli Chubanshe, 1992), p. 818.

177. Chen Jiyuan and Xia Defang, *Xiangzhen Qiye Moshi Yanjiu,* pp. 295–296.

178. *Xinhua,* February 8, 1994, in FBIS, *CHI/DR,* February 18, 1994, p. 24.

179. *China Daily,* April 19, 1994.

180. *China Daily,* January 7, 1994.

181. *Nongye Jingji* [Agricultural Economy], no. 7 (1993): 38. For a general description of these firms in the early years of Deng's reform, see Pat Howard, "Cooperation in a Market Context: The Impact of Recent Rural Economic Reforms in China," *Peasant Studies* 14, no. 3 (Spring 1987): 153–188.

182. *Nongmin Ribao* [Peasants Daily], April 14, 1994, in FBIS, *CHI/DR,* May 19, 1994, pp. 48–49.

183. *Chung-kuo Shih-pao* [China Times] (Taipei), August 1, 1994. Many Taiwanese business executives have entered into joint ownership with mainland Chinese entrepreneurs; thus, the Taiwan press is quite concerned with the state of township enterprises in China.

184. Wang Hanshen, "Nongcun Gongyehua Guochengzhongdi." Shequ Zhengfu: Quanli Yu Liyidi Fenghua [Community Government During the Process of Rural Industrialization: Differentiation Between Power and Interest], *Nongye Jingi* [Agricultural Economy], no. 8 (1992): 69–76.

185. Fei Xiaotong, "Zhongguo Chenxiang Fazhande Daolu" [The path to Chinese urban-rural development], *Xinhua Wenzhai* [New China Digest], no. 4 (1993): 8–13.

186. Qian Hang, "Guanyu Dangdai Zhongguo Nongcun Zongzu Yanjiudi Jige Wenti" [Concerning some problems on research of contemporary Chinese clans in the rural area], *Shehuixue* [Sociology], no. 3 (1993): 161.

187. Wang Hunning, *Dangdai Zhongguo Cunluo.*

188.   Potter and Potter, *China's Peasants,* chapter 12.

189.   Qian Hang and Xie Weiyang, "Zongzu Wenti: Dangdai Zhongguo Nongcun Yanjiude Yige Shijiao" [The clan problem: One vantage point for research on contemporary Chinese villages], *Shehuixue* [Sociology], no. 4 (1990): 128–132; Mao Shaojun, "Nongcun Zongzu Shili Manyande Xianzhuang Yu Yuanyin Fengxi" [An analysis of the present situation and causes of the spread of clan power in the countryside], *Shehuixue* [Sociology], no. 3 (1991): 110–115; Yin Zhaoqiang, "Nongcun Gongzuozhong Burong Hushide Jiazuwenti" [We cannot play down the clan problem in our rural work], *Shehuixue,* no. 6 (1992): 118–121.

190.   Qian Hang, "Guanyu Dangdai Zhongguo," p. 158.

191.   Wang Shulin, "Dangqian Nongcun Shehui," p. 40.

192.   Qian Hang and Xie Weiyang, "Zongzu Wenti: Dangdai Zhongguo"; and Gong Shuilin, "Xianjieduan Woguo Nongcun Jiating Tezheng Fenxi" [The current characteristics of rural families in our country], *Shehuixue* [Sociology], no. 5 (1990): 96–100.

193.   Wang Huning, *Dangdai Zhongguo Cunluo,* p. 321.

194.   Ibid., p. 377; and Gong Shuilin, "Xianjieduan Woguo Nongcun."

195.   David Gutmann, "Age and Leadership: Cross-Cultural Observations," in *Aging and Political Leadership,* ed. Angus McIntyre (Albany: State University of New York Press, 1988), p. 92.

196.   Mao Shaojun, "Nongcun Zongzu Shili."

197.   Yin Zhaoqiang, "Nongcun Gongzuozhong Burong."

198.   Qian Hang, "Guanyu Dangdai Zhongguo."

199.   Wang Huning, *Dangdai Zhongguo Cunluo,* pp. 291–581.

200.   Ding Yuanzhu, "Nongcun Shequ Yanjiu: You Jiandan Dao Fuzadi Shehuijiegou Tansuo" [A study of the rural community: An exploration of the change from simple to complex social structure], part 1, *Nongye Jingji* [Agricultural Economy], no. 12 (1992): 102.

201.   *Chung-kuo Shih-pao* [China Times], June 21, 1992, p. 10.

202.   Zheng Fangwen, "Nongcun Fengshanjiufeng Yinzhongshi Jiejue" [Rural disputes over graveyards should be given attention and solved], *Shehui* [Sociology], no. 4 (1983): 27–30.

203.   Tan Gengpin, "Nongcun Xiedou Heshiliao" [When will rural armed fights end?], *Shehuixue* [Sociology], no. 2 (1992): 145–146.

204.   *South China Morning Post,* May 18, 1993, in FBIS, *CHI/DR,* May 19, 1993, p. 41.

205.   Stephen Engelberg, "Carving Out a Greater Serbia," *New York Times Magazine,* September 1, 1991.

206.   Qian Hang and Xie Weiyang, "Zongzu Wenti: Dangdai Zhonguo," p. 130.

207.   Friedman, Pickowicz, and Seldan, *Chinese Village, Socialist State,* p. 211.

208.   Lin Shangli, "Cunluo Jiazu Wenhua Yu Zhongguo Shehui Xiandaihua" [The village-clan culture and modernization of Chinese society], *Fudan Xuebao* [Bulletin of Fudan University], no. 3 (1992): 41–43.

209.   V. O. Key Jr., *Public Opinion and American Democracy* (New York: Alfred A. Knopf, 1963), p. 150.

210.   Kriesberg, *Social Conflicts,* pp. 31–35.

211. Friedman, Pickowicz, and Seldan, *Chinese Village, Socialist State,* chapters 3 and 4.

212. J. R. Vincent, *Pollbooks: How Victorians Voted* (Cambridge, England: Cambridge University Press, 1967), p. 32.

213. Key, *Public Opinion,* p. 263.

214. Ibid. p. 151.

215. *Selected Works of Mao,* vol. 5, p. 125.

216. *Chen Yun Wenxuan, 1949–1956* [Selected Works of Chen Yun, 1949–1956] (Beijing: Renmin Chubanshe, 1984), p. 210.

3

WORKERS: REACTION AND AMBIVALENCE

Gradually the workers learned to offer passive resistance which, although never on a planned or organized basis, nevertheless became a serious problem for the regime.

—Robert Loh (1962)[1]

Older workers are full of misgivings.... They are afraid of being superceded before leaving their factories, which would amount to saying goodbye to bonuses and seeing their pensions fall. They support reforms, and yet they find the changes difficult to accept.... Younger workers, on the other hand, are full of contradictions.... They remain apprehensive because they believe that they,... not the cadres, are the targets of reform.

—*Economic Management* (1992)[2]

Unlike the peasants, whose opposition to the Party-state has been persistent, Chinese workers have undergone enormous changes in their attitudes toward the state (as the epigraphs show). Outwardly, workers carried on a class conflict with the state during Mao's time; workers, as the subordinate group, struggled against the state, as the superordinate group, over possession of goods and income opportunities.[3] In the post-Mao period, workers (primarily those in state-run firms) emerged as some of the strongest defenders of the old statist economy. Whereas peasants longed to be emancipated from the state, workers wanted the opposite. Chinese workers sought to protect their old relationship with the state in which the state served as chief patron. Ironically, it was the Party-state that wanted to emancipate itself from the patron-client relationship with the workers. Beginning in the 1980s, reports in the Chinese media appeared addressing the workers' feelings. These were expressed in statements such as "the reforms were directed at them" and "the leaders [were intent on] breaking the workers' 'iron rice bowls' [job security]."[4]

This chapter discusses the evolution of workers' attitudes toward the state—from class conflict to patronage-seeking. The main thesis postulates that the relationship between the Chinese Communist state and the workers is fundamentally an adversarial symbiosis. The major change in the state-worker relationship from Mao's to Deng's era is basically a change in emphasis: In Mao's time, it was the adversarial aspect that was prominent and in Deng's time, the symbiotic aspect. But this symbiosis between the state and the workers exists within the context of a patron-client relationship. Assuming different roles in their relationship, the state and the worker have divergent goals. The state's goal is more symbolic (ideological) than material: militant nationalism (making China a major military-industrial power, for example). The worker is more material than symbolic. The difference in goals partly accounts for the adversarial aspect of their relationship. At the same time, the state and the worker share some common interests. The state needs the worker to realize its nationalistic objectives. The worker needs the state to protect a privileged status and income against the background of an oversupply of cheap labor and extremely restricted life chances for the overwhelming majority of the population. Thus, the state-worker relationship in China is much more complex than the simple, zero-sum relationship between the state and the peasant.

Further complicating the state-worker relationship is the multifarious character of the working class. Jean Paul Sartre observed that "the working class is neither pure combativity, nor pure passive dispersal, nor pure institutional apparatus. It is a complex, moving relation between different practical forms."[5] Ira Katznelson characterized the working-class political culture in the United States as "schizophrenic," "with workers maintaining a fairly clear language of class division at work, while community politics is expressed through a language of ethnicity and territory."[6] Chinese workers are not exempted from these general characteristics. They are particularly prone to sectional and ethnic (or regionalistic) conflicts, as subsequent descriptions will show.

Based on the discussion so far, I will classify the manner in which workers expressed themselves in terms of class and sectional conflicts. Class conflicts refer to workers' conflicts with the state, as exemplified by the tension between workers and cadres. Sectional conflicts include both those within the working class itself (such as conflicts between the skilled and the unskilled and between the young and the old) as well those between workers and other subordinated groups in society, such as intellectuals, students, and self-employed workers. Figure 3.1 broadly classifies the workers' expressions into four periods on the basis of the relative prominence of class or sectional conflicts in each period.

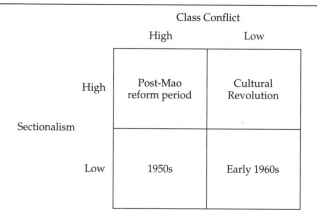

Figure 3.1　State and worker relationship

The Class Conflicts in the 1950s

To the majority of Chinese workers, especially those in the major coastal cities, the 1950s embodied a period of rapid change and anxiety. Although workers were generally guaranteed jobs by the state and enjoyed a new symbolic status (as members of the proletariat), these privileges were neutralized by other state actions, such as the extension of bureaucratic control into workers' everyday lives, elimination of an autonomous union, enforcement of austerity, and demands for extreme efforts on the job. On the surface, the state's impositions on workers were more involutionary than revolutionary, in contrast to the state's treatment of peasants. Nevertheless, from the workers' vantage point, the state's mobilization was quite revolutionary because workers were used to a much more autonomous and mobile way of life before the Communist takeover. By 1949, Chinese industrial workers had experienced thirty years of union activity, made up primarily of strikes for higher wages and better working conditions.[7] Thus, Chinese workers, especially those in modern cities such as Shanghai, Wuhan, Beijing, or Tianjin, understood the meaning and function of worker solidarity and unionization. During the days of run-away inflation and social chaos in 1947–1948, industrial workers were more successful than most other groups in protecting their interests through militant union activities. These were, in the overwhelming majority of cases, organized by non-Communist unions.[8]

The independent union tradition of Chinese workers was the first casualty of the CCP's rapid extension of bureaucratic control in the 1950s.

The CCP replaced the old unions with new ones in the "Democratic Reform" movement of the early 1950s. At the start these new unions were characterized by artificiality and status ambiguity. Most of the unions were organized by cadres with a minimal involvement of ordinary workers. Cadres were preoccupied with establishing the formal structure of unions rather than the stated aim of worker participation. In 1954 and 1955 the Chinese press described trade union organizations as "stupendous" and "overlapping." There were too many administrators and the working style of the unions was formalistic and bureaucratic. As one report put it: "The trade union has seriously estranged itself from the masses."[9] The new unions were an integral part of the Party-state, and as the process grew antagonistic, the workers and the state confronted one another directly.

The state carried out a seemingly unending series of campaigns designed to increase production and decrease worker benefits (using the excuse of sacrificing for socialism and the country). The first such campaign began as early as 1951. Workers' wages were reduced by compulsory savings while their working hours were increased.[10] As an extreme example of the state's demands upon the workers, the youth league press reported in 1956 that one group of students, which had gone to factories as members of a "mass supervision" team (supposedly to overcome "bureaucratism" in factory management), witnessed the following scene (translation not mine): "Owing to too much extra work, some workers were so exhausted that they lay in the ditches, and some were so fatigued ... they became dizzy and knocked their heads against electric wire pole[s] while walking in the streets.... Some workmen ... spat blood [due to] overwork."[11]

The conditions under which miners worked were particularly harsh, and a high rate of accidents and instances of political opposition were frequently reported.[12] That the workers put up with the state's extreme demands was perhaps only partly due to the absence of an independent union. The other major cause was the character of the labor force. It was in the 1950s that the state had recruited a large number of new workers from the countryside. From 1950 to 1958, the number of "staff and workers" in state firms increased from 5.1 million to 23.16 million. Most of the new workers were former peasants.[13] In the 1990s, the same extreme conditions exist in which migrant workers from the countryside were forced to work and live four decades ago.

Reacting to their plight in the 1950s, workers resorted to passive resistance, manifested in a kind of slowdown. Robert Loh, a former factory manager in Shanghai, reported: "Outwardly, the workers seemed animated with the zeal demanded by the authorities, but both the quantity and the quality of production fell noticeably."[14] Loh's testimony was corroborated by official Chinese press reports, one of which described the situation as follows: "Workers in general are late for work and early to go home, and always absent without leave; they break . . . regulations, disobey transfer orders and technical instructions, and resist . . . authority."[15]

One may recall that the 1950s was also a period of high state-peasant tension caused by collectivization. The state employed one terror campaign to deal with both the peasants and the workers—the campaign of "Suppression of Hidden Counterrevolutionaries" of 1955–1956. The extent of class conflict between workers and the state may be determined from the following report by Public Security Minister Lo Ruiqing in July 1955 (translation not mine):

> Counter-revolutionaries in the Wuhu Cotton Mill in Anhwei set fire to the mill and burned more than 23,000 spindles to ashes, causing a damage of some 1.6 million [*yuan*]. A counter-revolutionary worker in the petroleum wholesale station in Shanghai opened the oil tanks and deliberately let the oil flow into the river. When the Taihsuan Heavy Machinery Plant installed its only 5-ton steam hammer which could have produced 10,000 [*yuan*'s] worth of work each day, a counter-revolutionary worker purposely damaged it on the excuse of making a trial run. After a huge crack was discovered in the No. 20 tunnel on the Fengtai-Shacheng Railway, counter-revolutionary engineer Huang Tien-hai knowingly covered up the crack with cheap materials, scheming to cause a great disaster when the tunnel is opened to traffic. In the Hsiahuayuan No. 1 Coal Mine in Hopeh, counter-revolutionary chief engineer purposely adopted erroneous method of excavation to cause the accumulation of gas which led to a tragic explosion that killed 38 and wounded 156 miners, incurring a direct loss of more than half a million [*yuan*]. In a certain arsenal, counter-revolutionary assistant engineer secretly altered the blueprints for certain rifles, causing some 8,400 newly-manufactured rifles to be useless and another 509 to have a high degree of inaccuracy.[16]

As the chief of the political police, Lo naturally saw a "counterrevolutionary" conspiracy behind each of the incidents that he described. In reality, the multitude of industrial mishaps in the mid-1950s were most likely generated by an assortment of causes such as workers' exhaustion, low morale, inexperience of new workers, and, above all, cadres' indifference to workers' safety. Four months before Minister Lo's accusatory speech, Lai Jo-yu [Lai Ruoyu], head of the All-China Federation of Trade Unions (ACFTU), had publicly spoken about an alarming rise in industrial accidents. Lai said that the prevailing attitude of cadres and managers was that workers' safety was none of their concern. Cadres were interested mainly in increasing production and they sought to accomplish that by "increasing labor intensity and extending working hours." In some instances, reported Lai, "workers . . . worked continuously for 72 hours through additional shifts and working hours." Lai said that new workers were the chief victims of industrial accidents, constituting

60 percent of the casualties in some instances. An analysis of the accidents that occurred in 1950–1953 found that "gas or gunpowder explosions caused the greatest [number of] casualties." Death due to explosions accounted for 19.4 percent of all casualties.[17]

Given the general mood of workers, it is not surprising that workers' opposition to the state turned vocal and explicit during the Hundred Flowers campaign of 1957. The strongest opinion was expressed by union staffers. They were naturally the most intellectually inclined among the workers and felt keenly the CCP's perversion of the unions. The *Gongren Ribao* [Worker's Daily], an organ of the ACFTU, proclaimed that the union was in a state of crisis that was manifested in

> a steady alienation of the workers and staff from the union; the trustworthiness of the union among the masses becoming less and less; the functions of the union being difficult to perform; and the great majority of union staff having an "inferiority complex," being unwilling to carry out their work.[18]

Among the workers, the union was commonly referred to as "the worker control department," "the tongue of bureaucratism," or "the tail of administration." In the eyes of ordinary workers the union was indistinct from the CCP or management. After an extended tour to visit unions throughout China, a high-ranking official of the ACFTU told a reporter that a common occurrence observed among the striking workers in 1957 was their initiative in taking direct actions and ignoring the unions.[19] Even the head of the ACFTU, Lai Jo-yu, joined the critical union staff by declaring that unions should stand by the workers, "though the masses might have incorrect views." Lai's concern was to prevent workers from being alienated from the union. Lai admitted that the union had been put in a difficult position, between representing the interests of the worker and demonstrating consideration of the state's interests. He carefully avoided mentioning the union's subordination to the Party, as he frequently did before 1957.[20]

The quick mutation of unions in the Hundred Flowers campaign bespoke of two significant developments in mass opinion under a highly repressive state. First, any organization, even a cosmetic one such as the new union after 1949, is potentially important for political opinion and behavior. Backed by a union, Chinese workers are in a much stronger position than peasants are to express their opinions when an opportunity exists. The abrupt turn that unions made in the Hundred Flowers campaign, from a subordinate organ of the state to an independent entity, would repeat itself thirty-two years later, during the pro-democracy movement by the students in 1989. Second, although state repression caused people to stop public criticisms, privately, they found new and more effective ways to overcome repression. It became more difficult for the state to cope with subtle and pervasive opposition from workers from 1957 onward.

Next to the assertive role that unions assumed in the Hundred Flowers period was an outpouring of workers' resentment toward Party cadres. Loh reported that workers in his Shanghai mills posted crudely drawn posters showing cadres "as fat and bestial while the workers were emaciated, ragged and beaten down." The most common complaints directed at cadres by workers were the favoritism shown to Party members and the "unjust and undemocratic" conduct of cadres. In the eyes of many workers, the Party-state cadres were "ten times more arrogant than the previous capitalist owners had ever been."[21]

Mao's comments on worker unrest corroborated Loh's descriptions. Mao said that workers were primarily offended by some cadres who behaved even worse than the Guomindang. As a consequence, Mao said, workers became politically passive and sought mainly material benefits such as the so-called five big things: watches, bicycles, fountain pens, radios, and sewing machines.[22] Sociologically, the conflicts between Chinese workers and cadres were class conflicts. Fantasia wrote that class should be seen as a dynamic phenomenon "in which particular classes have no independent being, but are functions of their relationships to other classes."[23] Class conflicts between workers and cadres in the Chinese industrial system, which first became widely known in the Hundred Flowers campaign, persist today.

In addition to class conflicts between workers and the state, the unrest in 1957 threw into relief the multifarious character of the Chinese working class. Many of the workers' expressions in the "blooming and contending" activities of 1957 dealt with immediate issues such as wages and housing. Class conflicts were also mixed in with these socioeconomic complaints since many cadres were accused by workers of corruption in housing allocation.[24] In 1947, Chinese sociologist Ta Chen wrote: "The psychosocial reactions of the Chinese workingmen are more socioeconomic and less political."[25] Chen's description of the worker in China remained valid ten years later.

Sectionalism among Chinese workers made its first appearance in the Hundred Flowers campaign. At the time, the most prominent intra-worker conflict was between young and old workers. At the start of the "blooming" campaign, it was the young workers who rose in groups, staging strikes and creating other confrontations with authorities.[26] Young apprentice workers reacted not only to the general disparity in wages between them and the senior workers but specifically to a new wage policy that the state instituted in 1956. The new wage policy imposed a much finer gradation in ranking and pay differentials among workers. Differences in pay between young apprentices and skilled older workers increased. According to Tung Chi-Ping, whose younger brother was an apprentice worker then, apprentices were not paid enough even for their food and transportation. "He had to buy whatever working equipment was needed. He was given no assurance that at the end of his apprenticeship he would be offered a job." The life of an apprentice in the PRC, said Tung, was essentially as "a coolie."[27] Before their strikes, the young workers had already resorted to amorphous social protests such as high absenteeism, malingering, and inattention to work. The term *moyanggong* (dawdling along), which was primarily applied to peasants in collectives, was applied to the young workers also. Sharing the unenviable lot of apprentice workers were young female workers whose interests were often dismissed or ignored entirely by cadres. Among female workers, one group was especially active in protest activities in 1957; they were the ones moved by the state from the coastal areas to the interior. The strain experienced by these women was compounded by dislocation and maladjustment to their lives in the lesser developed interior provinces.[28] The activism of apprentice and female workers in 1957 showed that "diffused collectivities" such as age and gender groups, when combined with a class situation, can be the basis of worker solidarity, albeit localized.

In the final analysis, workers' protests in the Hundred Flowers campaign were primarily an expressive movement. They produced neither leadership nor organizations for the workers. Chinese workers were segmented; union staff and segments of workers each acted on their own. Articulation and mobilization of discontent occurred in localized and institutional settings. I found only one report of a worker's group attempting to widen their appeal to the society at large. Workers of one Shanghai machine-tool factory had formed an association with other discontented groups; they named the organization "Hardship-Resolving Society" (*pingnan hui*). This organization distributed leaflets to the public urging "dissatisfied people boldly organizing themselves to create power so to carry out struggle against the state."[29] For an authentic working class movement to grow in China two exogenous conditions are necessary: leadership by a militant group (often radical intellectuals) and a viable public opinion to lend moral support. Neither was available in 1957 or even in the 1990s. That a workers' movement was able to institutionalize itself in both England and the United States in modern times reflected the essential existence of these two external conditions.[30]

Rise of Sectionalism, Mid-1960s and 1970s

After the end of the Hundred Flowers campaign, the activism of Chinese workers ebbed. They dutifully turned out a high volume of output during the Great Leap Forward movement, but their morale was low. Among them, the prevailing view was that the Great Leap was just "a gust of wind." Workers treated the Great Leap with the same degree of indifference as they did the increase-in-production campaigns that came and went. Workers generally did not heed Mao's appeal to them to abide by the principle of "more, faster, better, and economical"; they were said to have wasted raw materials with abandon.[31] In the nationwide famine that followed the Great Leap, workers' spirits sank even lower. Absenteeism and work slowdowns occasionally occurred during this period.[32] The *Worker's Daily* in 1961 reported that workers displayed "a negative attitude toward labor" and that some had "indulged themselves in leisure-seeking."[33]. But amid the nationwide crisis of severe food shortages in the city and starvation in the countryside, both class and sectional conflicts among workers were rare.

However, unlike the peasants whose resistance against the state was toughened by the crisis in 1960–1962, workers' reactions to the famine tended to dampen their desire to confront the state. Instead, they seemed to have become more aware of their symbiotic relationship with the state after the crisis. From the 1960s until the late 1980s, class conflicts between workers and the state took a back seat, while sectional conflicts among workers came to the fore. Sectionalism among workers reached a peak during the Cultural Revolution (1966–1969) and remained at a high level throughout the 1970s, until Mao's death. Several plausible causes account for this major change in workers' attitudes. First, the disaster of the Great Leap restrained the state; gone were the days when the state could demand extreme efforts from workers. Second, workers adapted successfully to the statist economy by using it to their advantage. In China, the practice was known as "eating socialism." In other words, workers passed the time doing personal things, rather than working. Cadres were no longer intent on pressing workers to do a day's work; they were demoralized by the failure of the Great Leap and by strife among the Beijing elite. Instead, cadres themselves engaged in "eating socialism" through various corrupt deeds.[34] Third, the various measures undertaken by the state after the crisis of 1960–1962, in order to protect the interests of the urban population, made workers conscious of their close ties with the state.

In the crisis following the Great Leap, 28 million workers who had been recruited to work in the cities were forcibly returned to the countryside. The strategy was to reduce the state's burden by decreasing the urban population and the need for large amounts of basic provisions.[35] The state then strictly enforced a policy of stopping rural residents from moving to the city. Factories in the cities not only reduced their rate of recruitment but also confined the source of new workers to urban residents. A dual economy-and-society then emerged.[36] Workers and peasants were separated like two castes. Out of this dual economy and society, workers became more conscious than before of their dependence on the state for their privileged existence (compared with the peasants). Rather than confront a weakened state, workers devoted more of their time to intra-group conflicts, venting their grievances against the multiple status differences among them. Class conflicts did not disappear entirely but, on the whole, were secondary to sectional conflicts.

The new strategy of the workers became obvious in their reactions to the Cultural Revolution. After the initial period of "economism" (that is, demanding additional wages from management), workers were absorbed in factionalism and particularism. Factions among the workers of Shanghai, according to White, followed stratification lines.[37] In the interior of China, workers fought among themselves on the basis of territorial and regional divisions. Dissident writer Liu Binyan described fights between former Shanghai workers and native workers in the Sichuan city of Zhongqing that lasted from 1965 through 1975. Liu wrote that, within each of the two regional groups, workers further divided themselves into many small cliques, clashing with one another. Normal production was almost entirely suspended.[38]

The degrees of intra-worker conflicts and the mixture of class and segmental conflicts varied from one group to another. Five types of workers were particularly noteworthy for their intra- or inter-group conflicts: railway workers, steel workers, coal miners, dock workers, and young workers. However, in-depth information on any of the five groups is not available. I can only provide a general analysis of the unrest among these workers.

Among the five, the railway and steel workers belonged to China's "labor aristocracy," while the miners, dock workers, and young workers represented the underprivileged sections of the working class. The persistent militancy of the first two groups seemed to stem primarily from sectionalism. The unrest among the underprivileged groups was caused by both sectional and class conflicts. One common cause underlying the problems in all five groups was political incitement by the radical leaders in Beijing, headed by Mao's wife, Jiang Qing. But the radical leaders targeted those groups that were already in a state of high combativeness. In other words, there were various endogenous causes in these groups' militant activities in the 1970s.

Chinese railway workers had a strong proclivity for collective political actions. They were one of the most aggressive groups during the strikes in 1947–1949.[39] After 1949, the CCP staffed the railway work force with the most politically trustworthy people. The CCP frequently assigned demobilized soldiers to railway work. In China, anyone from a railway worker's family was regarded as wearing the badge of a "true proletariat" (*hongwulei*).[40] Railway workers were also highly conscious of their strategic role in the nation's economic and political life. At the same time, the veterans in China, like veterans elsewhere, tended to harbor many grievances against the state, which were due partly to their difficult adjustments to civilian life. It was not surprising that railway workers made economic demands on the administration as soon as the Cultural Revolution spread from the students to the workers. All these reasons must have induced the radical leaders to seek clients among railway workers for politically strategic reasons. Consequently, factional conflicts grew and remained out of control among railway workers throughout the 1970s.[41]

The unrest among steel workers seemed to be associated with the size of the steel factories and their internal organizations. Most of the Chinese steel plants, especially those in the Northeast, were built by Soviet advisers in the 1950s. They were large plants and operated on the Soviet principles of hierarchy and strict rank distinctions. For example, the Anshan Iron and Steel Company employed 100,000 workers and employees in 1957; in 1977 its technicians alone numbered 13,000.[42] U.S. scholar Randy Hodson and his colleagues found that "in large organizations, work groups are more likely to differentiate themselves from managers, clients, and other work groups than those in small organizations. Large organizations produce a more complex division of labor and more distinct groups within the organization."[43] Chinese press reports addressing the troubles among steel workers tended to confirm the finding of Hodson's group.

In the Anshan Iron and Steel Company, for instance, factionalization emerged along lines of generation and stratification, setting the young against the old, the unskilled against the skilled, and those lower in rank against those in higher ranks. These sectional conflicts were further aggravated by the radical leaders' installation of a new system of factory organization then known as the system of "two participations, one reform, and three-way combination" (that is, cadres' participating in productive work and workers' participating in management; reform of the irrational aspects of the factory system; and combination or unity among management, technicians, and workers). In Anshan, it was reported that this new radical system caused about 90 percent of old and skilled workers and technical staff to suffer political persecution.[44] In almost all the major Chinese steel plants then in existence, there were rapid turnovers of managerial and Party personnel. In the Benqi Iron and Steel Company (Liaoning Province), for example, 70 percent of the cadres had been transferred during the height of factional conflicts and intervention by the radical leaders.[45]

The turmoil among the three underprivileged groups—miners, dock workers, and young workers—stemmed from both sectional and class conflicts. Miners were particularly affected by class conflicts. Entire mines were frequently shut down and the national production of coal decreased significantly. It was estimated that the total output of coal in 1967 was 20 to 25 percent below that of 1966. A severe shortage of coal followed in the winter of 1967–1968.[46] In 1973–1974 the Pingdingshan mine in Henan, which supplied coal to five provinces and an estimated 1,700 state enterprises, stopped operation due to political conflicts between miners and cadres.[47] The chief cause of the miners' militancy was clearly the harsh and hazardous working conditions. In 1976, one group of coal miners in Jiangxi appealed to the nation in a wall poster that read: "We are human beings, not slaves." The poster then went on to describe the terrible working conditions that the miners had to endure (translation not mine):

> Although . . . fatigues, shoes, hats, and gloves are worn out, no new ones are available, simply because honor should be won and austerity practiced at the expense of workers' interests.
>
> Whenever a mine exudes water, to protect the safety of the mine the sluice will instantly be closed before all the workers have come out, disregarding the lives of class brethren.
>
> When a mine caves in, workers are forced to rescue machines first, an indication that machines are viewed as more precious than the lives of class brethen.
>
> Workers are forced to make voluntary contributions or to work overtime without reward, thus debilitating everyone and making them wan and gaunt.
>
> Veteran workers are not pensioned upon retiring. . . .
>
> Thirty percent of workers . . . live with the older and younger generation in a one-room house rather than in a brick house. Isn't our drudgery over the past years worth a table or a room?
>
> Over the past year the workers put forward more than one hundred proposals on how to prevent accidents from occurring in the mine and how to safeguard national interests and workers' safety, but none of them were accepted.
>
> Some of the mines . . . are still using 20-year-old machines.[48]

According to Hodson and colleagues, hazardous working conditions are among the most important determinants of workers' solidarity.[49] That is certainly borne out by the militancy of Chinese coal miners in the 1970s. Coal miners in peripheral provinces, such as in Guizhou and Yunnan, had the additional advantage of possessing tactical mobility, which strengthened their group solidarity.

Among the dock workers of Shanghai and Guangzhou, class conflicts were mixed with sectional conflicts. Chinese dock workers were historically the first to organize among themselves; their secret societies appeared as early as the seventeenth century. Their organizations were based on territorial and regional ties. Fights over turf were frequent before 1949. After the Communist takeover, the lives of dock workers improved minimally. During the 1957 "blooming" period, a union staffer exposed the harsh working conditions that the CCP cadres imposed on dock workers in Guangzhou. Cadres there had instituted a system of "flexible shifts," which required dock workers to work for sixteen hours a day; after two days of full-time work, the workers were given one day of rest. Many dock workers became ill and the absentee rate reached 60 percent.[50] They were among the most militant protesters at the start of the Cultural Revolution. In Shanghai, dock workers occupied public buildings.[51] In the 1970s, radical leaders set one section of the dock workers against another and also incited them to fight with cadres who wanted to restore the old system of flexible work shifts.[52]

Finally, the unrest among young workers surfaced once again in the 1970s as it had in 1957. Factionalism and the lack of discipline among young workers stemmed from fundamental political and socioeconomic crises in China. Their discontent represented a general political disaffection among the youth, which became noticeable after the Cultural Revolution. A second cause was the lack of social mobility. Many of the young workers living in major cities on the coast were high school graduates deprived of an opportunity to go to college. They went to work in the factories unwillingly. Sentiments like "[we] have no future" and "[our] hearts are not in [our] work" were quite common among them.[53] Young workers also resented bureaucratic control and institutionalized hypocrisy among cadres. They vented their anger in gang activities and general insubordination.

Workers in Early Reform Transition, 1977–1985

By the time Deng Xiaoping's administration took over China in 1979, it was confronted with widespread unrest and indiscipline among urban workers. Factional fights paralyzed many factories while the general mood of the workers was characterized by, as the Chinese press put it, "softness, laziness, and sloppiness" (*ruan, lan, san*).[54] It appears that workers obtained more from their passive resistance to the state than peasants did. As Liang Heng and Judith Shapiro described it, workers appropriated the normal working hours for private pursuits. The "wasted" time on factory floors was, for Chinese workers, an "opportunity gain"; they used the time to indulge in social exchanges with their colleagues and friends or to fulfill family obligations.[55] The peasants' amorphous social action, however, always carries an element of self-immolation since no matter how low agricultural production is in any year, the Chinese state will continue requisitioning the same amount of food from the peasants. The workers' work slowdown is a way, at least in the short-run, to gain personal well-being. "The standard of living of the nonprivileged [under socialism] is very low indeed," wrote Kriegel, "but at least they are not forced to submit to the demanding discipline of manual work."[56]

Chinese factories experienced a fundamental change under socialism. They became institutionalized—ends in themselves, instead of technical organizations created to mobilize human energies for economic gains.[57] As years went by and population pressure grew, the state relied more and more on factories, especially the large and medium-sized state firms, to solve the problem of providing employment. Workers treated factories as if they were extended families and acquired all kinds of social services. Within many state firms, a dense network of patron-client groups emerged. These personalistic alliances in Chinese factories, said Andrew Walder, gave workers the sense of having beaten "the system."[58] Chinese factories became self-contained and multifunctional social institutions, more *gemeinschaft* than *gesellschaft*. They were no longer expendable (as any factory in a market system is) and they resisted change. Unbeknown to many Chinese workers, while they carried on an adversarial relationship with the state, they had entered into a partnership in this new *gemeinschaft*. Workers took for granted their "cradle-to-grave" welfare and job security, treating it as their socialist entitlement.[59] To them, the state was always there to provide for them, no matter how dismal the guaranteed living was. The attitude of Chinese workers was described well by three scholars as follows:

> Heaven and earth may still govern survival for China's 800 million peasants, but the state guarantees subsistence to its assigned workers, no matter what conditions are. Whether they work conscientiously or loaf, whether the state enterprise makes or loses money, and even whether the enterprise operates at capacity or comes to a temporary standstill, these workers continue to receive their basic wage, their guaranteed grain allotment, and some fringe benefits which include free or part-paid medical care. Such security and benefits do not extend to workers in commune-run factories or in the growing number of collective and individual enterprises [in 1980s].[60]

This description also points out the differentiation among the workers. Those enjoying a state-guaranteed living were employed in state-owned firms. In the early 1980s, the total number of staff and workers in the state *industrial* firms was about 40 million, of which 30 million were industrial workers (*chanye gongren*).[61] The staff and workers in industrial firms constituted about 9 percent of all employed labor in 1981–1982.[62] In proportion to the rest of society, industrial workers were a privileged minority in socialist China.

However, the workers' dependence on the state for subsistence in no way dampened their interest in political protests if, in their opinion, such action would result in the material improvement of their lives. The transition years in the post-Mao succession (1978–1985) provided workers an opportunity, just as the Hundred Flowers campaign did, to express their social and economic discontent. There were plenty of reasons for workers to complain and protest. Majority of them had not had their wages adjusted since 1956, as Mao was opposed to material incentives for work. The living conditions of even the privileged workers, such as housing, were deplorable. In addition, there was virtually no occupational mobility for workers. The Cultural Revolution was instigated ostensibly for the purpose of ridding China of arrogant cadres and installing work-place democracy. In reality, cadres in factories remained as arrogant and indifferent to workers' lives as ever. Dissident journalist Liu Binyan described the predicament of the workers as follows: "In our personnel system there is not any individual freedom of changing employment. If a worker offends his boss who then makes things hard for the worker, the latter does not have the right to expose or contend with the cadre boss. What can the worker do? He can only put up with the wrong for a long time and meanwhile his family suffers with him."[63]

Many of the workers' reactions in 1978–1985 were the same as those in 1957: a quick rise of complaints over immediate socioeconomic issues, a universal resentment of cadres, strikes in peripheral areas, scattered demands for independent unions, and militancy among young workers. There were two new developments, however. One was the workers' knowledge of the Solidarity movement in Poland, and the second was an alarm—spread by a number of workers in large cities—that the old days of dependence on the state for a privileged life might be coming to an end.

The years from 1978 to 1980 were marked by a resurgent youth dissent movement, as exemplified by the "Democracy Wall" phenomenon in Beijing. A number of workers' used this opportunity to voice their discontent. This pattern of the workers, taking advantage of educated youths' dissent to air their own interests, was to repeat itself in the pro-democracy movement in 1989. One such example was a report published in the youth dissident journal, *Beijing Zhichun* (Spring of Beijing), on the housing situation of workers and staff of a large textile plant in Beijing.[64] According to the article, the housing complex was built in 1954 to accommodate 1,800 people. Twenty-five years later, the number of workers and staff of the factory had increased to 4,500, but the factory had added a mere two hundred square meters of new housing to the old building. An apartment initially designed for one family was now occupied by three, or even four, families. The crowded living quarters caused a host of social problems such as marital separations (because young mothers were housed in a special "mothers' dormitory"), adultery, incest, and juvenile delinquency.[65] It is, therefore, not true—as some authors have contended—that a culture of poverty in Chinese urban life did not exist.[66]

But workers reserved their most vehement criticisms for the cadres. Class conflicts between workers and cadres remained as intense as ever. The following excerpt from an essay written by a Guangdong worker is typical:

> Some said that the head of a factory is like a king. That might sound a bit melodramatic but it is worth deep reflection.
> In reality, the head of a factory controls every aspect of the lives of the staff and workers. He decides their admissions to the Youth League

or the Party, promotions, opportunities for advanced study, housing, transfers, changes of residence, going abroad, leaves of absence to visit families and relatives, marriages, and children's jobs. During the days of the Gang of Four, cadres at the lowest administrative units had the power to arrest, imprison, interrogate, torture, and even execute people. It was quite accurate then to refer to a cadre as a king. The cadres commanded troops—the militia. They possessed a judiciary—the [factory's] Office of Security. They had a prison system—the cattle pens [detention rooms during the Cultural Revolution]. Although these nightmarish days are over, is it possible that they might return?[67]

On the whole, workers resented the cadres' privileges. The cadres, wrote one Beijing worker, received pay without working and exploited the workers more than capitalists did elsewhere.[68] There was a noticeable emphasis on egalitarianism in the dissident workers' critique of the cadre system. One railway worker from Beijing, for instance, mentioned the Paris Commune as the model for a thorough reform of factory administration.[69]

With their dissatisfaction against cadres remaining strong, the articulate workers naturally demanded their own unions. The official ACFTU was as bureaucratic in the 1980s as it was in the 1950s. Its grass-roots organizations performed no meaningful functions. Some local union officials did not know the size of their membership, and others, when approached by members for welfare assistance, did not know how to carry out their work.[70] Union cadres in the 1980s were as timid as before, afraid of the Party's wrath but unafraid of workers' discontent. Union staff members who were popularly elected were quickly transferred by Party authorities to prevent them from working with their constituents.[71] In some cases, corrupt Party cadres used union funds to defray their personal expenses.[72] A group of workers in Wuhan City, which was active in unionizing in the 1920s, attempted to organize an independent union in 1980, modeled after the Polish organization Solidarity.[73] Like a flash in the pan, the demand for an independent union came and went, leaving no further traces except for the state's denouncement of it.

Some of the workers who protested in 1978–1980 were alert enough to sense the dire consequences of Deng's reform policy for workers. They were stationed in major cities such as Beijing, Shanghai, and Guangzhou. They sounded the first alarm suggesting that the era of symbiosis with the socialist state might end. These "backward-looking" workers boldly expressed their dissent against the reformers in the Deng administration. They were concerned about suggestions in the press for the state to adopt the principle of scientific management designed by an American, Frederick Taylor. The reformers blamed the inefficiency and anarchy in the factories on job security and egalitarianism, known in Chinese as the phenomena of workers' having "iron rice bowls" (*tiefanwan*) and "everybody's eating from the same big pot" (*chi daguofan*).[74] In response, a dissident worker maintained that the lack of discipline in Chinese factories was caused not by "iron rice bowls" but by cadres' "bureaucratism." The idea of one-sided emphasis on workers' discipline, said this critic, was misguided.[75] Another worker declared that what must be eliminated was the "iron command position" (*tiejiaoyi*) of cadres, not the "iron rice bowls" of workers. After all, according to this worker, the "iron rice bowl" stood for "the superiority of socialism"; otherwise there would be no difference between socialism and capitalism. The passivity and lethargy of Chinese workers, according to this dissenter, were caused mainly by irrational administration and cadres' "bureaucratism."[76]

While articulate workers joined movements led by dissenting intellectuals in Beijing and Shanghai for conservative purposes, those in the peripheral provinces staged strikes. The most noteworthy strikes occurred in Shanxi Province. In the provincial capital of Taiyuan, a series of demonstrations were organized by printers and steelworkers from December 1980 through March 1981. The printers even organized a political party in 1979, called the Chinese Democratic Party and, according to the government's charges against them, had proselytized their views through wall posters and pamphlets. They were reported to have gone to other provinces to recruit supporters. There were no details about this movement except for what the government chose to reveal in its indictment against the three striking leaders in 1981.[77]

The Taiyuan printers' political movement was soon succeeded by strikes and demonstrations among the 3,000 workers at the Taiyuan Steelworks in December 1980. The protest was sparked by the staff members and workers who lived away from their families and who had long-standing grievances against the management. Their initial demands were entirely economic, asking mainly for rights to bring their families to the city and for better housing arrangements. Their only "political" demand was to be able to elect their own representative, presumably to sit in the factory's management committee.[78] But the strike by this group showed potential for wider appeal, as they were soon joined by other steelworkers. Their initial economic grievances were expanded to include more issues. A journal, *Fengfan [The Sail]*, was published and other political demands were made. Slogans such as "Down with One-Party Rule," "[For the] Right to Decide Our Own Future," "For Liberty and Democracy," "Overthrow the Political Bureaucratic System," and "Down with Bureaucratism and Dictatorship" were expressed. The strikers were reported to have knowledge about the Polish Solidarity movement.[79]

One of the contributing factors to the labor unrest in Taiyuan was its large number of staffers and workers from other provinces. In the 1950s, the CCP had wanted to industrialize the Northwest and forcibly moved many staff members and workers from the industrialized eastern provinces of the country to northwestern places such as Taiyuan. The protesting workers in Taiyuan were probably encouraged by the returning-residents' movement then going on among the educated youths who had been forced to settle in the countryside by Mao's administration. During 1978–1981, a great majority of these youths had returned to the cities of their origins.

Labor unrest also took place elsewhere in China during this period. Anshan steelworkers in Liaoning Province called a strike against poor working conditions in 1981.[80] Chinese union officials had conceded to a visiting labor delegation from France in March 1981 that labor protests had occurred in several places.[81] But, like the peasants' turmoils in this period, the protests by the workers were all localized affairs. Taiyuan was peripheral to the industrial centers in northeastern and eastern China. Except for the strike in Anshan, there was no major strike activity in the industrial centers of eastern China.

The factories in the eastern region, however, were affected by the so-called young worker's problem (involving workers below thirty-five years old). The low morale of young workers had plagued Chinese factories since 1957. As mentioned earlier, the Cultural Revolution worsened the youth problem. To those youngsters who had been assigned factory jobs, the promised reform by Deng after 1978 was of no significance. They knew that their fate was sealed. They were left with nothing but feelings of bitterness and cynicism. According to a high-ranking Party official, young workers were "disgusted with politics, lacking revolutionary ideals, having no faith in the CCP or socialism, emphasizing instead concrete benefits, and displaying the attitude of wage labor"; they "obeyed no discipline, appropriated public property, and engaged in fights and rows."[82] The telltale sign of the young workers' political disaffection was their scorn for officially designated "advanced workers." It was reported, for example, that whereas among old workers 0.8 percent had won the title of "advanced worker," the proportion was 0.3 percent among young workers.[83] Numerous press reports in the early 1980s lamented the widespread practice of ostracizing and persecuting those who had been designated "advanced workers." Of the 126 "advanced workers" in the textile industry in 1981, sixty-six (52.4 percent) had been ostracized in their work places.[84]

Numerous opinion surveys of young workers concluded uniformly that the young were cynical, passive, and materialistic. A trade union survey of a Chongqing textile factory in 1981 found that over 80 percent of young workers (constituting 52 percent of all the staff members and workers in the plant) were interested mainly in "material benefits," rather than ideology or state affairs. The proportion of those who still believed in the CCP or in socialism was less than 2 percent.[85] A study of a Tianjin textile factory, where half of its work force was young, reported similar findings. Those said to be serious in work and hopeful about the future amounted to 15 to 20 percent.[86] In a confidential report of a study in a Xián bearing factory conducted by the Communist Youth League, young workers were asked for their personal beliefs and the most popular answer was: "With power a person can have anything." The motto with which the largest number of young workers expressed agreement was: "An honest fellow suffers losses in life."[87] It was no wonder that, among the most active youth dissenters in the 1978–1980 Democracy Wall phenomenon, a substantial proportion were factory workers such as the famous Wei Jingsheng.

The state responded to the unrest in this early reform transition by using both a carrot and a stick. In 1977 and 1979, for the first time in twenty years, approximately 40 to 46 percent of the workers received wage raises.[88] Walder's research, however, pointed out that wage reforms failed to lift the workers' morale and, in fact, caused new contentions and conflicts among them.[89] To deal with workers' indiscipline, the state formally legitimized the authority of the manager over the staff and workers. From then on, Chinese factories would be run on the basis of "one-man leadership." Even the Party secretary had to yield to the authority of the manager, as far as running the factory was concerned. These initial reform measures did not threaten the symbiotic relationship between workers and the state. But the government began to prepare the workers psychologically for an eventual break from their "iron rice bowls." In 1983, an experimental "labor contract" system was implemented in Sichuan Province. Meanwhile, the press published regular reports criticizing past practices of permanent employment and egalitarianism in wage policy.

Workers Under Accelerated Reforms, 1986–1994

Beginning in 1986 the state accelerated the pace of industrial reforms and workers felt even more keenly that their dependence on the state was becoming less tenable. In the brief period of three years, from 1986 to 1988, the state announced one measure after another, each designed to undermine the workers' security of employment. In 1986 the state formalized the "labor contract system" and with it, three other rules dealing with labor recruitment, dismissal of laborers, and unemployment insurance. In the same year, the national legislature began drafting a law on bankruptcy. Signaling the state's serious frame of mind, a small factory in the Northeast was declared bankrupt and its seventy-two staff members and workers became unemployed. The following year, the government shifted its attention to the problem of overstaffing in state firms and started a trimming campaign under the euphemistic title of "optimum regrouping of labor" (*youhualaodong zuhe*). In 1988, it was "discovered" that some 30 million people occupied redundant positions; the state determined that it would "shake off" these extraneous individuals.[90] An editorial in the newspaper *Worker's Daily* declared: "Unemployment is a positive way of increasing the economic results of our country's enterprises."[91]

Then, in 1988, a Bankruptcy Law was formally enacted by the National People's Congress. Legally speaking, the former symbiosis between the worker and the state was terminated. In reality, these reform programs were more bark than bite. The results of the labor contract system were disappointing to the reformers; "it had encountered 'all sorts of difficulties and problems,'" wrote Gordon White.[92] The reduction of redundant personnel moved at a snail's pace. By 1992, only 1 percent of staffers and workers had lost their jobs.[93] The government had declared approximately five-hundred state firms bankrupt by 1994. The total number of state firms to be eliminated was approximately 17,000.[94] Nevertheless, the reforms created a climate of anxiety among the workers and staff. For the first time since the founding of the PRC in 1949, the workers and the state seemed to be in a zero-sum relationship. What were gains for the government—such as economy in expenses and efficiency in production—meant loss of income and job security for the workers.

In 1993, the CCP convened an important meeting (the Third Plenary Session of the fourteenth CCP Central Committee Standing Committee) to announce that 1994 was going to be "the year of reform." The Party-state would go to great lengths to realize its previously announced reforms, such as the labor contract system and the elimination of excess labor. The government made it plain that it intended to have a labor market just as any other market economy had. Gone was the state's ideological reservation with respect to Marx's denunciation of a worker's "selling" his labor. Moreover, establishing a labor market was an integral part of the government's project of transforming the inefficient and unprofitable state firms into modern enterprises. In other words, the reformists in Beijing wished to change the state firms from institutions back into economic organizations, operating according to economic principles (that is, from the present *gemeinschaft* into *gesellschaft*). The present firms would be subject to a purge in which the inefficient ones would undergo a process of "closing down, suspending operations, mergers, or shifting to other product lines."[95] These policy statements were likely to remain unacted upon for sometime to come, given the fate of other reform decrees mentioned earlier. The government itself acknowledged tremendous difficulty ahead. The Party organ, *People's Daily*, described the obstacles to developing a labor market as "a hard nut to crack" and trimming excess workers and staff from state firms as "the biggest difficulty in the readjustment of the industrial structure."[96] Consequently, however, the growth of state industrial firms and their employees did

Table 3.1 Growth of Industrial Enterprises, Staff, and Workers

Year	Enterprises (unit: 10,000)	Staff and worker (unit: 10,000)
1980	8.34	3,245.8
1981	8.42	3,406.7
1982	8.61	3,502.7
1983	8.71	3,522
1984	8.41	3,592
1985	9.37	3,815
1986	9.68	—
1987	9.76	4,086
1988	9.91	4,229
1989	10.23	4,237
1990	10.44	4,364
1991	10.47	4,472
1992	10.33	4,521

Sources: "Social Labor Force by Sector" and "Number of Industrial Enterprises and Gross Output Value of Industry by Ownership," in *Zhongguo Tongji Nianjian* [Statistical Yearbook of China] of the following years: 1981, 1983, 1984, 1985, 1986, 1988, 1989, 1990, 1991, 1992, and 1993.

slow down, as Table 3.1 shows. In the first period of reform, from 1980 to 1985, state-owned industrial firms increased by 12 percent. But, from 1986 to 1992, the rate of growth declined to 6.7 percent. In the number of staff and workers, the percentage increase from 1980 to 1985 was 17.5. However, the figure was 10.6 percent from 1987 to 1992. The government seemed to be retrenching very gradually.

In the meantime, both internal and external conditions of state firms were changing rapidly and all of them threatened the workers' livelihood. The first among these conditions was the impact of other government policies, which forced many state firms to reveal insolvency. In 1994, the government enforced a new taxation system that abolished many tax shelters and imposed a new value-added tax. For many state firms—already saddled with debts, overstaffing, and large inventories—the real rate of the new tax amounted to 92 percent of their net incomes.[97] An estimated 40 percent of these firms incurred business losses in 1994.[98] Many firms drastically cut the wages of staff and workers, others could not pay wages at all. The number of press reports describing workers' hardships escalated. There were even accounts of workers' committing suicides.[99] In the long run, workers in inefficient state firms seemed to be doomed; either the state or the market would force these firms to close down.

The second condition was inflation and it cut deeply into workers' incomes. In 1987–1989, inflation reduced substantially the incomes of 30 to 40 percent of urban workers.[100] Jeanne Wilson reported that workers launched strikes and demonstrations, the largest involving 1,500 workers in a textile mill in Zhejiang Province.[101] According to Walder, inflation was one of the workers' primary grievances. It drove them to take advantage of the students' pro-democracy movement and to stage demonstrations in May and June 1989.[102] Workers' hardships returned in 1993 and 1994, reflected in an inflation rate of 25 percent. The rates of price increases in individual cities were even higher than the national average.[103] In Henan Province the provincial union found that 41 percent of the workers and staff suffered a decline in living standards due to inflation in 1993.[104] It is no wonder that there was a rapid rise in workers' protests from 1992 to 1994.

The third external change that impinged on state firms was the speedy proliferation of other types of enterprises, particularly joint ventures and foreign-owned firms. Table 3.2 shows that from 1985 to 1992 employees in state firms (all state firms included, not just industrial ones) rose by 21 percent, while those in joint ventures and foreign-owned firms increased by 3,793 percent and 2,940 percent, respectively. Although collective firms (primarily those owned by townships, counties, or municipalities) grew at a lower rate, they employed a substantial number of people. Many state firms were incapable of competing with the new firms that were much more adaptive to the market forces.

The official *China Daily Business Weekly* reported in 1994 that about half of the state-owned textile factories in thirty-nine major cities were operating at a deficit. In the first ten months of 1993 they lost US$182 million. The chief reason for the losses was competition from both foreign and domestic firms. In 1992, the township textile enterprises produced more than $11 billion worth of goods.[105] Even in Shanghai, where some of China's most advanced state firms are located, competition from non-

Table 3.2 Distribution of Staff and Workers by Types of Ownership, 1985–1992

Year	State-owned	Collective-owned	Joint ventures	Foreign-owned
1985	89,900,000	33,240,000	49,848	10,782
1988	99,840,000	35,270,000	280,380	25,645
1989	101,080,000	35,202,000	413,526	56,607
1990	103,460,000	35,490,000	575,468	83,904
1991	106,640,000	36,280,000	1,237,344	302,785
1992	108,890,000	36,210,000	1,908,580	304,009

Note: No data available for 1986 and 1987.

Source: Zhongguo Tongji Nianjian, 1993 [Statistical Yearbook of China, 1993] (Beijing: Guojia Tongjiju, 1993), pp. 97 and 109.

state enterprises forced some state companies to shut down and lay off workers and staff.[106] By 1994, the number of textile workers in Shanghai declined from 500,000 to 450,000 and was expected to shrink even further to about 250,000. The unemployed textile workers were said to have called themselves "the money trees of the 1950s, the bitter flowers of the 1990s."[107] The existence of other forms of enterprises not only endangered the job security of some state-firm workers but also caused envy and resentment among those who were still employed by the state. The average wages of *industrial* workers in state firms in 1992 were only 77 percent of the wages of those in foreign-owned or joint venture firms.[108]

In the face of all these ominous developments, the Party-state in Beijing sought to reassure state-firm workers and staffers. An article in the CCP's chief ideological journal, *Qiushi* [Seeking Truth], declared in May 1994:

> In the course of developing a socialist market economy, China's socialist system remains unchanged, the nature of the state remains unchanged, the working class being the leading class of the state remains unchanged, the working class being the class basis of the party remains unchanged, and the working class, as the master of its own affairs, remains unchanged.[109]

However, the context of these reassuring words was not very reassuring to the workers. The author wanted workers to support the government's project of turning state-firms into "modern enterprises." Other pronouncements by the CCP, designed to calm workers, were also equivocal. The *People's Daily* quoted Deng's remark to prove that the leaders in Beijing had no intention of abandoning state-owned firms. Deng was reported to have said: "As long as public ownership remains the mainstay of our economy, we will be able to prevent polarization." The essay went on to say that only selected industries would continue to be operated by the state. These include public utilities, infrastructure, communications, mines, and strategic industries. In other words, there would be a major retrenchment and restructuring of public enterprises.[110] For the majority of workers in state firms, the era of a worker-state symbiosis seemed to be rapidly coming to an end.

General Opinion of Workers

The reactions of Chinese workers to Deng's "shock treatment" in the late 1980s and early 1990s exposed fully the multifarious character of the working class. The attitudes and opinions of the workers may be analyzed on five levels: (1) personal, (2) institutional, (3) social, (4) system, and (5) cultural.

At the personal level, Chinese workers are concerned primarily with their economic well-being and that of their families. Perhaps the best evidence of this may be found in an article by a worker that was published in a dissident journal during the Democracy Wall movement of 1978–1980 in Guangzhou. The essay said in part:

> The Party Center has publicized the lofty goal of "four modernizations." It proclaims that by the year 2000 so many power stations, factories, and oil fields would be constructed. All of us rejoice at these. But for the workers there seems to be something missing [in these targets]. Why is it that our leaders have not set targets for upgrading people's living standard? *We laboring people stress practical things.* We are concerned with the "four modernizations." But we are also concerned with how much benefits the four modernizations might bring to us. (emphasis added)[111]

Changes subsequent to the publication of this essay certainly made economic issues more salient than ever for the working class of China. A poll of 50,000 staffers and workers in twelve cities and provinces was conducted in 1992–1993 by scholar Feng Tongqin of the Chinese Institute of the Workers' Movement (Zhongguo Gongyunyuan)—presumably an arm of the ACFTU tasked with training union cadres. The survey found that the three things to which workers and staffers gave their primary attention were (in descending order): personal income, the individual housing condition, and a company's welfare program. Addressing personal goals, the poll showed that 46 percent of the workers wanted "a stable and comfortable life" and "a happy family." These two conditions were given the highest priorities by the workers. Thirty-four percent of the technical staff and 31 percent of the cadres echoed the workers' desire for a life characterized by personal and familial well-being. In contrast, workers were least enthusiastic about nonmaterial goals, such as "serving society," "making the country strong and prosperous," and "realizing Communism." Only 35 percent of the workers mentioned these as their primary goals. The corresponding proportions among the technical staff was 48 percent and among cadres, 55 percent.[112]

Another survey of the opinions among various social strata by Lu Jianhua of the Chinese Academy of Social Sciences in 1992 corroborated Feng's findings. Workers in the second survey gave reforms in the following areas as their "primary concerns": wages, housing, social security, personnel system, and prices. The proportions of workers who experienced hardships were striking: 75.5 percent said that they had an unsteady income, while 75.3 percent said they had an unstable occupation. Lu's survey recovered 19,856 questionnaires from twenty-four cities and towns.[113]

On the institutional level, workers in large state-owned firms seemed to live in an environment of class conflict, sectionalism, and atomization. Given the factionalized situation in the factories in the 1970s, revelations from the polls and reports from field research are not surprising. Walder's study, for example, described workers as having divided themselves into two groups: (1) political activists who were allied themselves with the cadres (management), and (2) the rest of the workers. The relationship between the two was antagonistic.[114] This fundamental class conflict between cadres (as agents of the state) and workers was like a red thread that ran through virtually every study or reference to intergroup relations in Chinese factories.

It should be noted that this class conflict has a long history. It came into existence as soon as the CCP took over the factories in the early 1950s. In an essay on "contradictions within the working class" in the 1990s, a Chinese scholar concluded that the chief conflict was between the manager and the managed. The underlying causes were disparities in political and social status, power, and income. The ratios of pay and bonus between a worker and a cadre ranged from 1:10 to 1:117.[115] Mayfair Mei-hui Yang reported that the workers she interviewed pointed out that cadres always had the first opportunity to buy any goods that came into the factory before they were sold to other workers.[116] That the workers' image of Party members was less than complimentary was borne out in a poll of 1,362 workers and staff members in Beijing. Conducted by the Institute of Social Survey in 1988, the survey showed that 61 percent of the workers said "no" when asked whether Party members in general were "selfless and public spirited." Among Party members, 73 percent answered affirmatively.[117] Conflicts between workers and management (cadres) were fundamentally dissensual—the differences were in outlook and life chances. Compared to workers, the management had higher levels of education and a higher rate of membership in the CCP and the factory legislature (the so-called congress of workers and staff). The management also enjoyed a higher rate of job mobility than workers did. In response to questions, the management was much more oriented toward nonmaterial goals than were the workers.[118]

In addition to class conflicts, Chinese factories were rife with sectional conflicts. Yang's ethnographic study of a printing factory ("collectively owned," not state-owned) exposed a highly segmented situation inside the plant. Workers were divided along the lines of age, skills, status, and shops. Low morale pervaded the factory.[119] Feng's survey found that workers' views toward their coworkers were mixed. More than half of the workers (59 percent) deemed that their coworkers either did not fully apply themselves to their work or were "average" in accomplishing their tasks. Forty-one percent said that their colleagues fully applied themselves to their work. Feng also found that the staff and workers employed in foreign-operated firms or in joint ventures (primarily with U.S. and European businesses) were more positive toward their work and colleagues than were the workers and staff in state firms.[120]

The workers' identification with their firms also seemed tenuous. The 1988 poll by the Institute of Social Survey in Beijing found that workers seemed to be generally unconcerned with whatever problems their firms had. Forty-six percent of the respondents failed to name any problem in their enterprises. Only about 20.6 percent of those polled made any suggestions to the management on affairs concerning their plants. The 1993 study by Feng Tongqin delved deeper into workers' institutional identity. First of all, the workers' overall attitude toward the work itself was indifferent. When asked whether they were pleased as they arrived at work in the morning, the highest proportion (59 percent) picked the answer "so-so," 32 percent answered they were "pleased," and 9 percent said they were "fed up". Close to 26 percent of the workers sought transfer to other firms, but only one-third of the requests were granted. With respect to workers' interest in the affairs of their firms, Feng's study found that those in state firms were concerned more but got less satisfaction than did those in foreign-operated or joint venture firms. When the workers and staff in state firms were asked for their choice of employer if they were transferred to another job, 32 percent chose non-state-operated firms.

On the social level, Chinese workers behaved like any vested interest group—resentful of all those who earned more than they did. Scholar Bo Ningxiang reported that workers harbored grievances against the following groups: (1) professionals whose status and incomes were raised under Deng's administration, (2) those who worked in the service sector because their wages were higher, and (3) other workers employed in foreign-owned firms, joint ventures, and special economic zones. "At the beginning of our state," wrote Bo, "the workers felt proud of being called 'Big Brother the Worker,' but now their sense of superiority in the old days was replaced by a sense of loss."[121] Feng reported that the workers' resentment of private entrepreneurs was striking. When the workers as a whole were asked the question "Which type of people do you admire the most?" those who chose the answer "successful self-employed people" amounted to only 5.8 percent but, among workers in state firms, the percentage further declined to 4.9 percent.

On the system level, workers were ambivalent and conservative. Many saw Deng's reforms either being carried out at their expense or being directed at them. From the perspective of some workers, the so-called "optimum regrouping of labor" (trimming excess laborers) became the management's excuse to rid the factory of workers who had, in the past, offended management. In eliminating the "three irons" ("iron rice bowl," "iron position," and "iron wage"), workers maintained that the chief target was the workers' "iron rice bowls," not the cadres' "iron positions." Workers charged that in carrying out in-house reforms such as subcontracting, leasing out, and changing into share-holding companies, the management rarely considered workers' rights and interests.[122] For example, the vice-president of ACFTU complained in 1994 that in the campaign to convert state firms into modern corporations, "undue emphasis is laid on property rights relationship to the neglect of labor relationship and on funds and equipment to the neglect of the role of laborers in pushing productive forces forward." (translation not mine).[123]

Almost every poll has found that among various social groups the workers invariably accounted for the highest proportion of those who opposed post-Mao reforms. In Lu Jianhua's survey mentioned earlier, only 36.4 percent of the workers expressed agreement with the statement, "The necessary conditions having been obtained, reforms should be accelerated." The corresponding proportions among college students, peasants, cadres, and professionals were: 39.7, 44.3, 45.5, and 46.5 percent, respectively. There were practical and normative aspects to workers' opposition to reforms. Older workers felt that they had endured a hard life for a long time under Mao and that the Dengist state failed to appreciate their contribution to the country. Now that they were old, the reforms threatened to deprive them of their retirement benefits. Young workers both looked forward to and were afraid of the reforms. "To them," as one account put it, "the workers are always the subjects of experiments no matter what the reforms are, so they suspect that the ax is about to fall on them once again, this time, only to leave them out of work in the future."[124] In addition to these practical concerns, workers felt that the new and "modernized" system deprived them of their past sense of community. One report described the workers' sentiment as follows: "Employees start to feel that the entire operation, including themselves, is like a giant machine which operates meticulously and mechanically according to set procedures, putting them in a passive role throughout. Meanwhile, ideological and political work [of the state] teaches that the employee is the master of enterprise."[125]

On the cultural level, Chinese workers were predominantly of the "subject" frame of mind. The specific manifestations of this were: an authoritarian and personalistic perspective on leadership, an egalitarian view toward social relationships, and a very weak sense of individual rights. I must stress here that subsequent discussions are based on secondary sources and are interpretive in nature.

The Chinese worker's authoritarianism may be seen in the data presented in Tables 3.3 and 3.4. The information was gathered by Chinese scholar Zhang Panshi of the Sociological Institute of the Chinese Academy of Social Sciences.[126] It was based on a survey of workers in forty factories in fifteen cities, including Beijing, Shanghai, and Xiamen in 1990. The total

Table 3.3 Degree of Factory Staff and Workers Concerned About Management's Conduct

Very or relatively concerned	Very or relatively unconcerned	Indifferent
Factory leaders (96.6%)	Engineers (29.7)	Assistant engineers (24.8)
Shop cadres (75.8)	Ordinary workers (22.8)	Ordinary workers (23.7)
Political cadres (66.3)	Technicians,	Group leaders (20)
Group leaders (62.1)	accountants,	Engineers (19.8)
Technicians,	statisticians (21)	Technicians,
accountants,	Political cadres (17.9)	accountants,
statisticians (59.7)	Group leaders (17.8)	statisticians (19.2)
Assistant engineers (59.6)	Assistant engineers (15.5)	Political cadres (15.8)
Ordinary workers (53.9)	Shop cadres (11.4)	Shop cadres (12.8)
Engineers (50.4)	Factory leaders (3.3)	Factory leaders (0.0)

Note: The percentages in parentheses refer to those in each group expressing various degrees of concern.

Source: Zhang Panshi, "Qiye Lingdao Fangshi Yu Zhigong Jijixindi Diacha" [An investigation of firm leadership style and the initiative of workers and staff] *Shehuixue* [Sociology], no. 4 (1991): 123.

number of the workers interviewed was 5,396. Table 3.3 shows that, compared with other groups in the factory, the workers were relatively unconcerned with the management's leadership style. Workers ranked low in the category "very or relatively concerned" and high in "very or relatively unconcerned." The workers also occupied the number two position in the "indifferent" category. What is intriguing in Table 3.3 is that the attitude of engineers was close to that of the workers. One wonders if the engineers' indifference to factory leadership style is due to their having gained status in the post-Mao period.

Table 3.4 presents various groups' satisfaction with their leaders' democratic practice. Apparently, democracy is not a very meaningful concept to the workers. The positions of their answers were neither high nor low in the "very or relatively satisfied" and "indifferent" categories; the workers scored low in "very or relatively dissatisfied" category. Once more the answers of the technicians and engineers were very close to that of the workers. It seems that the "subject political culture" of the working class parallels the indifference or apathy of the technical intelligentsia. At the same time, there is a cultural chasm between the working class and the managerial class. Those in management—such as factory directors, shop leaders, and political cadres—were more concerned with leadership style and more critical of the degree of democracy inside factories than the workers or the engineers. In the industrial society of China, it there-

Table 3.4 Degree of Factory Staff and Workers Satisfied with
Management's Democratic Practices

Satisfied or relatively satisfied (in percentage)	Dissatisfied or relatively dissatisfied	Indifferent
Factory leaders (60)	Assistant engineers (42.2)	Engineers (39.7)
Shop cadres (46.6)	Political cadres (41.1)	Technicians,
Political cadres (39.2)	Group leaders (38.1)	accountants,
Ordinary workers (39)	Shop cadres (36.6)	statisticians (29.4)
Group leaders (38.4)	Factory leaders (36.6)	Assistant engineers (26.7)
Technicians,	Technicians,	Ordinary workers (25.9)
accountants,	accountants,	Group leaders (23.4)
statisticians (35.4)	statisticians (35.2)	Political cadres (19.6)
Assistant engineers (31.1)	Ordinary workers (35)	Shop cadres (16.7)
Engineers (26.5)	Engineers (33.9)	Factory leaders (3.3)

Note: The percentages in parentheses refer to those in each group expressing various degrees of satisfaction.

Source: Zhang Panshi, "Qiye Lingdao Fangshi Yu Zhigong Jijixindi Diaocha" [An investigation of firm leadership style and the initiative of workers and staff], *Shehuixue* [Sociology], no. 4 (1991): 123.

fore seems that there were three, instead of two, cultures: the "subject culture" of the workers, the separatist culture of the technical intelligentsia, and the participant culture of the management and cadres.

But the workers' view toward in-house democracy is actually more complex than the data in the two tables revealed, for the political views of the workers were highly personalistic. Thus, "democracy" as an abstract concept might not mean much to the workers, but if one translates democracy into personal terms, the workers' views are no longer ambiguous. For example, Zhang asked the workers whether their work morale would suffer if their factory director decided everything on his own: 44.6 percent answered affirmatively, 30.9 percent replied "it is hard to say," and 24.5 percent answered negatively (7 percent said they "will still work energetically" and 17.5 percent answered they would "work relatively energetically"). In overwhelming proportions, the workers preferred leaders who were personally solicitous and fair-minded in treating subordinates. The 1988 survey of Beijing workers and staff by the Institute of Social Survey cited earlier also lends some support to the thesis that workers personalize politics. When workers were asked to name major issues of concern, the political issues raised were entirely about conduct of the cadres: corruption, officials' profiteering, bad conduct of the children of officials, and dishonesty in government. The workers' personalistic image of politics is consistent with the Confucian tradition, which regards a good government as the extension of morally exemplary men.

The Confucianist and personalistic perspective of the Chinese working class is fundamentally embedded in the millenarianism of Chinese peasants. The core value of this millenarian view is egalitarianism, which is also strongly represented in Mao's thinking. The workers' preference for egalitarianism shows up almost everywhere. In 1985, the municipal government of Shanghai conducted a survey of 11,823 families for their views on wage reform. One question tested their tolerance for wage differential among different professions. The survey found that people's views were diverse. The highest rate of consensus was that 30.8 percent of the respondents allowed a differential of only ten *yuan*. However, researchers found that workers had the highest rate of agreement: 42 percent said that only a ten *yuan* differential should be allowed.[127] A 1986 ACFTU survey of 640,000 staffers and workers found that 56 percent did not like the price reforms; 38 percent disagreed with the policy of encouraging some people to become rich first; and 14 percent disapproved of individual businesses.[128]

In 1989, the publication *Zhongguo Fangzhibao* (China Textile) conducted an opinion survey of workers in 129 textile mills. In one mill, 74 percent of the workers expressed their anger at income inequity. They were especially resentful of four groups of *nouveau riches*: singers, "unscrupulous merchants," officials-turned-profiteers, and "haughty cadres."[129] The 1988 poll by the Institute of Social Survey in Beijing found that close to 80 percent of the respondents disagreed—or somewhat disagreed—with the statement "enterprises that are profitable deserve respect." Fifty-seven percent agreed or somewhat agreed with the statement "competition benefits only a minority." Workers' responses to the ambiguous statement "how hard one works should correspond to how much one gets paid" were intriguing. Fifty-six percent disagreed or somewhat disagreed, whereas 43 percent agreed or somewhat agreed. On the whole, evidence seems persuasive that the Chinese working class is strongly disinclined toward a competitive and meritocratic social system. Their preference is for a moralistic, egalitarian, and functionally diffused community. Chinese intellectuals who have had experience working in factories, therefore, often maintain that workers and peasants are culturally indistinct. One writer put it this way: "Most Chinese workers came from peasantry. Like that of peasants, the political culture of workers was of a compliant nature. Their willpower was weak and their vision, not broad. They were conscious primarily of things of immediate interest to them, rather than major issues such as reform."[130]

The millenarian aspirations of workers were naturally associated with their weak sense of personal rights. The 1988 poll by the Institute of Social Survey in Beijing probed the workers' concept of individual rights. The results astounded the pollsters. Over half of the respondents did not regard the following as violations of their rights: bribery, late arrival in meetings, dismissal, violation of rules and regulations, interference in one's private affairs, naming names in public criticism, and disinclination to associate with the masses. The workers seemed to have no meaningful sense of individual rights. The widespread workers' resentment against corrupt cadres now seemed not to have been caused by any sense of workers' rights having been violated; rather, their anger was directed at the cadres' having betrayed the spirit of an egalitarian community. The workers' stress on a moral community instead of individual rights is seen also in their view of interpersonal relationships. Almost 80 percent of the respondents in the 1988 Beijing survey agreed or somewhat agreed with the statement "to receive payment for helping a friend is embarrassing."

Specific Opinion in the Late Reform Period

In the light of the discussions so far, it is not surprising that labor unrest surged in the late 1980s and early 1990s. Now that the state was severing its umblical cord with the workers, the latter naturally fought back with increasing militancy. The late reform period is thus marked by a rapid rise of both class and sectional conflicts among Chinese workers. A national union official reported in 1988 that there were ninety-seven strikes in the previous year and forty-nine in the first six months of 1988.[131] Overall, the labor unrest from the late 1980s through the early 1990s displayed a prominent segmentary character, each group of workers fighting its own battle within a particular locality, much like the peasants who confined their small rebellions to their isolated rural communities.

In the late 1980s, unrest first occurred among the relatively privileged urban workers in large state firms. The high inflation in 1988–1989 triggered their protest activities. Workers did not join the students initially in the April–June 1989 pro-democracy movement. However, in mid-May, after workers perceived a split among the Party leaders, they turned out in increasing numbers to demonstrate on their own.[132] Walder correctly observed that the management acquiesced—and even supported—these demonstrations. Even while rebelling against the state, the workers displayed a subject political culture. There was at best a limited identification of interests between the workers and the student dissidents. The workers who demonstrated in the late 1980s did so more for negative reasons (especially their dissatisfaction with the post-Mao reforms) rather than because they approved of the students' new Westernized ideology. This was shown in a 1989 survey of 2,521 staffers and workers in an unnamed major Chinese city. The study found that 53 percent of the respondents were dissatisfied with the economic reforms, 36 percent expressed indifference, and 12 percent supported reforms. Since the poll was conducted not long after a major student protest movement in 1986–1987, the workers were asked about their views toward student protest. Their responses reflected serious internal divisions: 38 percent supported it, 37 percent opposed it, and 25 percent took no stand. However, the pollsters found a positive correlation between the degree of dissatisfaction with the reforms and support for the students. Among those supporting reforms, only 7 percent approved of student demonstrations. But among those dissatisfied with reforms, 53 percent supported the student protest.[133]

A few dissident workers emerged in the late 1980s, representing perhaps the beginning of a pan-worker movement, small and weak though it might be. In 1989, dissident workers in Beijing and elsewhere organized their own unions; the most famous one was the Workers Autonomous Federation in Beijing. Dissident unions appeared in major cities such as Shanghai, Changsha, Huhehot (Hohhot), Nanjing, Xian, Guizhou, Wuhan, and Hangzhou. The federations wished to operate openly and pledged to observe the constitution and the law of the state. The main purpose of the federations, according to Han Dongfang, the leader of the Beijing branch, was "to build an organization that can truly speak for the workers."[134] According to Jeanne Wilson, it was probably the fear of an expanding workers' movement that prompted the CCP hardliners to carry out the brutal crackdown.[135] Wilson's thesis is at least partially supported by the fact that the Beijing regime was particularly harsh toward those workers who joined the students in protesting and organizing. According to a report by the International Confederation of Free Trade Unions, "the severity of the sentences meted out to workers, . . . was based not on objective judicial criteria nor even on determination of guilt, but on political considerations, particularly union activity."[136] But even given the desperate situations that some of the workers were in, state repression could not stop workers' protests. There were 715 labor disputes, including strikes, from June through December 1989.[137]

A surge in labor turmoil occurred at the beginning of 1990. That year, there were 1,620 incidents of worker disputes involving some 37,450 workers.[138] Thereafter, unrest among the workers continued. In April 1994, a government report stated that labor disputes increased by 50 percent from 1992.[139] In mid-1994, incidents of industrial unrest were said to be occurring once or twice a week in the provinces of Hubei, Hunan, Heilongjiang, and Liaoning. The affected areas were in the depressed industries, including coal and textiles.[140] Worker militancy in the 1990s differed from that in the late 1980s in one respect: A more pluralistic composition existed in the ranks of worker protesters in the 1990s. Class and sectional conflicts now occurred both among the privileged and underprivileged workers. The second group was employed mainly in private or foreign-owned firms and joint ventures. The traditionally underprivileged and militant coal miners remained as restive as ever in the 1990s.

As discussed at some length earlier, workers in state firms were experiencing severe strain in the 1990s. Their conflicts with the state were reflected in an internal police document reporting on the instances of "illegal" civil disobedience throughout China in 1992. This document, entitled "Concerning Illegal Demonstrations, Assemblies, Strikes, and Boycotts in Localities, Villages, Factories, and Mines in 1992,"[141] was published by the Ministry of Public Security in 1993. Judging by the reports in the Chinese press and the sparse presence of police in the rural areas, it is safe to presume that the bulk of demonstrations and strikes mentioned in this document was staged by workers and staffers. In Table 3.5, I rank the

Table 3.5 Frequency of Turmoil in China, 1992

Province	No. of incidents	Population	Percent of urbanization	Per capita income[a]
1) Sichuan	78	107,218,173	20.25	$261
2) Jiangxi	52	37,710,281	20.40	214
3) Hunan	50	60,659,754	18.23	257
4) Anhui	43	56,180,813	17.90	241
5) Shaanxi	37	32,882,403	21.49	244
6) Shanxi	35	28,759,014	28.72	221.6
7) Heilongjiang	34	35,214,873	47.17	220
8) Xinjiang	33	15,155,778	31.91	250
9) Henan	32	85,509,535	15.52	216
10) Inner Mongolia	31	21,456,798	36.12	203.6
11) Hubei	30	53,969,210	28.91	243.7
12) Hebei	29	61,082,439	19.08	262.6
13) Liaoning	29	39,459,697	50.86	274
14) Guangxi	26	42,245,765	15.10	277.5
15) Guizhou	26	32,391,066	18.93	226
16) Guangdong	23	62,829,236	36.77	414
17) Zhejiang	22	41,445,930	32.81	351
18) Qinghai	19	4,456,946	27.35	242
19) Yunnan	18	36,972,610	14.72	252
20) Jilin	15	24,658,721	42.65	217
21) Shandong	13	84,392,827	27.34	267
22) Beijing	13	10,819,407	73.08	340
23) Ningxia	12	4,655,451	25.72	235
24) Gansu	12	22,371,141	22.04	241
25) Fujian	11	30,048,224	21.36	306.5
26) Jiangsu	11	67,056,519	21.24	292
27) Tianjin	8	8,785,402	68.65	292.5
28) Shanghai	2	13,341,896	66.23	396

[a]1990 figures from New China News Agency (*NCNA*), May 20, 1990.

Note: No data available from Hainan and Tibet.

Source: For turmoils, *Cheng Ming*, no. 185 (March 1, 1993): 19.

provinces and three municipalities (Beijing, Tianjin, and Shanghai) in the order of instances of turmoil (combining all the activities of civil disobedience in the police reports). I also provide data on population, urbanization, and per capita income.

The first notable feature in Table 3.5 is the low frequency of disturbances in the fast-growing eastern provinces, which include Shandong, Jiangsu, and Zhejiang. Moreover, the economically underdeveloped provinces, where ethnic minority groups reside, also rank low in the frequency of turmoil. Representative of these areas are Gansu, Ningxia, Yunnan, and Qinghai. The provinces that experienced the most turmoil were mostly the interior provinces in central China, with Sichuan (the most populous province in China) heading the list (see Map 3.1). The plight of Sichuan reflects the social stress and strain in the central provinces as a whole. They suffered from an unproductive economy combined with a population problem. Table 3.5 reveals that, statistically, the instances of turmoil are significantly correlated only with the size of the population, the Pearson product-moment coefficient of correlation is 0.56 (those with urbanization are -0.389 and per capita income, -0.358).[142] Excluding the three municipalities and Tibet from the list (for lack of per capita income figures) and applying regression analysis turned up similar

Map 3.1   Ten Top-Ranked Provinces in 1992 Turmoil

results: beta for population size and turmoil is 0.55; for urbanization and turmoils, 0.0345; and for per capita income and turmoil, −0.34.[143] The correlation between population size and turmoil in the Chinese provinces has similarities with the situation in the United States during the racial disturbances in the 1960s. Louis Kriesberg wrote:

> Spilerman. . . studied racial disorders in the United States between 1961 and 1968 and found that the absolute number of nonwhites in a city was by far the single most important factor in accounting for disorders. . . . Presumably, the grievances of blacks were sufficiently diffuse in the society and rioting a widely enough accepted form of expression that the more blacks there were available, the more incidents that might trigger a riot would occur and the more people there were available for rioting.[144]

David Snyder further refined Seymour Spilerman's analysis by finding that riots could be more adequately explained by the availability of persons, times, places, and occasions to assemble.[145] However, specific data such as these are not available in the case of turmoils in Chinese provinces. In subsequent analysis, I shall correlate the instances of turmoils as recorded in Table 3.5 with the population and economic conditions of Chinese provinces. The following interpretations are necessarily partial since I do not have information on the cultural or behavioral variables underlying the turmoils.

To examine further the regional differences in turmoil, Table 3.6 compares the proportions of population in three major regions of China and

Table 3.6 Proportion of Turmoil and Population in Three Macroregions of China, 1992

Macroregion	Turmoil (%)	Population (%)
Nine coastal provinces (Hebei, Liaoning, Shandong, Jiangsu, Zhejiang, Fujian, Guangdong, Guangxi, Hainan)	24	39.64
Nine central provinces (Shanxi, Inner Mongolia, Jilin, Heilongjiang, Anhui, Jiangxi, Henan, Hubei, Hunan)	43	36.82
Nine western provinces (Sichuan, Guizhou, Yunnan, Tibet, Shaanxi, Gansu, Qinghai, Ningxia, Xinjiang)	32.5	23.53

Note: Hainan and Tibet are counted here but not in Table 3.5 since the figures here include only population and frequency of turmoil.

the prevalence of turmoil. The nine coastal provinces (Hebei, Liaoning, Shandong, Jiangsu, Zhejiang, Fujian, Guangdong, Guangxi, and Hainan) have 39.6 percent of the total Chinese population but 24 percent of the turmoil. The nine central provinces (Shanxi, Inner Mongolia, Jilin, Heilonjiang, Anhui, Jiangxi, Henan, Hubei, and Hunan) have 36.8 percent of the population and 43 percent of the turmoil. The nine western provinces (Sichuan, Guizhou, Yunnan, Tibet, Shaanxi, Gansu, Qinghai, Ningxia, and Xinjiang) have 23.5 percent of the population and 32.5 percent of the turmoil. In other words, turmoil is "overrepresented" in the central and western provinces.

The interior provinces of China are more agrarian than industrial, and the social unrest in these areas probably reflects a portion of the grim situation in the countryside (discussed in the previous chapter). The proportion of agricultural output in the total value of industrial and agricultural outputs in 1991 were: 20 percent in the eastern provinces, 27.7 percent in the central provinces, and 38 percent in the western provinces.[146] It was from the central provinces, such as Sichuan, that large numbers of migrants came. In industry, factories in the western and especially in the central provinces of China were primarily large state firms that dealt in producer goods and were, technologically, of Soviet vintage. Several provinces in the central region, such as Sichuan, Hunan, Shaanxi, Henan, and Hubei, were the sites of so-called Third Line construction (*sanxian gongye*) in the mid-1960s through mid-1970s. Fearing attack by the United States or the former Soviet Union, the state ordered approximately 2,000 firms removed from the coastal areas to the interior. Most of these were involved in strategic industries. These state firms became the backbone of heavy industry in the central provinces and were now critically affected by post-Mao reform.[147]

Table 3.7 compares the rank of each province in the frequency of turmoils and the composition of its industrial firms—proportions of light versus heavy industry. The important point is that virtually all the firms in heavy industry are state-owned. Table 3.7 exposes the fact that, of the provinces occupying the top thirteen ranks in turmoil, eleven (the exceptions being Hunan and Anhui) have more heavy than light industrial firms. As the previous discussion has shown, it is the large and medium-sized state firms that are going through a severe crisis. In the lower group of fourteen provinces in Table 3.7, eight have more light than heavy industrial firms. Chinese press reports and scholarly writings clearly show that state firms in the interior provinces are chiefly responsible for the workers' distress. These firms share some common characteristics: producer-goods industry, obsolete equipment, excessive consumption of energy, autarky, and an underemployed and poorly educated work force. They were referred to, in China, as a "rice-eating industry" (*chifan gongye*), meaning that their growth depends on state appropriations; they have great difficulty adapting to market forces in the post-Mao period.

Table 3.7 Rank Order in Turmoil and Type of Industry in Chinese Provinces

Province	Rank in turmoil	Light industry (%)[a]	Heavy industry (%)[a]
Sichuan	1	27	33.3
Jiangxi	2	23	30.6
Hunan	3	36.6	28.7
Anhui	4	36.2	34.4
Shaanxi	5	24.5	36.8
Shanxi	6	16.8	55.4
Heilongjiang	7	23.2	52.4
Xinjiang	8	30.4	31.4
Henan	9	31.6	38
Inner Mongolia	10	24	35.8
Hubei	11	34.5	39.2
Hebei	12.5	23.3	31.4
Liaoning	12.5	19.8	52
Guangxi	14.5	27.3	25.6
Guizhou	14.5	22.7	31.17
Guangdong	16	52.6	24.6
Zhejiang	17	39.1	23
Qinghai	18	18	49.6
Yunnan	19	30.8	28
Hainan	20	26.6	12.8
Jilin	21	26	42.8
Shandong	22	27.4	26.4
Ningxia	23.5	19.5	53.5
Gansu	23.5	17	51
Fujian	25.5	33	22.2
Jiangsu	25.6	35	31
Tibet	27	3.4	9.4

[a]Percentage in total value of industrial and agricultural output for 1991.

Sources: Zhongguo Jingji Nianjian, 1992 [Almanac of China's Economy, 1992] (Beijing: Jingji Guanli Chubanshe, 1992). Also, *Cheng Ming,* no. 185 (March 1, 1993): 19.

Under Deng's reform, the state significantly reduced appropriations to these firms and many of them were on the verge of bankruptcy. For example, the Sichuanese industry was predominantly tooled for munitions production, but its equipment was largely obsolete. Those with up-to-date technology constituted only 18 percent. Firms in Sichuan were saddled not only with excess workers and staff but also with low-quality labor force. Over half of the staff and workers (63 percent) had only a junior middle school education, and the number of redundant laborers in state firms in 1991 was between 500,000 and 600,000. Sichuan state firms were burdened by a lack of funding, the high price of energy, and their own inability to make products that could compete profitably in the market.[148] In 1994, about half of the state firms suffered deficits.[149] The provincial government now wanted to sell both profitable and unprofitable state firms to foreign investors.[150] Reflecting the people's distress, an editorial in a Sichuan newspaper admitted in June 1994: "Compared with the past, the present contradictions among the people are more conspicuous, widespread, and complicated."[151]

In 1994, the hardcore central provinces that were ranked relatively high for turmoil in the 1992 police reports were once more plagued by social unrest, especially workers' demonstrations. These provinces were Sichuan, Shaanxi, Shanxi, Hubei, and the western frontier region of Xinjiang.[152] Meanwhile, the northeastern province of Liaoning, ranked twelfth in Table 3.5, came to the fore in 1994 in terms of worker militancy. The provincial capital of Shenyang has a concentration of state firms, many of which were in financial difficulty in late 1993. In March 1994 Shenyang saw workers' protests of various types, some declaring their intention to enlist 10,000 people and charter a train to go to Beijing to petition the central government. In the petition by the staff and workers in the chemical industry, politically charged slogans were printed such as: "Factories belong to the working class," "Down with the new aristocracy," and "Down with the new bureaucratic bourgeoisie."[153] In other words, workers' discontent reflected a general social stress. In 1994, mass disturbances had again been reported in Sichuan and Hubei; troops were mobilized to deal with them.[154] The central region of China seemed to be the focus of Chinese socioeconomic crisis in recent history. During the height of the Cultural Revolution from January 1967 through July 1968, large-scale "armed struggles" *(wu dou)* took place in Shanxi, Shaanxi, Anhui, Sichuan, Hubei, Henan, and Jiangxi.[155]

While the formerly privileged workers and staff in state firms led the protest movements in the interior provinces, it was the underprivileged workers in the joint ventures and foreign-owned factories who played the main role in the strikes and demonstrations in the eastern provinces in the 1990s. The Chinese government provided widely inconsistent information on the numbers of foreign-owned firms and joint ventures and the numbers of Chinese employees in these firms. The official *Fazhi Ribao*, (Legal Daily) for example, reported in 1993 that there were, by the end of 1992, 84,000 "foreign-funded enterprises" employing approximately 4.8 million Chinese staff members and workers. This figure is inconsistent with the one given by the State Statistical Bureau as presented in Table 3.2. But this much is clear. First, these so-called foreign firms were primarily owned by Chinese from Taiwan and Hong Kong. They were short-term investments in labor-intensive industries.[156] Second, a substantial number of the workers in these firms were rural migrants, especially women. An ACFTU survey in 1991 and 1992 of 914 foreign-funded firms showed that women accounted for 50.4 percent of the total 160,000 employees.[157] Third, the indifference of the overseas Chinese investors to the welfare of their workers, along with local government's connivance, prevented workers in these companies from being fully unionized. In 1994, about 12 percent of these "foreign-owned" firms had unions.[158] According to a Chinese researcher based in Hong Kong, "It's not a matter of law. Resistance from government and party authorities [against unions] has been strong because they are afraid that unions will scare off investors."[159] Naturally, the rural character of this transplanted labor force made it even more difficult to organize.

Many reports have now been written about the inhuman conditions in these overseas Chinese-owned factories.[160] The workers were overworked, physically abused, underpaid (including indefinite delays in payment), and made to live in squalor. Accidents occurred frequently in these plants. The government reported that there were 206 major industrial fires in 1993—one-tenth were in foreign-funded enterprises.[161] In the Special Economic Zone of Shenzhen, 134 industrial fires were reported in 1993, of which 116 took place in "foreign-funded" factories.[162] In June 1994, a building collapsed in a factory in Shenzhen operated by a Chinese businessman from Hong Kong. Eleven were killed and nine were injured.[163] As mentioned earlier, of all the variables, hazardous working conditions account significantly for solidarity among workers. Thus, labor disputes in these overseas Chinese-operated firms rose precipitously in 1993–1994. In these two years in Shenzhen, there were 1,100 labor disputes, strikes, and slowdowns. Ninety percent of these happened in "foreign-owned" firms.[164] In Shanghai, it was reported that in 1991, the municipal labor arbitration organizations handled seventy cases of major labor disputes in foreign-owned firms. In 1992, the number increased to 111.[165]

In the 1990s organizations were formed spontaneously among workers in the "foreign-funded" firms. One source reported that there were, in 1994, over eight hundred such workers' organizations in Shenzhen alone. They resembled traditional secret societies more than modern unions, and their methods of resistance, judging from informants' descriptions, were the Luddite type.[166] But one dissident labor group in Shenzhen was in the early stages of organizing a modern union. It published a newsletter entitled *Workers' Square*. In its initial issue, this publication stated: "The improvement of working environments, improvement of living conditions, shortening of hours and increase of wages will not be bestowed on us. . . . It's something we must fight for. If we unite, we will become a strong force." However, the government arrested the editors of this publication.[167]

In Shanghai, some labor organizations were organized with the encouragement of the Chinese management in the foreign-owned firms. One account described these organizations as follows: "The unofficial groups went under different names: A welfare society in a Taiwan enterprise, a recreation club in an American enterprise and a workers' committee in a European enterprise."[168] Workers in these overseas Chinese-operated firms were repeating the activities of their predecessors in the early 1920s. At that time, Chinese workers struck against Japanese-owned factories in Shanghai and elsewhere, protesting poor pay, cruel treatment by Japanese foremen, and hazardous working conditions. Female textile workers were no less militant than male workers.[169] The Chinese labor union movement seemed to have remained where it began some seventy years ago.

Among the underprivileged workers, the coal miners persisted in their class conflicts with the state. Working conditions did not improve under Deng's administration; in fact, they had probably declined. Deng's policy of decentralized economic development caused local governments to increase pressure on the miners to accelerate production and to pay little or no attention to their safety or health. James Dorian reported that an estimated 5 million people were employed at more than 120,000 collectively and individually run mines in China. "Nearly 10,000 coal miners were killed in accidents in 1991. In the nation's statistics on accidental deaths, only traffic fatalities outrank mining."[170] In the first three months of 1994, a total of 724 miners were killed in accidents, compared with 1,058 for the whole of 1993.[171] In May 1994, it was reported that some 20,000 coal miners in Shuangyashan and Jiamusi in Heilongjiang Province had staged a strike.[172] However, some of the strikes were provoked by the state's forced closing of unproductive miners, driving many miners out of work.[173] In 1993 alone, the government planned to dismiss 140,000 miners.[174]

State Reaction to the Workers' Movement

Finally, the increasing militancy of workers in the late 1980s and early 1990s, especially those in foreign-owned firms, forced the hand of the government. Through propaganda and legislation, the state sought to convince workers that their rights were not overlooked. The government launched a publicity campaign to stress new and substantive roles that official unions would play in the transformed state firms. Workers would have the right to organize their own unions in the new modern enterprises.[175] The government also announced that a labor code was being drafted for use in foreign-funded firms. The State Council decreed in April 1994 that all workers in foreign-owned firms must be unionized by the end of the year.[176] The Chinese press maintained that the ACFTU played an important role in drafting new laws and regulations safeguarding workers' rights. It was reported that three union leaders were on the

Standing Committee of the National People's Congress, allegedly involved in labor legislation.[177] In her field research, Anita Chan reported that the ACFTU felt underappreciated by the workers for its role in drafting new labor laws and codes in 1993 and 1994.[178]

The most important labor legislation was undoubtedly "The Labor Law," which was enacted by the National People's Congress in July 1994. It took the government almost forty years to enact this law; the first draft was completed in 1956. Hailed as a breakthrough, the law has thirteen chapters and 107 articles. Specifically, there are six aspects of the new law designed to protect workers' rights. They are a labor contract system, a limit upon overtime working hours, minimum wages, vocational certificates for skilled workers, social insurance to guard against unemployment and injury, and labor arbitration.[179] The law gives special protection to the rights of women workers. For example, maternity leave should not be less than ninety days, and women should not do heavy work during pregnancy.[180]

The fact that the new labor law was conceived almost forty years ago suggests that its final enactment in 1994 was due less to the state's initiative and more to workers' public opinion—including the dissidents' movements. In this perspective, the many informal unions or workers' groups that sprang up in the 1990s achieved their purposes, at least partially. The question now is whether the state will truly carry out the law. If not, then the new labor law will intensify workers' conflicts with the state, the exact opposite of the law's intended purpose.

Conclusion

The overall reactions of the Chinese working class to the Party-state since 1949 can be understood on two levels: the cultural level and the status level. On the cultural level, the workers' political views and actions were like the peasants', as some Chinese scholars suggested. The workers stressed immediate socioeconomic issues and relied on amorphous social action to express their preferences. They practiced what James Scott called "routine resistance"—"a never-ending attempt to seize each small advantage and press it home, to probe the limits of the existing relationships, to see precisely what can be gotten away with at the margin, and to include this margin as a part of an accepted, or at least tolerated, territorial claim."[181]

On the status level, Chinese workers differed from the peasants. The fact that the workers were "included" in the Party-state scheme of national reconstruction after 1949 caused the birth of a tradition among them, a tradition that they militantly defended in the post-Mao period. Such a custom was absent among the peasants who welcomed the reforms in the post-Mao era. By tradition, I mean a particular ethos of a group that emerges out of social interaction. As Craig Jackson Calhoun put it, we should see tradition "less in terms of antiquity and communication across generations than in terms of practical, everyday social activity."[182] Such a tradition imparts to a group its distinct identity, which makes collective action possible and effective. In ordinary times, wrote Calhoun, tradition has conservative effects on a group. "But in times of rapid change, this very conservatism may make traditional communities politically radical, even revolutionary."[183] The discussion in this chapter provided ample evidence of such a tradition in the Chinese working class—the "iron rice bowl," egalitarianism, "eating socialism," and the symbolic status of being the masters in a "workers' state." Much of the militant workers' movements in the late 1980s and early 1990s was motivated by a defense of this working class tradition, a perfect example of the "radicalism of tradition."

The different reactions of the workers and the peasants exposed once more the irony of "enacted change." The Chinese Communist Party-state, its propagandistic claim of the peasants' being part of the proletariat aside, regarded the peasants as conservative and reactionary. The state's exclusion of the peasantry from the "construction of socialism" consequently made the lives of the peasants so intolerable that they became a force for change and modernization in the post-Mao period. The state thought of the workers as the true proletariats who would spearhead the socialist transformation of China. The "privileged" status of the working class under Mao turned the workers into a conservative force resisting the Dengist state's modernizing programs.

Notes

1. Robert Loh, *Escape from Red China* (New York: Coward-McCann, 1962), p. 110.

2. *Jingji Guanli* [Economic Management], no. 15 (October 15, 1992): 42.

3. My notions of class and class conflict are partly informed by Max Weber, *Economy: An Outline of Interpretive Sociology, and Society:* vol. 2, ed. Guenther Roth and Claus Wittich (New York: Bedminster Press, 1968), pp. 926–940; and James C. Scott, *Weapons of the Weak* (New Haven: Yale University Press, 1985), pp. 290–300.

4. Bo Ningxiang, "Xianjieduan Woguo Gongrenjieji Neibumaodun Jibianhuaqushi Qianxi," [A preliminary analysis of the trend of internal contradictions among our country's working class] *Shehui Kexue* [Social Sciences], no. 6 (June 15, 1993): p. 26.

5. Quoted in Rick Fantasia, *Cultures of Solidarity: Consciousness, Action, and Contemporary American Workers* (Berkeley: University of California Press, 1988), p. 17.

6. Ira Katznelson, *City Trenches: Urban Politics and the Patterning of Class in the United States* (New York: Patheon, 1981), as cited in Fantasia, *Cultures of Solidarity*, p. 218.

7. Mao gave the figure of 4 million industrial workers in a speech to the Supreme State Conference on October 13, 1957; see *Mao Tse-tung Ssu-hsiang Wan-sui*, [hereafter, Wan-sui], no. 2, Beijing, 1969; reprint, Washington, D.C.: Center for Chinese Research Materials, 1969) p. 135. For a comprehensive record of the Chinese labor movement before 1949, see Chung-kuo Lao-kung Yung-tong-shih Pien-tsuan-wei-yuan-hui, *Chung-kuo Lao-kung Yung-tong-shih* (CLYS) [History of the Chinese Labor Movement], vols. 1–5, (Taipei: Chung-kuo Lao-kung Fu-li Chu-pan-she, 1959).

8. S. Bernard Thomas, *Labor and the Chinese Revolution: Class Strategies and Contradictions of Chinese Communism, 1928–1948* (Ann Arbor: Center for Chinese Studies, University of Michigan, 1983), pp. 249–261; and Elizabeth J. Perry, *Shanghai on Strike: The Politics of Chinese Labor* (Stanford, Calif.: Stanford University Press, 1993).

9. "6th Meeting of ACFTU 7th Executive Committee Presidium Reaches Decision on Trade Union Work of Engineering Company of Ministry of Building," *New China News Agency (NCNA)*, March 20, 1955, in *Survey of China Mainland Press (SCMP)*, no. 1024, p. 27; see also "Several Problems Existing in Basic Trade Union Organs," *Gongren Ribao* [Worker's Daily] (hereafter, GRRB), February 9, 1954, in *SCMP*, no. 763, pp. 23–25.

10. Lynn T. White III, *Policies of Chaos* (Princeton: Princeton University Press, 1989), p. 116; similar references may be found in Loh, *Escape from Red China*, and Tung Chi-Ping and Humphrey Evans, *The Thought Revolution* (New York: Coward McCann, 1966).

11. Li Yuan-hung, "Youth League Supervision Posts: Discourses and Practices," *Zhongguo Qingnian Bao*, September 2, 1956, in *SCMP*, no. 1375, pp. 14–19.

12. An Ming, "Sabotage by Counter-Revolutionary Elements in Industrial and Mining Enterprises and Transport and Communications Systems," *Renmin Ribao* (hereafter, *RMBR*), July 3, 1955, in *SCMP*, no. 1092, pp. 15–17; and "Counter-Revolutionary Ring in Hunan Mines Smashed," *NCNA*, September 7, 1955, in *SCMP*, no. 1133, p. 46.

13. Ma Xia, "Sanshiduonianlai Woguode Guoneirenkouqianyi Jijinghoude Zhanwang" [Migration in our country for the past thirty years and its future prospects], *Renkouxue* [Demography], no. 3 (1987): 65.

14. Loh, *Escape from Red China*, p. 110.

15. *Xinhua Ribao* [New China Daily], (Chongqing), July 22, 1953.

16. *Guangming Ribao*, July 29, 1955, cited and translated in Shih Ch'eng-chih, *People's Resistance in Mainland China, 1950–1955* (Hong Kong: Union Research Institute, 1956), pp. 106–107.

17. Lai Jo-yu, [Lai Ruoyu], "Correctly Implement Party Policy of Labor Protection," *GRRB*, February 20, 1955, in *SCMP*, no. 1024, pp. 30–34.

18. *GRRB*, June 20, 1957.

19. Li Feng, "Pa-ch'ien-li-lu 'tsou-ma-kuan-hua' chi," [An Eight-thousand-li's trip and observations], *NCNA*, May 9, 1957, in *Hsin-hua Pan-yueh-kan*, no. 11 (1957): 73.

20. *GRRB*, May 8, 1957, in *Hsin-hua Pan-yueh-kan*, no. 11 (1957): 72.

21. Loh, *Escape from Red China*, pp. 299–300.

22. *Wan-sui*, no. 2, pp. 182 and 227.

23. Fantasia, *Cultures of Solidarity*, p. 14.

24. "Zhigong Sushe Wei Shenme Jinzhang?" [Why is houseing for staff and workers in short supply?] *RMRB*, November 19, 1957; see numerous Chinese press reports on this subject in microfilms of the Union Research Institute (Hong Kong), no. 1413313, at the Center for Chinese Studies, University of California at Berkeley.

25. Ta Chen, "Basic Problems of the Chinese Working Classes," *American Journal of Sociology* 53 no. 3 (1947): 188.

26. See, for example, *Shanxi Ribao*, January 18, 1957; *RMRB*, January 21, 1957; *Jiefang Ribao* (Shanghai), February 5, 1957; *Zhejiang Ribao* (Hangzhou), June 28, 1957; *Xinwen Ribao* (Shanghai), May 16, 1957; *Jiefang Ribao* (Shanghai), June 22, 1957; *Chongqing Ribao* (Chongqing), September 22, 1957. Reprints of these papers are available in Union Research Institute microfilms at the Center for Chinese Studies, University of California at Berkeley. See also, White, *Policies of Chaos*, p. 135.

27. Tung and Evans, *The Thought Revolution*, p. 53.

28. *GRRB*, June 1, 7, 8, and 11, 1957.

29. *Jiefang Ribao* (Shanghai), July 13, 1957.

30. John Foster, *Class Struggle and the Industrial Revolution* (London: Weidenfeld and Nicolson, 1974); and Joseph G. Rayback, *A History of American Labor* (New York: Macmillan, 1966).

31. Hsu Ming, "Cheng-ch'an Chieh-yueh Yung-tong-chung-ti Chi-ke-ssu-hsiang-wen-ti," [Some thought problems in the campaign to increase production through practicing thrift] *Hsin-hua Pan-yueh-kan*, no. 14 1959: 30–33.

32. "Trade Unions and Industrial Workers," *China News Analysis*, no. 482 (August 23, 1963).

33. *GRRB*, October 1, 1961.

34. Liang Heng and Judith Shapiro, *Son of the Revolution*, (New York: Random House, 1983), chapter 19.

35. *RMRB*, July 14, 1981.

36. Ma Xia, "Sanshiduonianlai Woguodi Guoneirenkouqianyi," p. 66.

37. White, *Policies of Chaos*, p. 187.

38. Liu Binyan, *Wo-ti Jih-chi* [My diary] (Hong Kong: Ming Pao Publishing, 1988), p. 14.

39. *Chung-kuo Lao-kung Yung-tung-shih* [History of the Chinese labor movement], vol. 4 (Taipei: Chung-kuo Lao-kung Yung-tung-shih Pien-tsuan-wei-yuan-hui, 1958), chapters 4–9.

40. This is common knowledge in China. See, for example, the career of the dissident labor leader Hang Dongfang in *South China Sunday Morning Post*, March 13, 1994, in FBIS, *CHI/DR*, March 15, 1994, pp. 43–46. After his discharge from the army, he was assigned to railway work. See also physicist Hsu Chia-luan's [Xu Jialuan] description of the family background of the dissident astrophysicist Fang Lizhi in *Shijie Ribao* [World Press Journal], January 16, 1987.

41. *RMRB*, March 16, 1977. Also, "Reaction to Fa-Chuan Among the Working Population," *China News Analysis*, no. 998 (May 2, 1975): 5–7.

42. *RMRB*, December 20, 1977.

43. Randy Hodson, Sandy Welsh, Sabine Rieble, Cheryl Sorenson Jamison, and Sean Creighton, "Is Worker Solidarity Undermined by Autonomy and

Participation? Patterns from the Ethnographic Literature," *American Sociological Review* 58, no. 3 (June 1993): 411.

44. *RMRB,* December 20, 1977.

45. *RMRB,* November 14, 1977.

46. Colina MacDougall, "What About the Workers?" *Far Eastern Economic Review,* October 3, 1968, p. 69; Colina MacDougall, "A Propaganda Leap," *Far Eastern Economic Review,* March 20, 1969, p. 531.

47. *RMRB,* October 28, 1977.

48. "Campaign to Repulse the Right Deviationist Wind to Reverse Previous Verdicts: Posters for and Against," *Issues and Studies,* no. 11 (November 1976): 106–107.

49. Hodson et al., "Is Worker Solidarity Undermined," p. 412.

50. Li Feng, "Pa-ch'ien-li-lu," p. 74.

51. "Urgent Notice," *RMRB,* January 12, 1967, in *Current Background,* no. 818, p. 6.

52. *RMRB,* February 1, 1974; July 5, 1977; and April 14, 1978.

53. "Industrial Workers, Part Two: A Stricter Rule—Why?" *China News Analysis,* no. 941 (November 23, 1973): 4, quoting from broadcasts from *Radio Gansu,* April 4, 1973. See also Martin K. Whyte and William L. Parish, *Urban Life in Contemporary China* (Chicago: University of Chicago Press, 1984), chapter 8.

54. Interested readers might wish to consult the Chinese press in 1977; there were daily reports about turmoils in the factories.

55. Liang and Shapiro, *Son of the Revolution,* chapter 19.

56. Annie Kriegel, "The Nature of the Communist System: Notes on State, Party, and Society," in *The State,* ed. Stephen Graubard (New York: W. W. Norton and Company, 1979), p. 146.

57. I am following Selznick's distinction between organizations and institutions; see Philip Selznick, *Leadership in Administration* (Berkeley: University of California Press, 1984), chapter 1.

58. Andrew G. Walder, *Communist Neo-Traditionalism* (Berkeley: University of California Press, 1986), chapter 8.

59. According to Korzec and Whyte's analysis of the Chinese publication *Selected Documents on Labor Wages,* there was actually no absolute job security for the staff and workers. But they read the documents too literally; in China, practice deviated widely from principles. By all accounts, before Deng's reforms, Chinese workers and employees assumed that they were entitled to job security. See Michel Korzec and Martin King Whyte, "Reading Notes: The Chinese Wage System," *China Quarterly,* no. 86 (June 1981): 248–273.

60. Ivan D. London, Miriam London, and Ta-ling Lee, "Prospects and Dilemmas of Chinese Workers," *Workers Under Communism,* no. 1 (Spring 1982): 19.

61. The figure of industrial workers is based on a report by Rong Yiren in *RMRB,* March 10, 1981, p. 2; the figure of the workers and staff is from the report by Lu Lupin in *RMRB,* April 23, 1981, p. 5.

62. Calculated from State Statistical Bureau, *China: Statistics in Brief, 1984* (Beijing: New World Press, 1984).

63. Liu Binyan, *Baogao Wenxuexuan* [Selected reports] (Beijing: Beijing Chubanshe, 1981), p. 14.

64. "The Spring of Beijing" was the original translation by the publisher of the Chinese journal, not mine.

65. Wei Minqing, "Tamen Yaoqiu Xiuxidiquanli" [They demand the right to have rest], *Beijing Zhichun* [The Spring of Peking], no. 6 (June 17, 1979), in Case Team for the Collection of Mainland Underground Publications, comp. *Ta-lu Ti-hsia K'an-wu H'ui-pien* [Collection of mainland underground publications] (hereafter *TLTH,*), book 7 (Taipei: Institute for the Study of Chinese Communist Problems, 1982), pp. 109–113.

66. Whyte and Parish, *Urban Life in Contemporary China*, chapter 6.

67. *Renmin Zhishen* [Voice of the people] (Guangzhou), February 1979, p. 6. I had acquired a number of these dissident journals while visiting the Universities Service Center in Hong Kong in August 1982.

68. *Kexue Minzu Fazhi* [Science, democracy, and rule of law], no. 16 (June 30, 1979), in *TLTH,* book 17, pp. 86–87.

69. *Kexue Minzu Fazhi* [Science, democracy, and rule of law], February 15, 1979, in *TLTH,* book 8, pp. 272–287.

70. See reports in *Fuyin Baokan Zhiliao-Gongrenzuzhi Yu Huodong* [Duplicated press and journal materials on workers' organizations and activities] (hereafter, *FBZ-GYH),* no. 11 (1981): 23; no. 1 (1982): 64; and no. 4 (1982): 19.

71. *FBZ-GYH,* no. 9 (1981): 31–32.

72. *FBZ-GYH,* no. 10 (1981): 20.

73. Hu Chaoshen, "Jizhenghefayang 'Er Qi' Geminchuantong" [Inherit and carry on the revolutionary spirit of 'February 7'], *Changjiang Ribao* [Yangzi Daily], February 4, 1981, in *FBZ-GYH,* no. 1 (1981): 3. See also Reuter's dispatch from Beijing, dated December 10, 1981, as published in the overseas Chinese newspaper *Yuandong Ribao* [Far Eastern Daily] (San Francisco), December 12, 1981.

74. For a description of workers' "eating socialism," see Liang Heng and Judith Shapiro, *Son of the Revolution* (New York: Vintage, 1993), pp. 220ff.

75. Bu Wei, "Yaojilu, Buyao 'Jiangong'" [Discipline is desirable; work surveillance is not desirable], *Renmin Zhishen* [Voice of the people], nos. 12–13 joint issue (December 1979), in *TLTH,* book 16, pp. 192–193.

76. Xiao Min, "Gongren Jiugaiyou 'Tiefanwan' Ganbu Buyinzuo 'Tiejiaoyi'" [The worker ought to have the "iron rice bowl," the cadres ought not to have the "iron command position"], *Renmin Zhishen,* nos. 12–13 joint issue (December 1979), in *TLTH,* book 16, pp. 194–196.

77. *Ming Pao,* March 7, 1981.

78. *Fengfan* [The sail], December 1980. I had read an issue of this journal while visiting the Universities Service Center in Hong Kong in 1982.

79. Brief reports on the Taiyuan steelworkers' demonstration were published in *Ming Pao* (Hong Kong), March 2 and 6, 1981. It was also referred to in Miriam London and Ta-ling Lee, "The Young Democratic Movement in China," *Wall Street Journal,* August 11, 1981.

80. *Ming Pao,* March 2, 1981.

81. *Ming Pao,* March 23, 1981; also "China Magazine Reports Workers Staged Disorders," *New York Times,* April 14, 1981.

82. Yu Yannan, "Zhengque Guji Woguo Gongrenjiejidi Xinyidai" (Correctly appraise the new generation of the proletariat of our country) *Hongqi,* no. 17 (1982): 29.

83. Yu Yannan, "Geng Daguimodi Kaizhan Xianjing Shengchanzhe Yundong" [Once more carry out large-scale labor emulation campaigns], *Hongqi*, no. 22 (1982): 31.

84. *GRRB*, May 11, 1982, in *FBZ-GYH*, no. 3 (1982): 18.

85. Han Xiya, "Jiaoyuhao Xinyidai Shigonghuigongzuode Zhongdaketi" [Educating the new generation well is an important task of the union], *GRRB*, February 26, 1981, in *FBZ-GYH*, no. 2, (1981): 15–17.

86. *RMRB*, March 1, 1982.

87. Gongqingtuan Xianshiwei Xuanchuanbu Xian Baoshi Zhoucheng Chan Tuanwei [Youth League Committee of the Xian Gem-Bearing Factory, Propaganda Department of the Youth League Committee of Xian City], "Yige Gongchang Qinggong Renshenguandi Diaocha" [An investigation of the views on life of young workers in a factory], *Qingnian Yanjiu* [Study of Youth], (1982): 9–12.

88. Xinhua Tongxunshe Guonaizhiliaoshi, ed., *Shinian Gaige Dashiji, 1978–1987* [Major events in a decade of reforms, 1978–1987], (Beijing: Xinhua Chubanshe, 1988), p. 179.

89. Andrew G. Walder, "Wage Reform and the Web of Factory Interests," *China Quarterly*, no. 109 (March 1987): 22–41.

90. *GRRB*, September 28, 1988, in FBIS, *CHI/DR*, October 12, 1988, pp. 46–47.

91. Ibid., p. 47.

92. Gordon White, "The Politics of Economic Reform in Chinese Industry: The Introduction of the Labor Contract System," *The China Quarterly*, no. 111 (September 1987): 385.

93. *China Daily*, June 13, 1992.

94. The number of bankruptcies is from *Wen Wei Pao* (Hong Kong), October 29, 1994, in FBIS, *CHI/DR*, November 2, 1994. The state firms targeted for a purge were large and medium-sized ones, based on information in *Zhongguo Tongji Nianjian, 1993* [Statistical Yearbook of China, 1993] (Beijing: Zhongguo Tongji Chubanshe, 1993), p. 417.

95. *Ming Pao* (Hong Kong), August 19, 1994, in FBIS, *CHI/DR*, September 20, 1994, p. 27.

96. *RMRB*, July 29, 1994, in FBIS, *CHI/DR*, September 28, 1994, p. 40.

97. This information is from a special essay written by Yang Peixin, member of the PRC's Center for Research on Development of the State Council, for the Taipei newspaper *Chung-kuo Shih-pao* [China Times], May 16, 1994.

98. *Zhongguo Tongxun She*, October 27, 1994, in FBIS, *CHI/DR*, November 3, 1994, pp. 43–44.

99. *Ming Pao* (Hong Kong), August 19, 1994, in FBIS, *CHI/DR*, September 20, 1994, p. 27.

100. *RMRB*, April 10, 1988.

101. Jeanne L. Wilson, "Labor Policy in China: Reform and Retrogression," *Problems of Communism* 39, no. 5 (September-October 1990): 59.

102. Andrew L. Walder, "Workers, Managers, and the State: The Reform Era and the Political Crisis of 1989," *China Quarterly*, no. 127 (September 1991): 467–492.

103. *Zhongguo Tongxun She*, April 20, 1994, in FBIS, *CHI/DR*, May 9, 1994, p. 45.

104. *Hsin Pao* (Hong Kong), March 9, 1994, in FBIS, March 11, 1994, p. 38.

105. *China Daily Business Weekly*, June 19–25, 1994, in FBIS, *CHI/DR*, June 20, 1994.

106. *Ya-chou Chou-k'an* [Asia Weekly] (Hong Kong), August 28, 1994.

107. *Wen Wei Pao* [Wen Wei Press] (Hong Kong), February 4, 1994, p. A3.

108. Based on the figures given in *Zhongguo Tongji Nianjian, 1993*.

109. *Qiushi*, no. 9 (May 1, 1994), in FBIS, *CHI/DR*, June 14, 1994, p. 37.

110. *RMRB*, September 12, 1994 in FBIS, *CHI/DR*, September 20, 1994, pp. 50–53.

111. *Renmin Zhishen* [Voice of the people], no. 3 (1979).

112. Feng Tongqin, "Zhongguo Zhigong Zhuangkuande Fengxi Yuyuce, 1992–1993" [Analysis and forecast of the mood of Chinese workers and staff, 1992–1993], *Shehuixue* [Sociology], no. 4 (1993): 85–95.

113. Lu Jianhua, "Yijiujiuernian Shehui Gejieceng Dui Shehuixinshide Jiben Kanfa" [The basic views of various social strata on social conditions in 1992], *Shehuixue* [Sociology], no. 4 (1993): 76–84.

114. Walder, *Communist Neo-Traditionalism*, chapter 5.

115. Bo Ningxiang, "Xianjieduan Woguo Gongrenjieji Neibumaodun Jibi-anhuaqushiqianxi" [A preliminary analysis of the internal contradictions among the working class of our country, its changes, and prospects], *Shehui Kexue* [Social Sciences], no. 6 (1993): 25–27.

116. Mayfair Mei-hui Yang, "Between State and Society: The Construction of Corporateness in a Chinese Socialist Factory," *The Australian Journal of Chinese Affairs*, no. 22 (July 1989): 34.

117. Dong Min, "Gongrende Kunhuo He Xiwang," [Hope and confusion among workers], *Weidinggao* (Beijing), no. 10 (1989): 54–64, in *FBZ-GYH*, no. 2 (1990): 134–144.

118. Feng Tongqin, "Zhongguo Zhigong Zhuangkuande."

119. Mayfair Mei-hui Yang, "Between State and Society," pp. 31–60.

120. However, Feng clarified, in a separate interview with Taiwan reporters, that by foreign or joint-venture firms he meant those operated by Western business executives on a long-term basis. See *Chung-kuo Shih-pao* [China Times] (Taipei), June 26, 1994.

121. Bo Ningxiang, "Xianjieduan Woguo Gongrenjieji," p. 27.

122. Ibid, p. 26.

123. *Zhongguo Xinwen She*, March 22, 1994, in FBIS, *CHI/DR*, April 1, 1994, p. 59.

124. *Jingji Guanli* [Economic Management Monthly], no. 15 (October 15, 1992): 42.

125. *Jingjiwenti Tansuo* [Exploration of Economic Problems], no. 6 (November 3, 1992): 49–51.

126. Zhang Panshi, "Qiye Lingdao Fangshi Yu Zhigong Jijixinde Diaocha" [An investigation into the leadership style and initiative of the staff and workers], *Shehuixue* [Sociology], no. 4 (1991): 122–126.

127. Wen Lianfan, "Gongzi, Renmin Guanzhudi Redian" [Wage: The focus of people's serious attention], *Shehui* [Sociology], no. 6, (1987): 14–16.

128. "Survey Shows Workers Support Reforms," *GRRB*, in *Beijing Review* 29, no. 46 (November 17, 1986): 27.

129. *Chung-kuo Shih-pao* [China Times], October 30, 1989.

130. Yuan Zhimin, "Muqian Zhongguode Sigujieceng"[Four strata of present-day China], *Jingjixue Zhoubao* [Economic Weekly], April 24, 1988. My interviews with a score of Chinese scholars who worked in factories during Mao's time corroborated Yuan's views.

131. "Official Says Strikes Result of Economic Policy," *South China Morning Post* (Hong Kong), September 3, 1988, in FBIS, *CHI—DR*, 6 September 1988, p. 36.

132. Walder, "Workers, Managers and the State." In late May 1989, I also witnessed the workers of Xian demonstrating in an organized fashion. They rode their factories' trucks and held broad banners identifying their work units.

133. Jianhua Zhu, "Cong Bumangaige Dao Tongqing Xueyun" [From discontent to revolt? An empirical study of Chinese urban workers on the eve of the 1989 pro-democracy movement], *Dangdai Zhongguo Yanjiuzhongxing Lunwen* [Papers of the center for Modern China], vol. 3, no. 8 (August 1992): 11–14.

134. "Chinese Workers Receive Harsh Sentences: ILO Reports on 91 Cases," *Asia Watch*, March 13, 1991, p. 3.

135. Jeanne L. Wilson, "'The Polish Lesson': China and Poland, 1980–1990," *Studies in Comparative Communism*, vol. 23, nos. 3–4 (Autumn-Winter 1990): 274.

136. "Chinese Workers Receive Harsh Sentences," *Asia Watch, p.* 3.

137. *Chung-kuo Shih-pao* [China Times] (Taipei), August 30, 1991, citing an Agence France Press (AFP) cable from Beijing, dated August 29, 1991. The AFP report was based on an internal CCP document.

138. *Chung-kuo Shih-pao* [China Times], August 30, 1991; this report was based on an *AFP* dispatch from Beijing, dated August 29,1991, citing a confidential report of ACFTU.

139. *China Daily*, April 30, 1994.

140. *South China Morning Post*, May 17, 1994, in FBIS, *CHI/DR*, May 17, 1994, p. 28.

141. The report on strikes and demonstration sin 1992 was published in the Chinese journal *Cheng Ming* (Hong Kong), March 1993, p. 19. *Cheng Ming* specializes in Chinese affairs and its articles are frequently translated and published in the FBIS, *CHI/DR*.

142. I am grateful to my colleague Professor Eric Smith for advice on these statistical computations and interpretations.

143. I am grateful to my student Allen Shen for computing and advising about the regression analysis.

144. Louis Kriesberg, *Social Conflicts* (Englewood Cliffs, N.J.: Prentice-Hall, 1982), p. 135.

145. David Snyder, "Collective Violence Processes: Implications for Disaggregated Theory and Research," in *Research in Social Movements, Conflicts, and Change*, ed. Louis Kriesberg, vol. 2 (Greenwich, Conn.: JAI Press, 1979), pp. 35–62.

146. My data are from *Zhongguo Jingji Nianjian, 1992* [Almanac of China's Economy, 1992] (Beijing: Jingji Guanli Chubanshe, 1992).

147. For Chinese scholars' discussion on the Third Line construction and these firms' current crises, see Xiao Min, "Shilun Sanxiangongye Chanyejiegou Tiaozheng" [On adjustment of the composition of the Third Line industry], *Gongye Jingji* [Industrial Economy], no. 7 (1989): 89–93; and Li Xiaofan,

"Sanxiangongyedidai: Zhongguojingjidi Qianzai Chenzhangdian" [The area of Third Line industry: The developmental potential of China's economy], *Gongye Jingji* [Industrial Economy], no. 1 (1992): 130–131. Also, *New York Times*, December 15, 1991.

148. For an analysis of the industry in Sichuan, see Liu Deyang, "Sichuansheng Gongyeqiye Jingjixiaoyide Fengxiji Duice Shilu" [An analysis and possible solution of the industrial firms in Sichuan], *Gongye Jingji* [Industrial Economy], no. 7 (1988): 19–24; and "Sichuan Gongye Jingji Xiaoyixianzhuang Jitigaotujing" [The present condition of industrial efficiency in Sichuan and paths toward its improvement], *Gongye Jingji* [Industrial Economy], no. 10 (1991): 151–158.

149. *Chung-kuo Shih-pao* [China Times] (Taipei), September 8, 1994. This Taipei newspaper is privately owned and has resident correspondents in China, just like any major U.S. newspaper.

150. *Zhongguo Xinwen She*, April 25, 1994, in FBIS, *CHI/DR*, April 28, 1994, pp. 87–88.

151. *Sichuan Ribao*, June 3, 1994, in FBIS, *CHI/DR*, June 22, 1994, p. 38.

152. *Cheng Ming*, June 1, 1994, in FBIS, *CHI/DR*, June 6, 1994, pp. 18–20.

153. *Cheng Ming*, April 1, 1994; for an English translation of this report, see FBIS, *CHI/DR*, April 14, 1994, pp. 27–29.

154. *IRAR-Tass*, November 6, 1994, in FBIS, *CHI/DR*, November 7, 1994, p. 25.

155. Chao Tsung, *Wen-ke Yung-tong Li-ch'eng Shu-lueh* [An account of the "Great Proletarian Cultural Revolution"], vols. 2, 3, and 4 (Hong Kong: Union Research Institute, 1974, 1975, and 1979).

156. *Zhongguo Tongxun She*, February 4, 1994, in FBIS, *CHI/DR*, February 10, 1994, pp. 41–42; also Feng Tongqin's essay in the Taipei newspaper *China Times*, June 26, 1994.

157. *China Daily*, July 6, 1994, and July 23, 1994. For a Western reporter's account on these workers, see *Wall Street Journal*, May 19, 1994.

158. *China Daily*, July 15, 1994.

159. *South China Morning Post*, June 14, 1994, in FBIS, *CHI/DR*, June 14, 1994, p. 31.

160. *Fazhi Ribao*, August 25, 1993, in FBIS, *CHI/DR*, September 21, 1993, pp. 48–51; and *Liaowang*, no. 5 (January 31, 1994), in FBIS, *CHI/DR*, March 3, 1994, pp. 32–41.

161. *Zhongguo Tongxun She*, February 4, 1994, in FBIS, *CHI/DR*, February 10, 1994, p. 41.

162. *Chung-kuo Shih-pao* [China Times], July 9, 1994.

163. *Xinhua*, June 6, 1994, in FBIS, *CHI/DR*, June 7, 1994, p. 48.

164. *South China Morning Post*, March 25, 1994, in FBIS, *CHI/DR*, March 25, 1994, p. 68.

165. *Chiushih Nientai* (Hong Kong), April 1, 1994, in FBIS, *CHI/DR*, April 6, 1994, p. 20.

166. *Tangtai* (Hong Kong), March 15, 1994, in FBIS, *CHI/DR*, April 5, 1994, pp. 43–44.

167. *South China Morning Post*, June 13, 1994, in FBIS, *CHI/DR*, June 13, 1994, pp. 30–31.

168. *Eastern Express*, March 31, 1994, in FBIS, *CHI/DR*, March 31, 1994, p. 28.

169. *Chung-kuo Lao-kung Yung-tong-shih* [History of the Chinese Labor Movement], vol. 1 (Taipei: Chung-kuo Lao-kung Yung-tong-shih Pien-ch'uan Wei-yuan-hui, 1958).

170. "Mining in China: A Threat to Safety, Environment" *East-West Center Views,* January-March, 1994, p. 3.

171. *AFP,* May 8, 1994, in FBIS, *CHI/DR,* May 9, 1994, p. 51.

172. *Lien Ho Pao,* May 21, 1994, in FBIS, *CHI/DR,* May 23, 1994, p. 39.

173. Sheryl WuDunn, "The Layoff Introduced to Chinese," *New York Times,* May 11, 1993, p. A4.

174. *Chung-kuo Shih-pao* [China Times], August 17, 1993, p. 11, citing a report in *China Daily,* August 16, 1993.

175. *China Daily,* April 23, 1994, in FBIS, *CHI/DR,* April 25, 1994, p. 49.

176. *China Daily,* June 29, 1994, in FBIS, *CHI/DR,* June 30, 1994, p. 40.

177. *Xinhua,* May 27, 1994, in FBIS, *CHI/DR,* May 31, 1994, pp. 56–57.

178. Anita Chan, "Revolution or Corporatism?—Workers and Trade Union in Post-Mao China" (in Chinese) *Dangdai Zhongguo Yanjiu* [Modern China Studies], no. 4 (1994):4–28.

179. The full text of the law is in *Xinhua,* July 5, 1994, in FBIS, *CHI/DR,* July 19, 1994, pp. 18–26.

180. *China Daily,* July 23, 1994, in FBIS, *CHI/DR,* July 25, 1994, p. 33.

181. James C. Scott, *Weapons of the Weak* (New Haven: Yale University Press, 1985), p. 255.

182. Craig Jackson Calhoun, "The Radicalism of Tradition: Community Strength or Venerable Disguise and Borrowed Language?" *American Journal of Sociology* 88, no. 5 (1983): 895.

183. Ibid., p. 898.

4

POLITICAL ATTITUDES AND BEHAVIOR OF STUDENTS: CYCLES OF PROTESTS

The Chinese people have been deceived. When they courageously drove out the imperialists and the Chiang Kai-shek gang, they put their trust in the wrong man. We used a robber's knife to drive out another robber. When one robber had been killed, we gave the knife to the other one.

—Wall poster at Beijing University, 1957[1]

In the last forty years, we got rid of the Guomindang and welcomed the Communist Party. And since then, with all the power struggles and changes in the Party leadership, all we really got each time was a hungrier devil in exchange for a full-bellied one.

—Beijing University student, 1989[2]

In early April 1989, I saw a wall poster entitled "Echo of May Fourth: The Call of Our Times" at the so-called triangular area of Beijing University (Beida hereafter)—the campus plaza for student activity. The author of the poster lamented the fact that seventy years after the May 4, 1919, student movement, China "was still under the shadow of feudalism," and he concluded, "History mocked us mercilessly." After the state mercilessly put down the student pro-democracy movement two months later, a young Chinese scholar echoed the sentiment expressed in that student poster by telling a Hong Kong reporter: "The times have gone backward. I feel that Chinese intellectuals in the late twentieth century are sharing the same fate of those in the late nineteenth century. The intellectuals at the present are like another generation of K'ang Yu-wei's and Liang Ch'i-ch'ao's. The Communist Party has taken China back by a century."[3]

The statements of these two young Chinese intellectuals call attention to the fact that since the turn of the century, Chinese history has seen cycles of student protests. Dates of memorable student movements have been recorded in Chinese history books: May 4 (1919), May 30 (1925), December 9 (1935), and December 1 (1945).[4] Each date represents not only a major student movement but the occurrence of a particular national crisis at the same time. The establishment of the PRC in 1949 did not bring student activism to an end. From the mid-1950s to the pro-democracy movement in 1989, more memorable dates of collective student protest were written into Chinese history, such as the April 5, 1976 demonstration at Tian'anmen Square (*"Si Wu"*) and the June 4, 1989 massacre (*"Liu Si"*). Specifically, from the founding of the PRC to the reform era under Deng Xiaoping, four cycles of student protests occurred: during the Hundred Flowers campaign in 1957, the Cultural Revolution in 1966–1969, the Democracy Wall episode in 1978–1980, and the pro-democracy movement of 1986–1989.

Although students in modern and contemporary China have yet to achieve their declared goals of establishing science and democracy in the nation, student movements have had more immediate political impact than those of the workers or the peasants. Student movements have a "broadcasting" effect, which is usually absent from those by the workers or the peasants. We have mentioned earlier that the 1978 Democracy Wall episode induced some worker activists to join student dissidents. The 1989 pro-democracy movement even inspired clan wars in Jiangxi. Due to students' skill in mass communication and their habit of moving about to unite with their colleagues, student movements tend to precipitate a "revolutionary bandwagon effect," drawing in other social groups. Because of the students' unique status as potential successors to the present elite, their movements tend to push the elite into a quandary. Neither concession nor repression seems a viable option to a state confronted with a large-scale student movement. Consequently, students are likely to precipitate a severe elite split over how to cope with the protesters. Above all, student movements are always a reliable indicator of major crises within a country. For all these reasons, the significance of student activism is not diminished by its often failed outcomes. In this chapter, I shall analyze the dynamics and genesis of student movements after 1949. My emphasis will be on the interpretation of general student activism in contemporary China rather than on a description of each movement.

Main Points of Conflict

Since the following discussion on the conflict between the students and the Party-state necessarily draws information and insights from the more articulate and active elements of the student generation, I must first address the question of how representative these student leaders were. It has been suggested that Chinese student activists, such as Lin Xilin (Lin Hsi-lin) in 1957 or Wang Dan and Wuer Kaixi in 1989, were "oddballs" among the students, as were the U.S. student radicals in the 1960s and 1970s, such as Bernadette Dohrns or members of the "Weathermen" group. However, this assertion bears scrutiny. First, one must make a distinction between these activists' means and the values that they articulated. Although the student leaders may be regarded as "oddballs" because of the radical means they employed, the basic values they expressed could not have been so "odd" as critics suggested, otherwise no mass movement would have occurred. As Karl Mannheim pointed out, in every generation there are the active, the intermediary, and the isolated segments among the young. It is the active group that articulates the *Zeitgeist*.[5] Second, time also serves as a test of the representative nature of the student activists. There is a fundamental difference between the U.S. student radicals in the 1960s and their counterparts in China. Whereas student radicalism in the United States petered out after the end of the U.S. involvement in the Vietnam War, student movements in China grew larger in scale over the years. Moreover, the basic values of these movements remained identical, as later discussion will show. Obviously, Chinese student activists were more representative of their cohorts than were their American colleagues. Third, one also might judge the degree of representation of student activists in China by the reaction of the state. For example, the student protest in the Hundred Flowers campaign in 1957 provoked the Maoist regime to fundamentally alter university education. Eventually, the state suspended university teaching altogether for the decade from 1966 to 1976. If the activists were merely "oddballs," the state presumably would not have responded in such a radical way. However, I have no intention to gloss over the fact that Chinese students are internally differentiated. "Within any generation," Mannheim wrote, "there can exist a number of differentiated, antagonistic generation-units. Together they constitute an 'actual' generation precisely because they are oriented toward each other, even though only in the sense of fighting one another."[6] In the discussions to follow, I shall take into consideration the internal differentiation of Chinese students from period to period.

In retrospect, Chinese university students have persistently expressed four major values over the four decades of Communist rule. It was also over these values that students have come into conflict with the Party-state. The first one is the students' longing to be incorporated into a new political system—one that is based on liberal values of constitutionalism, civil liberties, representation, and mass participation. As years went by, different groups of students have expressed these values in varying terminology. In the early 1950s, students thought that the Communist Party represented these liberal values since it was fighting the Nationalist Party in the name of democracy.[7] The failure of the CCP to fulfill its promises of democracy and constitutionalism was one of the major causes of the student protest in the Hundred Flowers campaign of 1957.[8] The students' initial support of the Cultural Revolution stemmed partly from their perception (mistakenly, it turned out) that this campaign was to establish a genuine electoral system. For example, the students then were attracted to the organizational principles of the Paris Commune of 1871. Mao and his leftist associates trumpeted the Paris Commune at the start of the Cultural Revolution, obviously for propaganda purposes. In 1967, Shanghai students called their first citywide Party-state organization the "Shanghai Commune." During the 1970s, the most famous youth underground wall poster was the "Li Yizhe" wall poster of 1974. The title of this poster—"Concerning Socialist Democracy and the Legal System"—testified to the persistence of liberal values, at least among the more active educated youth.[9] In the Democracy Wall movement of 1978–1980, democracy and human rights were the primary issues in the speeches and publications of the young dissidents.[10] The 1986–1987 student protest was triggered by perceived election irregularities, and the 1989 movement was explicitly identified by its participants with the symbols of science and democracy—representative of the May 4, 1919, movement.[11]

The second value that Chinese students have articulated persistently is to achieve an egalitarian and just society. Their conflict with the Chinese state was perhaps a part of the universal tension between the young and the established order. Samuel Eisenstadt attributed this type of conflict to the youth's emphasis on the "creation of and participation in future-oriented collectives" and the reality of the "growing institutionalization of such values."[12] Following the Hundred Flowers campaign, students showed a strong resentment against social stratification and bureaucratization. They spoke out against the system of ranks, privileges, and nepotism. Since the days of the Cultural Revolution, the homespun "theory of bureaucratic class" had been widely spread; it was originally advocated by a radical youth group from Hunan during the concluding phase of the Cultural Revolution. As the chapter on the working class showed, workers protesting against a plant closure in Shenyang in 1993 shouted the slogan: "Down with the Bureaucratic Class!"[13] At least part of the cause of the Chinese students' stress on an egalitarian society is due to the CCP's own propaganda line. Officially, the CCP has always identified itself with an image that harked back to its early days. The Party was then a revolutionary and youthful mass movement that enjoyed the reputation of being group-spirited, egalitarian, and idealistic. This public image of the CCP acted as a powerful magnet to the students in China before 1949. The same picture of the Party probably accounted for Chinese university students' strong support of the new state in the early 1950s. Since then, Party propaganda has persisted in describing the CCP in such an idealistic manner, although the reality is otherwise. One of the chief slogans used by the Maoist regime to launch the Hundred Flowers campaign was characterized by its emphasis on antibureaucratism. Mao and his left-wing associates repeated the antibureaucratic propaganda again at the start of the Cultural Revolution, through the symbol of the Paris Commune. But the official propaganda has been at a significant variance from the students' experience. The disparity between the state's words and its deeds has served to intensify the students' sense of a "revolution betrayed."

The third value that Chinese students have espoused continuously is for the right to enjoy independent expression. Both the adolescent status of the students and the totalitarian system under which they lived fueled the youths' desire for autonomous articulation. As psychologist Erik Erikson pointed out, adolescent youth experience identity crises, and one of the ways for them to cope with the turmoil is articulation.[14] The totalitarian order that the CCP established ran counter to the youthful spirit for autonomy and expression. Since the mid-1950s, almost every youth protest movement in China has rallied against the Communist Party's suppression of free speech and association. Students have accused the Party-controlled press of telling lies and have derided the impotence of the representative organs of the state such as the "democratic parties" or the parliament—the National People's Congress. By their own actions, students have expressed their strong desire for autonomous articulation, such as by displaying posters *(dazibao)*, publishing underground journals, and organizing associations. The rapid spread of Red Guard organizations and Red Guard papers in the Cultural Revolution bespoke of the students' ability and strong desire for independent expression of views. In the 1970s, the intellectual youth of China did not stop associating and articulating on their own—even though the repressive power of the state was at an all-time high. The "Li Yizhe" group was proof of that. In the post-Mao period, no sooner had the Dengist state removed the "Democracy Wall," than it was confronted with open student demonstrations and wall posters on campuses.

The fourth value that Chinese students have tenaciously adhered to since the 1950s is toward modernism—professionalism, meritocracy, and achievement-orientation. This value has been particularly embraced by those from the "middling classes" of Chinese society, such as urban employees and modern professionals. The CCP could not fit these groups readily into their Marxist class categories. The youngsters from these families obviously thought that they might employ these modernist values to overcome the strong ascription-orientation of the CCP. The ultimate goals of these students were mobility and autonomy. The concrete manifestation of the modernist values among the students was their desire to major in science and technology, instead of in the humanities and social sciences. However, the Maoist regime subjected the students to a protracted campaign of disorientation. On the one hand, the Party-state affirmed the spirit of science; on the other hand, the Party made repeated attempts to dampen students' enthusiasm for science and technology.

The post–1957 campaign of "Be Both Red and Expert" was an example of the state's campaign of disorientation. After the debacle of the Great Leap, the fractured leadership in Beijing gave students contradictory signals. In 1961, reacting to the withdrawal of Soviet specialists in China, top CCP leaders Zhou Enlai and Chen Yi openly called on universities to stress education in science and technology, pledged respect for scientists and technical specialists, and promised support for research and development. Their promises lifted the spirit of students and scientists—but only briefly.[15] Mao soon struck back. To neutralize the impact of Zhou's and Chen's ideas among students, the Maoists made the U.S.-educated rocket scientist, Qian Xuesheng, tell students publicly not to think of him as their model.[16] Qian's 1965 essay in the youth league newspaper exposed the general mood among students engaged in higher learning. He reported that among these students there was the attitude described as "getting by in politics, obtaining a solid professional skill, and living a good life." A popular saying among the students was: "Let us follow Qian Xuesheng's path." Qian maintained that he had disavowed his own career pattern. According to one former student, Qian's article failed to impress college youths. Those who read Qian's essay responded by saying that Qian himself symbolized the "first expert, then red" approach. He became a famous rocket specialist in the United States and then returned to China. He was admitted into the Communist Party and appointed to head the rocketry development project.[17].

While these contradictory signals from the Party-state naturally confused the students, the increasingly restricted mobility of the young (since the 1960s) disillusioned and angered them. The line of division was sharpened between the privileged few (primarily children of high-ranking Party-state officials) and the mass of high school and university graduates who were sent to the countryside to work alongside the peasants. In the post-Mao period, those Chinese students specializing in science and technology were at first shocked to learn how far behind China was, compared to the scientific and technological advancement of the West. Subsequently, they regarded the totalitarian political system of the CCP as the chief cause of China's backwardness.[18] For the bulk of Chinese college and university graduates, the lack of career opportunities in science and technology is probably the key to the difference in political behavior between Chinese and Soviet youths. While the educated youth in the former Soviet Union also displayed political disillusionment after the death of Stalin, there was no militant youth movement in Russia as there was in China. To the Russian youth, a career in science and technology was still open under socialism.[19] In

China, modernism and the spirit of science were overwhelmed by ascription, especially in Mao's time. The intellectual youth in China tended to bear the brunt of the Communist Party's political ascription.

Bases of Conflicts

As mentioned earlier, conflicts between the Party-state and Chinese university students have been going on for over thirty years and are becoming larger in scale. One may be inclined to ask whether there are deeper causes of the state-youth conflicts in China. Here, I suggest a cultural theory for the conflicts. Table 4.1 lists the four levels of this theory: values, norms, roles, and situational facilities. From values to situational facilities, the variables become more specific or immediately connected with the student movements in each period.[20] The premise of my theory is that student and state conflicts are primarily dissensual. That is to say, the Chinese state and the students disagree over values "pertain[ing] to ways of life or goals that are intrinsically meaningful and valuable" for each party.[21] In other words, they disagree over ultimate ends.

The most fundamental cause of the value conflicts between students and the Party-state is generational difference, which in this case is more than just the customary sense of a "generation gap." The generation that Mao, Deng, and their colleagues represented was not only older than the students but, more importantly, belonged to a generation unit (borrowing Mannheim's concept) quite different from that of the student activists

Table 4.1 Dynamics of Student–State Conflicts in China

Specificity ↕	Values	Generational conflict: Generation gap and conflicts between generational units—neotraditionalists versus modernists	Subgroup differentiation ↕
	Norms	Social mobility: Universalism versus particularism and achievement versus ascription	
	Role	Youth as political successor	
	Situational Facility	Resources, movement characteristics, mobilization, and participation	

after 1949. Mao and Deng were part of the neotraditionalist generation unit that rose to political prominence in the 1920s and 1930s. The modernist generation unit, the one that spearheaded the May Fourth Movement in 1919 (those who demanded science and democracy), was politically submerged in both the Communist Party and the Nationalist Party. The cultural differences between these two generational units in the 1920s were obscured by the nationalism of the time.

During the ensuing revolution, the neotraditionalist group inside the Communist Party rose to power. Mao and Deng were examples of the ascendance of the neotraditionals. (In the Guomindang, the rise of Chiang Kai-shek was a part of the same process.) Robert North and Ithiel de Sola Pool's study of the composition of the CCP's central leadership from the 1920s onward revealed the following trend: "At first there was a goodly sprinkling of men from professional or intellectual families—men who gave the initial ideological impetus. Along with these, and increasingly dominant, however, was a group consisting of sons of peasants or sons of landlords."[22]

The neotraditionalists brought with them strong influences of traditional Chinese politics, such as autocracy and charisma. The Marxist-Leninist ideology provided the neotraditionalists in the Communist Party with concrete socioeconomic programs and a doctrinal rationalization. But the cultural core of the PRC was traditional autocracy. Tim McDaniel defined autocracy as personal power "uncontrolled by competing powers and unconstrained by fixed law." "Autocratic rulers put their trust in individual men, not in formalized procedures or organizations."[23] There is little doubt that Mao's political style was an example of autocracy par excellence.[24]

The process of armed struggle before 1949 further solidified the power of neotraditionalists inside the CCP.[25] Following the creation of the PRC, Maoist neotraditionalism clashed with modernist values. Representative of these values were the division of labor, structural differentiation, and pluralization of culture and authority. At an even deeper level, Mao's neotraditionalism came into conflict with the tenets of what Robert Lane called "a knowledgeable society." According to Lane, the members of a knowledgeable society "are guided (perhaps unconsciously) by objective standards of veridical truth and, at the upper levels of education, follow scientific rules of evidence and inference in inquiry," and "devote considerable resources to this inquiry and thus have a large store of knowledge."[26] It was in the Westernized Chinese universities in major cities such as Beijing, Tianjin, Nanjing, and Shanghai that liberal and modernist values of a knowledgeable society resided. Student activists before and after 1949 were socialized in the liberal and modernist tradition of these universities. Their conceptions of knowledge and education were at variance with the neotraditionalists in the Communist Party, especially Mao. The core of Mao's view toward knowledge and education was an overwhelming emphasis on the concrete. Thus, in the campaign of "cultivating successors to revolution," Mao said to his nephew: "You students know nothing. You cannot tell the differences among horse, cow, sheep, chicken, dog, pig, rice, grain, bean, wheat, corn, and millet. You have no knowledge whatsoever."[27] After voicing this critique, Mao ordered all university students to spend a substantial amount of time doing farm work in the countryside as part of their university education.

In the 1970s, Mao also made major universities create "rural branches." The various programs implemented by Mao after 1957 to restructure higher education were designed to accomplish a single objective—to pattern Chinese education after the experience of children of lower classes. Students were thus subjected to a short duration of learning, lack of commitment to the value of education, limited choice in occupation, and blurring of generational differences (forcing youth to live adult lives).[28] It is clear that Mao's philosophy of education and understanding of knowledge were a faithful reflection of his own experience. His programs were bound to encounter conflict among university students and intellectuals in major Chinese cities.

Generational conflicts in China after 1949 differed from those in the West. Generational conflicts in the West were due to different perspectives toward new problems at the time. The older generation tended to treat new problems with the value perspective of their generation, while the young generation treated problems in the new or current perspectives.[29] However, in the PRC, generational conflicts were due to different cultures, not just differences in perspectives. At each historical epoch since the mid-nineteenth century, the modernists in China renewed their battle with the neotraditionalists. The repeated failures of the modernists were the most powerful causes for continuing the battle into the distant future.

Conflicts between the state and the students at value level necessarily were carried over to norms. Since 1949, a major cause of tension between the CCP and university students revolved around universalistic norms and achievement-orientation. Formally, the CCP did not reject these modern norms, but it put a particularistic qualification on it. According to the CCP, universalistic and achievement norms applied only to those who were politically qualified. This CCP perspective was succinctly expressed in the official statement: "We emphasize class status, but not exclusively so; what we stress is political behavior" (*Women yu chengfenlun, buwei chengfenlun, zhongzai zhengzhibiaoxian*). But the CCP defined "political behavior" with flexibility and vagaries, such as "serving the people," "mingling with the workers and peasants," "taking the stand of the proletariat," or "meeting the need of the revolution." The Party-state and its agents (the cadres) interpreted the meaning of "political behavior" as they saw fit. Universalism and particularism now became quite blurred. Former journalist Liu Binyan described the practical result of the CCP's equivocation over universalistic and achievement norms as follows:

> In evaluating a person a premium was put on superficial matters, such as his family, social connection, seniority, political status, past record, and so on, not on his true worthiness. This means that a person was judged independently of his performance and actual contribution.
>
> A strange thing then happened: A person found that his performance and contribution were used to oppose him. His real virtues and talent were not taken into account in others' judgment of him; these were even used against him.[30]

The CCP's equivocation over universalistic norms could not have been entirely due to the social background of the neotraditionals. Self-interest was another possible cause for the CCP leaders' *practical* rejection of universalism and achievement orientation. The former revolutionaries lost their opportunity to acquire an advanced education (or even any schooling at all). Now that revolution was over, the members of the CCP were fearful of being penalized if they lived up to their proclaimed goals of "science and democracy." The practical result of the CCP's denial of universalism was persistent corruption permeating the Party and was one of the focal points of conflicts between the state and the students. As Arnold Rogow and Harold Lasswell wrote, "A background of severe deprivation may encourage the use of power in corrupt forms as a means of acquiring and maintaining environmental control."[31] Moreover, the fact that the CCP victory in 1949 was hard-won gave the former revolutionists a strong sense of rectitude, even while perpetrating deeds that would normally be regarded as corrupt. When Deng publicly conferred status to intellectuals in the 1980s, he was confronted by a critical view (apparently from old Party members): "We fought for the revolution, intellectuals sat out the revolution" (*Women da tianxia zhishi fenzi zuotianxia*).[32]

The conflicts between Chinese university students and the Party-state also reflected the students' role confusion. Mao's pronouncements about the youth as political successors included both idealistic and distrustful views of the young. For example, at the start of the Great Leap campaign, Mao seemed to believe reports about the alleged fantastic feats of some students, such as writing a history book on world literature in four days and nights.[33] In November 1959, Mao was alarmed by the speech of U.S. Secretary of State John Foster Dulles on the possibility of the Communist states' undergoing a peaceful mutation. Mao called on the CCP to put the cultivation of "successors to revolution" on their agenda, to make sure that China "would not change color" after the old revolutionists were gone.

But Mao's views of the young generation were clearly ambivalent and, on the whole, contained more contempt than respect for the young. On the one hand, Mao praised the energy and intelligence of the young; he said that many heroic figures in Chinese history achieved their successes while young. On the other hand, Mao voiced his disdain for the young. That he regarded the current young generation as ignorant has already been mentioned. In 1965, Mao told French author André Malraux that the youth was "showing dangerous tendencies" and "must be put to test."[34] In the same year Mao expressed his basic mistrust of the young generation to Edgar Snow. Mao said that the present youth "knew nothing about the old society at first hand. Parents could tell them but to hear about history and to read books was not the same thing as living it."[35] Mao was afraid that, after his death, the "youth could negate the revolution and . . . make peace with imperialism."[36]

Mao's doubts about the young were apparently shared by many CCP members. Both Mao and Deng had to impose themselves on the rest of the Party-state to implement, let alone accelerate, generational succession in their times. However, neither of these two paramount leaders set personal examples for generational succession. Turner and Killian pointed out that those who experienced a protracted revolution or social movement developed a sense of their "owning" the movement. "The more bitterly fought the battle for a movement's goals, the greater is the tendency for the movement's activists to place the attainment and maintenance of power above the evaluation of their consistency with the value objectives."[37] One wonders if Mao's distrust of the young generation might not have been an unconscious rationalization for not willing to let the young succeed him. At the same time, the tensions between the young and the old revolutionaries in the PRC also reflect a general problem of succession in modern technological society. Bruno Bettelheim pointed out that, in traditional society, generational succession was smooth since it was dictated by the rise and fall of physical strength. As old men's physical strength waned, it was succeeded by young people's rising physical power. In a modern society, "the life-assuring labor was performed by others," such as technology. The young must fight for their rights and obligations while the old view the young with suspicion. "Why should the older generation voluntarily abdicate if it has nothing to gain by it and loses nothing by holding on?"[38]

Situational Facilities

I have discussed the major cultural conflicts between Chinese students and the Party-state. But my cultural theory of state-student conflicts does not explain the form of student articulation. To deal with that, one needs to discuss the unique situational facilities to which students have access and that enable them to organize mass movements with relative ease. I shall discuss the situational facilities of Chinese students in the two contexts: (1) intergroup differences (that is, contrasting students with peasants and workers); and (2) the neutralization of totalitarian control. Unlike the workers and peasants, Chinese students adopted a confrontational approach in their conflicts with the state. The first important cause of this difference is that Chinese students had little or no use for the amorphous social action that suited workers and peasants well. Being young, Chinese university students had not yet become a part of the production system, so they did not have the option of using aggregate productive conduct to express their opinion. The second cause of the students' confrontational reaction to the state was their environment. The campus provided the milieu for informal association, so students could organize a collective protest more readily than either the workers or peasants. Although workers were also in a natural association—the plant, they were weighed down by the practical concerns of providing for their families. Students were relatively free of these concerns. Each group found the form of articulation that best suited its daily routines.

Nevertheless, Chinese students were repeatedly able to evade or overcome heavy bureaucratic control by the state and to organize mass protest movements. This was due to other situational facilities dealing with resources, characteristics of student movements, mobilization, and participation. First of all, student movements relied on intangible internal resources for their movements. One such resource was the students themselves. "People are the primary intangible resource," wrote Jo Freeman, and "social movements are low in tangible resources, especially in money, but high in people resources."[39] Like the poor people's movements in the United States, the collective actions by Chinese students were built on indigenous resources, drawn from their own constituency, not from elites.[40] Students gave their own and, in some cases, their families' time, labor, money, and equipment to their movements. However, once their movements were publicly launched, students were likely to benefit from external resources, even from the elites.

Second, Chinese student movements were primarily value-oriented and many of the students' actions were also for expressive purposes. These movements were somewhat similar to the so-called New Social Movements in Western Europe in the 1960s and 1970s that were motivated by new and post-industrial values.[41] U.S. social scientists' stress on rational-instrumental considerations in social movements is not as relevant in understanding Chinese student movements or the European New Social Movements.[42] If one determined the likelihood of organizing collective protests primarily on rational-instrumentalist grounds, then there would never be any such action in a highly repressive state such as the

PRC. European scholars' stress on the formation of a common identity and a new cultural trend as the main catalysts for collective action is much more germane to analyzing the student actions in China than the rationalist-utilitarian approach of the U.S.-based "resource mobilization" school. The latter approach is best suited to societies with weak social controls.[43] The values or cultural orientation of Chinese students also meant that their movements were self-sustained. In the United States, the dynamism of a social movement may have to depend on a special interest group to keep it alive in a time of low activity or "abeyance."[44] However, Chinese student movements were kept alive by a strong commitment to modernist values on the part of a hard core of student activists who were reborn in every student generation. These activists were, in turn, supported by a general cultural identity among university students. When the right time or opportunity came, the activists could always count on the general identity of the students to support them.

As to the source of students' values, in Mao's time the idealistic aspects of Marxism itself provided a counter-ideology within the official ideology. "The very cultural symbols on which Communist party rule is based—Marxist ideology, the ideals of socialism, and the promise of a Communist utopia—also support independent public expression," so wrote Goldfarb.[45] Another source of cultural inspiration to the students was the CCP's appropriation of some pre-Communist cultural traditions, such as the May 4, 1919, movement. After 1949, May 4 was designated by the PRC as Youth Day. In other words, Chinese students did not have to design a totally new ideology to inform their movements. After Mao's death, Deng's open-door policy unwittingly provided the students with an intellectual boon.

Yet another characteristic of Chinese student movements is the dependence on opportunities for expression granted by the state itself. The two cycles of student movements—the Hundred Flowers campaign of 1957 and the Cultural Revolution of 1966–1969—were started originally by Mao, thinking that he could count on supportive public opinion to accomplish partisan purposes. In both instances, the students turned the tables on Mao and developed independent oppositional movements. After Mao's death, the 1978 Democracy Wall movement appeared partly due to Deng's tacit encouragement, since he was then locked in a power struggle with the Maoists.[46] Thereafter, students seemed to take the initiative themselves, instead of waiting for state authorization. But even the large demonstration in 1986–1987 happened partly because there was some movement among top CCP leaders for political reform. As Charles Tilly pointed out, there were advantages to using officially sponsored occasions to express independent opinions, such as attracting potential participants (even including some elites), gaining publicity, and assuming legality.[47] But this dependency of Chinese student movements on elite sponsorship (wittingly or unwittingly) also set a definite limit to student actions. Whenever the authorities closed ranks and applied repression, student movements subsided. Thus, student movements in China exhibited the same "waves of mobilization" as did those in Eastern Europe before the final collapse of the socialist regimes. However, Chinese students did not rely on professional social movement organizations (SMO) as the Europeans did.[48] The Beijing regime's repressive power and the segmentation of the Chinese social structure precluded the existence of SMOs in China.

There are additional attributes pertaining to the mobilization and participation of Chinese students in protest movements that account for the state's failure to prevent them. For example, the mobilization for student protests depended primarily on internal and informal means. Chinese students relied on a high degree of group consciousness to rally supporters, rather than on the "selective incentives" stressed by U.S. scholars of the "resource mobilization school."[49] As pointed out earlier, the students had already developed a tradition of collective protest by 1949. The CCP unwittingly contributed to the students' consciousness of their protest tradition by appropriating the symbols of pre-1949 student movements. Various types of cultural conflicts between the generations naturally enhanced Chinese students' awareness of their being a distinct social group.

Similarly, there was little need for student activists to carry out a planned campaign of "consensus mobilization"—a concept favored by some Western sociologists specializing in social movements (especially Bert Klandermans). "Consensus mobilization" describes "a deliberate attempt by a social actor to create consensus among a subset of the population."[50] According to Sidney Tarrow, "consensus mobilization" may be taking place in cultural trends, community and social networks, and ideological processes among individuals and groups.[51] The activities that Tarrow stressed were the ones that Chinese students always counted on for consensus mobilization. Students interacted on a daily basis. China's congested dormitories offered even more opportunities for contact and discussion. Since the Hundred Flowers campaign, students also had firm control over their own mass medium—the wall poster, which successfully escaped the state's seemingly totalistic control. The wall posters may be regarded as equivalent to a deliberate attempt at consensus mobilization. Almost every student protest in China began with wall posters on campus. Chinese students tended to engage more in "consensus mobilization" *after* the first stage of their movements, not before. For a movement to rise to the surface, students counted on the power of a general mood—a kind of implicit or latent consensus that might be activated by any precipitant, such as the death of a popular leader (as in the case of Hu Yaobang in April 1989).

Chinese students also used informal means of recruitment for their movements, such as friendship and informal associations.[52] European scholars' research confirmed the importance of informal recruitment for the mobilization of collective actions. "Political enterpreneurs will be unlikely to organize joint political actions, possibly because an effective system of repression prevents the emergence of a well-organized opposition," wrote Karl-Dieter Opp and Christiane Gern on the protest movement in East Germany in 1989.[53] They found that friendship was an important means of mobilizing people to participate in protest movements. Klandermans and Dirk Oegema identified an association between ideological motivation and the importance of informal recruitment. They reported: "The more important ideological incentives are in a movement, the more informal networks linked to the movement act as guardians of the principles by forcing people to act according to their principles."[54] Their finding was fully borne out in Chinese student movements, as exemplified by the 1974 "Li Yizhe" episode. Finally, the polarized relationship between the state and student activists in universities since the mid-1950s was a source of mobilization. Hirsch commented that if members of a group have already developed a high degree of collective consciousness, then polarization can have a strong positive impact on participation. "The protesters will respond to threats as a powerful, angry group rather than as isolated, frightened individuals."[55] Deng Xiaoping's threat to brand the protesting students as "counterrevolutionaries" in April 1989 made more students participate in the pro-democracy movement than before.

As in mobilization, the forces that drew Chinese students to protest movements were not necessarily cold calculations of gains or losses for themselves, as set forth by Mancur Olson's "rational choice" school of thought.[56] Given the failed record of student movements since 1919, one would not expect Chinese students to keep demonstrating, as the "rational choice" theory would lead one to think. European scholars' stress on a sense of group solidarity and identification with the goals of protest as the primary motivations for participation in a movement is equally valid for Chinese student movements.[57] From the Hundred Flowers campaign to the 1989 pro-democracy movement, Chinese student activists often traveled from campus to campus to rally students and appeal to their common cultural identity. These activities were described either as "lighting fire" (in 1957) or "linkup" (during the Cultural Revolution). In 1989, students from all over China arrived at Tian'anmen Square in droves for the explicit purpose of showing solidarity with the Beijing students. One might deduce some distant utilitarian logic from the student actions in 1957 or 1989, but, in fact, the most immediate reasons for their participation were intangible—a sense of group solidarity and the desirability of the movement's goals.

Cycles of the Student Movement

In the ensuing discussions, I shall present a *brief* analysis of each of the four cycles of the student movement from 1949 to the 1990s. My focus will be on the main trends in student attitudes and behaviors, not on descriptions of the cycles in detail.

First Cycle, 1950–1957: Onset of Disillusionment

This initial cycle of student activism is perhaps most noteworthy for the rapid change in the youth's mood—from euphoria to disillusionment. But the students were also internally differentiated; the main division was between the politically active and the inactive. The latter were primarily interested in acquiring the knowledge and skills necessary for modern professions. But when the first cycle ended with the conclusion of the Hundred Flowers campaign in 1957, both student groups were politically disaffected. At the same time, the state still retained a degree of support from provincially oriented students, known ironically among the Chinese as "Activists" *(jijifenzi)*. (I shall capitalize this term from now on to refer to these loyalists among the students, to distinguish them from politically active but dissident students).

By all accounts, university students were the most enthusiastic in welcoming the Communists' establishment of the PRC. It was reported in February 1949 that students in Beijing were "solidly behind the new regime" and that they took "every opportunity possible to show their loyalty to it."[58] But this superficial appearance of support was deceiving. A sizable number of students held the mistaken notion that, although they did not come from "proletarian" families, they might still fulfill their dual goals of gaining social mobility for themselves and serving their country. They could accomplish that by being specialists in science and technology, or so they thought.[59] In contrast to these students were the political enthusiasts, some of whom had already joined the propaganda corps of the army.

By the mid-1950s, the student mood had changed radically—from idealism to disillusionment. The young people primarily reacted to the tight bureaucratic control that the Party-state sprang on them and the CCP's overwhelming stress on ascriptive norms, such as assigning each student a class status. Students' life chances then were determined by class; achievements were irrelevant. The Communist youth league leader, Hu Yaobang, reported in August 1955 that the mood among the young was characterized by pessimism and anxiety. Some resisted the Communist Party's class discrimination of them by organizing among themselves.[60] Some of the literary works then reflected the youths' disillusionment with the "new" order of things, especially the bureaucratic phenomenon. For example, one of the most famous works was the short story entitled "The Young Newcomer in the Organization Department" written by Wang Meng, then twenty-two years old. Wang depicted formalistic and bureaucratic behavior among old Party cadres who betrayed their youthful ideals and were now indifferent to the interests of the public. Condemned by the authorities, Wang's story received positive response from the reading public. In one month alone (September 1956), the journal that published Wang's story received 1,300 letters commenting on the novel.[61]

This general mood of resentment accounted for the surge of student activism in the Hundred Flowers campaign in May 1957. For the first time, the generation gap between the Chinese Communist leaders and the students was bared. The historical agenda fought for by the old revolutionists was no longer of concern to the new generation in 1957. Mao acknowledged this stark reality by stating: "It seems as if Marxism, once all the rage, is currently not so much in fashion."[62] The students also were divided. The dissidents were the most articulate and active in organizing and criticizing the Party-state. Natural student leaders emerged, such the famous Lin Xilin (Lin Hsi-lin) and Tan Tianrong. The main thrust of their criticism of the CCP was the familiar "revolution betrayed" thesis. Students such as Lin and Tan were formerly ardent supporters of the CCP, especially Lin who had been groomed by the CCP for future political leadership.[63]

Lin's case was not unique, however. A former student at Lanzhou University (in Gansu Province) reported that the most critical publication there came from the teaching assistants and lecturers of the Marxist-Leninist Research and Teaching Section of the Northwest Teachers' College.[64] The reactions of Lin, Tan, and other activists in the provinces were similar to those of student dissidents in Eastern Europe at about the same time. According to Lipset, an opinion survey of students at the University of Warsaw reported that "those students who were most committed to socialism and its egalitarian ideals were much more likely to have actively participated in the demonstrations against the regime in 1956, than were those who had less faith in, or were opposed to, socialism as a goal."[65]

The student movement during the Hundred Flowers campaign also highlighted the major division among them: dissidents versus supporters of the Party-state. The first group was later labeled the "Rightists" and the second, the Activists. According to a former student from Lanzhou University, after the start of the Anti-Rightist campaign the boundary between the Activists and the "Rightists" was sharply drawn. Each associated only among their kind, but the Activists—primarily members of the CCP and the Communist Youth League—displayed high spirits while the "Rightists" were depressed.[66] Since the Communist Party relied on ascriptive norms to recruit members, it may be inferred that the Activists were those either of "noble birth" (children of high-ranking CCP leaders) or of "true proletarian" background (workers or peasants).

Insight into the mentality of the Activists might be gained by citing just one example. In 1989 I interviewed a former Activist who participated in the Hundred Flowers campaign. He came from a "middle peasant" background in a northern province. After high school graduation, he failed a college admission test and was idle at home when the Communist army "liberated" his rural town in 1947. Two years later, he read for the first time, Mao's essays, "On the People's Democratic Dictatorship" and "Report on an Investigation of the Peasant Movement in Hunan." He found that the ideas in these two essays were agreeable. Upon a second application, he was admitted by Beida in 1949. The Activist studied some of the theoretical works of Marx, Lenin, and Mao. He was most taken with their emphases on equality. This Activist also compared the Communist cadres favorably with the corrupt Nationalist officials during the period before 1949. He was greatly impressed by the Party's execution of two corrupt cadres in Beijing in the "Three-Anti" campaign of 1950. When student dissenters criticized the CCP during the Hundred Flowers campaign, the Activist did not approve of such criticism. He felt that freedom should not exist without some limitations. In his opinion, a new regime must take resolute measures to deal with certain problems and, generally speaking, the state should act "with the force of a thunderbolt" (*leiting wan jun*). However, the Activist admitted that his political role made him a pariah among the students. He had very few true friends, and students in general would not speak their minds when he was present.

It was clear that a wide intellectual gap existed between the Activist and student leaders such as Tan and Lin. The Activist was culturally closer to the neotraditionalist leaders, such as Mao, than were the dissidents, such as Lin and Tan. The ideology of the dissidents was closer to the "science and democracy" spirit of the May Fourth movement. One does not expect the Activist to be able to make the following analysis that was done by Lin Xilin in 1957:

> Marxism tells us that all social phenomena have their social and historical origins. The problem of Stalin is not the problem of Stalin the individual; the problem of Stalin could only arise in a country like the Soviet Union. . . . China is the same. . . . I hold that the socialism we now have is not genuine socialism; or that if it is, our socialism is not typical. Genuine socialism should be very democratic, but ours is undemocratic. I venture to say our society is a socialist one erected on a feudal foundation.[67]

In other words, the Hundred Flowers campaign revisited the conflicts between two generational units—the neotraditionalists and the modernists—as they first appeared in the era of the May Fourth movement in 1919. However, during that period there was nationalism to unite the two units and mask their cultural differences. In 1957, nationalism was replaced by class and the conflicts between the two generational units intensified.

The years between the first and second cycles of the student movement, from 1958 to 1964, may be termed the period of "abeyance." Taylor defines "abeyance" in social movements as "a holding process by which movements sustain themselves in nonreceptive political environments and provide continuity from one stage of mobilization to another."[68] In the United States, such abeyance is made possible by a special agency characterized by temporality, purposive commitment, exclusiveness, centralization, and culture.[69] But in China, no independent youth agency existed to hold the movement together, waiting for another opportune moment. However, the state served as the equivalent of such an agency. Unwittingly, the Chinese state kept the youth movement alive by its failure to demobilize the youth.

In these intervening years, the Maoist state took up two measures to deal with the students. One was to undermine the students' facility of mobilization by reducing their time spent in formal learning. Students were required to spend lengthy periods in the countryside doing hard farm labor. The second measure was designed to persuade young people to identify themselves totally with Mao and to be willing tools of Mao. To this purpose, the Maoists designated a neotraditionalist youth model—a dead soldier named Lei Feng. The youth were instructed to emulate Lei Feng, who had no other purpose in life except to serve Mao. However, both measures failed to achieve their intended purposes. Former students from China testified that Lei Feng was subject more to doubt and scorn than to belief. Many regarded Lei a "docile tool" and expressed the view that "those who emulated Lei Feng were banal."[70] As Bettelheim pointed out, "the parent who sees his child's main task in life as the duty to execute his will or to justify his existence" will surely cause more conflicts between the generations.[71] Mao's attempt to pervert university education by requiring students to spend more and more time in farm work, provoked elite dissension and failed to dampen students' desire for acquiring modern knowledge.[72] The cultural chasm between the Maoist state and university students remained as wide as ever. It is this cultural distance that kept the student movement alive.

Second Cycle: The Cultural Revolution, 1966–1969

The second cycle of the Chinese student movement—the Cultural Revolution—repeated much of the first cycle. It began with Mao's authorization and the first stage was marked by student euphoria. Students participating in the Cultural Revolution were also split into two large units: the ascriptionists and the achievers. The first group consisted of the children of high-ranking Party-state leaders, heirs of the New Class. The second group was composed of youngsters from a nonproletarian background. Students belonging to the second group had the same commitment to universalism and meritocracy as did their counterparts in the 1950s. The behavior of these two generational units reflected closely their class interests. This is perhaps a major distinction between the first and the second cycle. In the second, the *initial* conflict between the two generational units among the students was more explicitly class-oriented than that of the students in the Hundred Flowers campaign. The most important reason for this was the state's promotion of class viewpoint, which began at the end of the Hundred Flowers campaign. The formal title of the Cultural Revolution was, after all, "The Great *Proletarian* Cultural Revolution."

Another reason for class orientation was that in 1966, the young heirs of the Party-state elites had reached adolescence and were conscious of their position as the New Class of China. The conflicts between the two generational units at first revolved around the right to participate in the Cultural Revolution. The ascriptionists naturally wished to reserve the right exclusively for the New Class. The achievers wanted to extend the right to a broader group of the population, including themselves, of course.[73] As in 1957, outstanding spokespersons emerged among the achievers, not among the ascriptionists. The most remarkable articulator among the achievers was eventually martyred—a Beijing youth named Yu Loke who was later executed by the leftists. Yu wrote the famous thesis "On Family Status" *(Chushenlun)* in 1966. He might be regarded as one of the first youth dissidents in the Cultural Revolution. Yu's thesis championed universalism and achievement orientation.[74] There was a third, albeit marginal, youth group in the Cultural Revolution—the former students who were sent away to settle in the countryside. Although they were active in group conflicts, these youths mainly played the role of reminding the others, especially the achievers, that the fate of downward mobility awaited them.[75]

In the end, the Cultural Revolution accomplished one result that was contrary to the original intent of the Maoists. The common experience of all the youth groups in the Cultural Revolution actualized the generational phenomenon. According to Mannheim, young people may be "located" in the same generation but not really constitute an actual generation. "The location as such only contains potentialities which may materialize, or be suppressed, or become embedded in other social forces and manifest themselves in modified form."[76] For the generational phenomenon to happen, the youth must participate in the common destiny of their times. Mannheim wrote: "We shall therefore speak of a *generation as an actuality* only when a concrete bond is created between members of a generation by their being exposed to the social and intellectual symptoms of a process of dynamic destabilization" (original emphasis).[77] It is in this sense that the Cultural Revolution is unique in its impact on the youth of China, the students in particular. The Cultural Revolution began with differentiation among the youth and it ended with a degree of common identity among them. From then on, the adolescents in the Cultural Revolution would be referred to in China as the "Cultural Revolution Generation" *(wengede yidai)*. Their most distinct intellectual outlook was political disaffection, as shown in the pronouncements of the Hunan-based dissident group Shenwulian. According to Shenwulian, a "Red Capitalist Class" had emerged in China and perpetrated class exploitation.[78] It is ironical that Mao's Cultural Revolution turned the first post-1949 generation of adolescents against the CCP. One would think that this generation ought to have been Mao's most ardent supporters.

"Abeyance," 1970 to 1977

The interim period between the end of the Cultural Revolution in 1969 and Mao's death in 1976 was a period of "abeyance" in the youth movement. I shall replace "students" with the broader term "youth" for this period, since the educational system was in disarray and the majority of "students" was scattered throughout China by the Maoists. The youth movement was kept alive during this period by three social and political conditions. The first of these was youth disaffection following the Cultural Revolution. It constituted what Klandermans and Oegema called "mobilization potential"—"a group of people with a common identity and a set of common goals."[79] The second condition was the Maoists' perpetuation of a highly polarized political situation on campuses and in society. For example, the Maoists kept a small group of coopted students both as their propaganda corps and as a potential reserve force for insurrection. These students were drawn primarily from Beida and Qinghua University (a technological university). The Maoists extended their power struggle with the established CCP elite by organizing mass campaigns in universities, factories, offices, and villages. In their last campaign in 1976, the Maoists mobilized their student clients at Qinghua, Beida, and some provincial universities for a somewhat watered-down second Cultural Revolution. Tens of thousands of wall posters were said to have appeared at Qinghua and Beida.[80]

Outside of the universities, there was a much larger population made up of former students discarded by Mao after the Cultural Revolution. The great majority of this second youth group was scattered in the vast countryside and condemned to oblivion.[81] But a portion of them was employed in state-operated factories in cities. It was among this section of former students that a dissidence movement grew stronger as time passed by. The famous "Li Yizhe" wall poster of 1974 was created by this youth group.

The third condition that kept young people in a state of unrest was the spread of political disaffection from the Cultural Revolution generation to the youth in general. The main cause of this was the lack of opportunities for the young.[82] The "hard grievances" (those affecting a fraction of the population having suffered from disturbing changes in their lives) of the former Red Guards in the Cultural Revolution were transformed into "soft grievances"—generalized discontent that developed over time.[83]

As proof of the dissident youths' popular base (groups such as "Li Yizhe" were not necessarily "oddballs," as critics might claim), one needs only to mention the spontaneous demonstration and riot on April 5, 1976, at Tian'anmen Square in Beijing. This sudden outburst of mass opinion was, in retrospect, the precursor of the pro-democracy movement of 1989. The core of demonstrators on April 5, 1976, was composed of the young, but it mobilized a mass following among citizens of Beijing. One Western eyewitness reported: "They were old, young and middle-aged, civilian and military, worker, cadres and peasants. But the high literary tone of many of the poems [posted at the square] suggested that there was a fair proportion of intellectuals among them. Young people jostled to copy the poems down."[84]

Retrospective accounts by former participants revealed that there was an extensive "micro-mobilization" among the residents of Beijing before the outburst on April 5. In small groups, among friends and relatives, and in factory shops, people talked about their anxiety, resentment of the Maoists, and sadness over the death of Zhou Enlai months earlier. "Diffused collectivities" played a crucial role in the onset of the demonstration.[85] Once again, the youth movement was kept alive—not by any special agency as in U.S. social movements, but by the state's own political culture of conflict and polarization and by rising public discontent in China.

Third Cycle: Democracy Wall, 1978–1980

The Democracy Wall episode in Beijing marked the start of youth movements in the post-Mao era. On the surface, the Democracy Wall was the youths' own Hundred Flowers campaign; it was not deliberately started by the CCP. The young dissidents simply capitalized on a short-lived crack in the political monolith (Deng Xiaoping was staging a political comeback and Mao's holdovers were resisting him). Nevertheless, the campaign signified that the youth protest in China was developing a momentum of its own; hereafter, the Party-state was on the defensive, as far as the state-youth relationship was concerned. Gone were the days when the CCP manipulated students for its own partisan purposes.

"Who formed the nucleus of the Democracy Wall?" asked a young dissident writer. He later replied to his own question: "The majority of them were those among the victims of the persecutions by Lin Biao and Jiang Qing, who refused to remain silent."[86] The leading group seemed to consist of participants in the April 5, 1976, movement; some of them were imprisoned shortly after that. Undoubtedly, a handful of the activists were children of the Party-state elites and were using public opinion to assist their parents' power struggle within the CCP. They were the authors of the wall posters calling for the rehabilitation of Deng Xiaoping. But once the poster movement got started, it created a social contagion. Masses of people, educated youth in particular, took the opportunity to express their views.

The main force behind the Democracy Wall seemed to be declassed youth. They were the "veterans" of the Cultural Revolution. The modal attitude of these youth was a deep sense of political alienation. They resented the fact that they were used and then cast away. Almost all of them were city youth; during the Cultural Revolution, they traveled around the country, idealistically emulating the historic Long March. They were shocked by the horrible living conditions of the peasants and the plight of former students who had been sent to the countryside.[87] To these youngsters, the Maoist state had not only used them with cynicism but had also represented institutionalized falsehood. Another strong reason for these young dissidents' political alienation was their dead-end careers. After the termination of the Cultural Revolution, these youths became student-turned-workers, just like the members of the "Li Yizhe" group in 1974. Like their less fortunate colleagues in the countryside, these educated youths never accepted their declassed status. The lackadaisical atmosphere in Chinese factories provided a conducive environment for these youths to organize dissident activities.

Table 4.2 shows that almost all of the authors of dissident journals during the Democracy Wall period were declassed middle-school graduates; all of them listed their current occupations as workers. They were in their adolescence when the Cultural Revolution erupted in 1966, the youngest of them being nine years old. Their education was prematurely terminated or preempted. Nevertheless, they were the more fortunate school dropouts, for they were able to live in the city and their livelihood was assured by the state's rationing system. Most of their former classmates were not so lucky and were sent to the rural or frontier areas. Although my data on the family status of these young editors were limited, it is known that they came from middle-class backgrounds. In the final issue of the youth journal *April Fifth Forum*, editor Xu Wenli revealed that the members of the journal's editorial staff were from families of workers, "revolutionary martyrs," employees, and intellectuals. A small number hailed from the rank of middle or lower-level cadres. There was no one from families of high-ranking Party or state leaders.[88] Even the members of *The Spring of Beijing* were mostly from families of middle-ranking cadres. The personal backgrounds of these writers were consistent with those of their predecessors in the Hundred Flowers campaign and the Cultural Revolution. The dissident movement was both a generational and a middle-class phenomenon.

Table 4.2 Social Background of Dissidents in the Democracy Wall
             Movement, 1978–1979

Name	Age	Education	Occupation	Father's occupation
Fu Shenqi	25	Middle school	Worker	Worker
He Qiu	31	Middle school	Worker	—
Liu Huigang	33	High school	Worker	Professional
Liu Qing	29	University	Worker	Former army officer
Sun Feng	—	—	Worker	—
Wang Rongqing	36	—	Worker	—
Wang Xizhe	31	Middle school	Worker	—
Wei Jingsheng	29	High school	Worker	Cadre
Xu Wenli	36	High school	Worker	Doctor
Yang Jing	33	Middle school	Worker	—
Zhong Yueqie	21	—	Worker	Cadre

Sources: Chi Chih, "'Ch'ing-nien Min-chu-pai' Ch'ing-nien Huo-tung Ta-shih Chih-yao,"
Ch'i-shih Nien-tai, no. 6 (1981),:15–17; Miao Shuo, "Peking Min-pan Kan-wu Hsien-ku'an,"
Cheng Ming, no. 2 (1980),:44–43; Wei Jingsheng, "A Dissenter's Odyssey Through Mao's
China,"*New York Times Magazine*, November 16, 1980, pp. 134–143; Liu Huigang, "Wo Wei
She-me Tou-shen Min-chu Huo-tung," *Hai-wai Hsueh-jen*, no. 2 (1981):23–32.

The wall posters and journals published during the Democracy Wall
movement summarized the substance of the new youth subculture.[89]
They expressed the diverse interests of Chinese youth, interests that had
long been denied by Mao and the CCP. Politically, these private publications revealed fine distinctions among the intellectual youth. The writers'
ideas ranged from those of neo-Maoist utopian socialists, pro-Deng
reformists, pro-Yugoslavia revisionists, to Westernized liberal democrats.
But their diversity was also constrained by a common generational culture. They were "bound by a common thread—the conviction that
progress in China and democracy [were] inseparably linked."[90] They all
championed the freedoms of speech, press, association, and demonstration, the right to strike, and the rule of law, as guaranteed formally by the
Chinese constitution. The values espoused by the modernist generations
of May 4, 1919, were the same as those of China's youth in 1978–1980.

It is a gross irony for Mao and Deng's generation that the dissident
youth in 1978–1980 identified with the old generation; however, the
youths identified only with the modernists among the old revolutionaries. The history of the PRC reversed itself. The old revolutionaries who
came to power in 1949 failed (or, more accurately, were culturally unable)
to create a politico-socioeconomic environment that was significantly different from that of the 1920s. Thus, the Democracy Wall movement and
the student protest that followed shamed the old revolutionists in Beijing.
The polarization between the students and the state, which was first

exposed in the Hundred Flowers campaign, remained as intense as ever under Deng's administration.

From "Youth" Back to "Student"

The Democracy Wall movement seemed to have left university students out in the cold. This was largely due to the paralyzed nature of universities in the 1970s. During the Democracy Wall movement, university students were preoccupied with restoring normalcy in their lives. The first national admission test for higher educational institutions in more than a decade was held in November 1977. Approximately 5.7 million eligible youths took the test.[91] The returned students' first spontaneous collective action was to protest against army occupation of campuses.

But university students did not sit entirely on the sidelines during the Democracy Wall period. Chen Jo-hsi [Chen Ruoxi] reported that in 1979 university students published approximately forty journals. The substance of these student journals was identical to the wall posters and journals published during the Democracy Wall. The student publications dwelled on the horrors of the Cultural Revolution and exposed the misdeeds and perquisites of the "bureaucratic class."[92] In late 1979, as the Democracy Wall movement was being repressed by Deng, the students proclaimed that the torch of political protest had been passed to their hands. Students from thirteen universities gathered to plan a youth journal called *This Generation (Zhei Yidai)*. Although the state rushed to nip the journal in the bud, students managed to publish half of the first issue in November 1979. The opening page of *This Generation* strongly confirmed the generational phenomenon by declaring:

> This generation has already been described in many ways: wounded, confused, held-up, reflective, or combative. All sorts of sayings [about the youth] are being heard. But history, solemn history, has found an honorable date to describe the youth today. If it were not for the event on April 5th [1976], our children would look back at this generation and say: "They turned in a blank test paper!" A shameful blank test paper, masking a strong and resolute appearance of this generation. This generation has its own way of life. This generation has its own thoughts and feelings. So this generation has its own sacred mission.[93]

By identifying themselves with the April 5, 1976, demonstrators, the returned students demonstrated to the country that they were more action-oriented than the Democracy Wall activists, who were primarily articulators. University students quickly tested the sincerity of Deng's political reforms by contesting local elections in 1979. Those in Shanghai, Changsha (capital of Hunan Province), and Beijing were particularly active.[94] The Beida students lost no time in reviving its tradition of activism. In

December, twenty-two Beida students drafted a law to insure freedom in publishing. The draft was, in turn, endorsed by some six hundred students. The Beida students went to the defense of Bai Hua, the writer of the novel *Unrequited Love (Ku Lian)*, who was in danger of being persecuted by the military (Bai was employed in the propaganda office of the army). Students put up wall posters to give moral support to Bai. One such poster called on the public to take the stand that, in the future, when one person was being persecuted, tens and thousands of people ought to go to his or her defense.[95] These campus reactions in 1978–1980 strongly indicated that the student movement had returned to haunt the Dengist state.

"Abeyance" in the Mid-1980s

Following the Dengist state's suppression of the Democracy Wall, there followed an uneasy period of abeyance in student movements in the mid-1980s. In retrospect, the years from 1980 to 1985 served to build up the student mood for the great outburst in the fourth cycle of 1986–1989. Once again, the state itself was partly responsible for keeping the students mobilized for action. First, the Dengist state probably attempted to shift the onus of student unrest to the students themselves by commencing a press campaign to discuss "the youth problem." This campaign, in turn, became a full-scale exposé of the young generation's alienation from the Party-state. In post-Mao China, the reactions of the young were virtually identical to the attitude of the Soviet youth after de-Stalinization.[96] The main manifestations were political apathy and cynicism, disinterest in political ideology, self-orientation, and the worship of Western values.[97] There were also pathologies among the young: a significant number of crimes committed by juveniles and various symptoms of depression (including suicides).

It was during this national discussion on the youth problem that the state, for the first time since 1949, became fully cognizant of a generation gap. The CCP youth league journal, *China Youth*, focused the reader's attention on the generation gap. The sentiment of university students was exemplified by the following essay entitled "Letter to Our Father's Generation," which appeared in *China Youth*:

> Ever since the time when I became more aware of things, you taught me to write "Long Live" and sing the song of "The Great Savior." Although you proclaimed yourself an atheist, you nevertheless held a golden idol before me, when I began learning to walk. You knew well the principles stated in *The Communist Manifesto*, but you held high above my head a person who was no different from you and me—a citizen. You said that he was the sun and we were the multitude and that we depended on the sun to grow. We were not supposed to feel the need to think for ourselves.

Father, once you were as pure and honest as nature. Just when did you learn the art of embellishment and use very simple colors to picture reality? Some families were so poor as to possess nothing more than a few broken bowls and in some villages women and children begged in droves. But you talked glibly with assurance, painting a picture of prosperity and hopefulness. Was that your way of expressing the steadfastness of your faith? No. That was impertinence under the guise of being nice, blasphemy under the guise of sincerity, and libel out of good intention. Father, I felt ashamed for your sake.[98]

To this deep alienation of the youth, the old revolutionists responded with contempt and some empathy. For instance, a high-ranking CCP leader wrote in the authoritative *People's Daily:*

Generally speaking, they [the youth] did not appreciate China's sufferings in the past. Neither did they feel personally affected by the hard-won victory that the Communist Party achieved for China. They did not have a deep feeling for the positive role that the thought of Mao Zedong played in the revolution and construction of China. They had no direct experience of rapid developments in every sphere at the beginning of our state. But they did experience destructive deeds committed by Lin Biao and the Gang of Four, defects and mistakes in our Party's work, a long period of turmoil, interruptions in production, lack of improvement in the living standard of the people, and rise of corruption.[99]

Given these mutually alienating sentiments between the old revolutionists and the intellectual youth, the strategies that Deng adopted to firm up his leadership added fuel to fire. Deng resorted to what Max Weber calls "office charisma" and "hereditary charisma" to stabilize his rule.[100] The first kind of charisma was used by Deng to deal with the public at large. There his emphasis was upholding the sovereignty of the Party. Deng used the second kind of charisma to deal with members of the CCP. Thus, Deng endorsed and actively promoted the authority of "old cadres." As an example of Deng's "office charisma," he repeatedly stressed the point that no one was allowed to challenge the authority of the CCP even though the Party had made "some mistakes" in the past. Deng maintained that the CCP was a self-correcting and self-sufficient institution.[101] Given the widespread disaffection of the youth, Deng's conception of an aloof and self-righteous state was destined to clash with the intellectual youth.

As China's economy developed rapidly in the late 1980s, new types of strain were added to the students' sense of alienation. The major ones were feelings of relative deprivation, resentment of political corruption, a sense of loss and anomie, and shame over national backwardness. Opinion polls found that, while youth or students acknowledged the economic achievement of the Deng administration, they felt that their lives did not improve and were very dissatisfied.[102] University students in Beijing dramatized their economic hardship by going to Tian'anmen Square to demonstrate for more state funding for education; some graduate students even set up a shoe-shine stall at the square to impress upon the public their impoverishment.[103] Students' and young intellectuals' feelings of relative deprivation were particularly sharp in 1987–1989, as inflation plagued the national economy. In the spring of 1989, as the two national legislative bodies—the Chinese People's Political Consultative Conference (CPPCC) and the National People's Congress (NPC)—convened, the press was full of reports on the delegates' discussions about a "crisis in education." The legislators reported that a large number of students in primary and secondary schools were dropping out because of their view that "learning was useless."[104] The parliamentarians maintained that some college graduates were working as street sweepers.[105] More and more teachers and young faculty were quitting the teaching profession in favor of more lucrative occupations. A report in the *Guangming Daily*—which specialized in educational and intellectual matters—said that in about ten years, the "young teachers"(those under forty) in Chinese universities would assume the main responsibility of teaching. But these days many of them could not concentrate on their work because of economic hardship. If they had a choice, many would leave.[106] The legislators and intellectuals of China blamed the government for the hardship that young intellectuals had to endure. Throughout these public discussions one fact was mentioned frequently: The Chinese government spent only 2.6 percent of the gross national product (GNP) on education. It was also pointed out that developed countries spent 6 to 8 percent of the GNP on education and some developing nations spent 4 to 5 percent.[107]

Like the workers and peasants, students were particularly resentful of political corruption. In a survey of 1,762 students in seventeen higher educational institutes in Beijing, Tianjin, Shenyang, and Dalian in 1983–1984, the students were asked about their views on political priorities. Table 4.3 presents the students' answers. Students favored eliminating corruption as the first priority. "Style of work of the Party" (*Dangfeng*) in Chinese stood for the honesty and integrity of officials. The second priority was the reform of the political system. The pollsters explained: "In open-ended questions, students expressed their strong disapproval of deviant Party work styles, hatred for immoral social practice and economic crimes, and wish for democracy and rule of law."[108]

The various social deviances that accompanied rapid economic growth grated on the minds of the intellectual youth. A personal experience is worth recounting here. On March 28, 1989, I was among the audience at a symposium at Beida, which was sponsored by the campus Communist Youth League as part of the celebration of the seventieth

Table 4.3 Students' Views on Political Priorities
              (in percentage)

Rectify the style of work of the Party	32.5
Carry out structural reform	20.3
Improve national finances	15.1
Reform the cadre system	8.3
Make full use of the functions of intellectuals	7.9
Change social morality	6.6
Develop democracy and rule of law fully	6.2
Punish economic crimes	3.1

Source: Zhao Zhixiang, Wu Yan, Liu Dixin, and Lu Chao, "Guanyudaxueshengde
Renshengguan Zhuangkuang He Tediande Yanjiu," *Shehuikexue Chanxian*, no. 1
(1984):117–122.

anniversary of the May Fourth (1919) movement. It was an open forum
and any student, faculty, or staff member could go to air their views.
Throughout the whole morning, students' talks were dominated by two
themes: They saw no progress in Chinese politics and society from 1919
to the present, and they were severely depressed by the various anomic
phenomena in the nation. Some of the phrases that the students used to
describe the current national atmosphere were: "dejection in spiritual values" *(jingsheng jiazhi kumen zhuangtai)*, "a shifting and unstable mood"
(biandi dongdang xinli), "running-away psychology," *(taodi xinli)* "attitude
of having a last meal," *(zuihou wancandi xinli)* "grab a handful [and run]"
(laoyiba), and "cheating" *(pian)*. The students gave me the impression that
China was on the brink of self-destruction. They made dire forecasts such
as: "the whole race is disintegrating" *(zhengge minzu wajiezhong)*, "the
[Chinese] race lacks a cohesive power" *(meiyou minzu ningjuli)*, and "the
[Chinese] race is faced with the most serious crisis for several centuries"
(minzu weiji jibainianlai zuiyanzhongdi). Chinese students were apparently
still caught up in a spiritual void and desperately in search of a new and
explicit *weltanschauung*.

The students were ashamed of China's overall national underdevelopment. They vented their hurt national pride on Japan, for Deng's new
economic policy caused a large influx of Japanese loans and business
executives to China. On September 18, 1985, about 1,000 students from
Beida and Qinghua University gathered at Tian'anmen Square, protesting
against the economic relationship between China and Japan. The protest
was ostensibly provoked by Japanese Prime Minister Yasuhiro Naka-
sone's visit to a Shinto shrine for the war dead in August. The date—
September 18—also marked the fifty-fourth anniversary of Japan's
invasion of Northeast China in 1931. On September 12, 1985, a wall poster
appeared at Beida; the text demanded the government to declare

September 18 a national day of shame and called on all students to remember the dead in the war of resistance against Japan. The poster also accused Japan of reviving militarism and invading China economically.[109] Like their counterparts in the May Fourth movement of 1919, the protestors of September 18, 1985, turned their wrath on the Chinese government for its "servile" attitude toward Japan.

The anti-Japan protest was not confined to Beijing; similar demonstrations occurred in Xi'an (Shaanxi), Chengdu (Sichuan), and Wuhan (Hubei). In Xi'an, students from ten universities and colleges participated; the protesters numbered 50,000. They shouted slogans, such as "oppose the revival of Japanese militarism," "oppose economic encroachment," and "stop the revival of the Northern Warlords." In Sichuan, students destroyed a Japanese-made car.[110] To the students, every aspect of the national situation in the late 1980s reminded them of the May 4, 1919, movement—disunity, an unresponsive and illegitimate government, political graft, national backwardness, and the government's appeasement of Japan. Once more, the polarization between the state and the students as well as the general public mood in the mid- and late 1980s kept both student unrest and militancy alive.

As the strain on students grew in the mid- and late 1980s, so did their numbers and density, thus facilitating collective actions. From 1977 to 1988, the number of higher educational institutions increased from 404 to 1,075; the number of students also rose from 625,000 to 2,000,000, breaking all records of growth in the history of Chinese higher education.[111] However, Chinese universities were concentrated in a limited number of modern cities. Table 4.4 presents the degree of concentration of colleges and universities in China's major cities. Student demonstrations occurred in all of the eighteen cities in 1986–1987 and also in 1989. An official report after the 1989 demonstration stated that student protest took place in some eighty cities, involving six hundred universities and 2.8 million students.[112] Undoubtedly, the heavy concentration of students in a few cities facilitated mobilization by easing communication, providing normative support, and insuring a degree of anonymity for many ordinary participants in the movements.

Fourth Cycle: Pro-Democracy Movements, 1986–1989

Given the restive mood of the students in the mid-1980s, the surge of student movements in 1986–1987 and 1989 should surprise no one. This fourth cycle of student protest unfolded in two phases. The initial phase was the 1986–1987 movement and the derived phase was the 1989 pro-democracy movement. The basic causes of the two movements were the same, but the initial phase produced a demonstration effect on the derived phase. Consequently, the second movement was much larger in scale and better organized.

Table 4.4 Colleges and Universities in Selected Chinese Cities
in the 1980s

City	Number of colleges and universities
Beijing	67
Shanghai	51
Xian	32
Tianjin	28
Guangzhou	27
Changchun	26
Shenyang	24
Wuhan	24
Harbin	23
Nanjing	20[a]
Chengdu	12[a]
Hangzhou	11[a]
Kunming	10[a]
Changsha	9[a]
Taiyuan	8[a]
Heifei	8[a]
Guiyang	8[a]
Lanzhou	8[a]

[a]1982 figure; all others are 1988 figures.

Sources: Zhongguo Gaodeng Xuexiao Jianjie (Beijing: Jiaoyu Kexue Chubanshe, 1982);
Zhongguo Jingji Nianjian, 1988 [Almanac of China's Economy, 1988] (Beijing: Beijing Jingji
Guanli Chubanshe, 1988)

The student collective protest of 1986 began at the China University of Science and Technology (popularly known as Keda) in the city of Hefei, Anhui Province, on December 5. It was provoked by students' anger at the local Party's interference with the election of deputies to the district people's congress. In 1980, the CCP's rigging of a local election caused a student demonstration in Changsha, Hunan Province. Apparently, the CCP failed to learn (or was unwilling to learn) the elemental truth about public opinion: What the government has led the public to believe in, the public will demand. Elections had become a real issue among the intellectual youth since 1980. In that year, the CCP made the National People's Congress amend the national constitution to outlaw the "four bigs" (*sida*)—"speaking out freely, airing views fully, holding great debates, and writing big-character posters." The "four bigs" were invented by Mao at the outset of the Cultural Revolution as part of his tactic of mobilizing students to support the Cultural Revolution. The Democracy Wall activists made full use of the "four bigs." To suppress the Democracy Wall movement, Deng made the parliament abolish the "four bigs" and promised genuine local elections as a trade-off. It was the state's reversal on its word to implement elections that provoked the students to protest in 1986.

The first student demonstration in Hefei drew more than 1,000 participants. By December 9, the number of protesting students rose to 3,000, and they rallied behind the principle of the Democracy Wall dissident Wei Jingsheng: "No modernization without democracy!"[113] Soon the Anhui movement spread to other cities, including Beijing and Shanghai. Altogether, eighteen to twenty cities saw student demonstrations from December 1986 to the end of January 1987.[114] The government's allegation that less than 2 percent of the 2 million college students were involved was not credible. In Shanghai alone, it was estimated that 50,000 students participated in the demonstrations.[115] Like the students at Hefei, those in Shanghai targeted the election system and broke into the People's Congress building and the city hall.[116] Students as far south as Yunnan and as far north as Lanzhou also demonstrated.

There were three noteworthy characteristics of the 1986–1987 student movement; the first two concern the students and the last one, the state response. The first was that the protests began in an impoverished, economically marginal province and then spread to the traditional centers of student radicalism (Beijing and Shanghai). This was historically unprecedented. It showed that the mobilization potential for a Chinese student movement existed far beyond the few modern cities in the country. The second important feature was the bridging of the generation gap between the young and the old. The students were inspired and supported by several senior Chinese intellectuals, including some from the CCP propaganda establishment. The most well-known figure was the astrophysicist Fang Lizhi, a professor at Keda.[117] But before the student outburst in Anhui, there was already a spate of articles in the press advocating Western-type democracy—they were written by Party-affiliated ideologues. The most prominent figure was Su Shaozhi, director of the Institute of Marxism-Leninism and Mao Zedong Thought of the official Academy of Social Sciences. Su wrote that a genuinely democratic political system must be based on the people's ability to exercise the rights of freedom of speech, the press, assembly, association, procession, and demonstration. Su maintained that, without these civil rights, "feudalism" in Chinese politics could never be eradicated. By "feudalism," Su meant current deviances, such as corruption, nepotism, incompetence, red tape, anti-intellectualism, and contempt for public opinion.[118]

In October, 1986 an important academic conference was convened in Beijing on political structural reform. The conference communiqué called for political pluralism and a genuine national legislature.[119] Even the CCP-controlled Communist Youth League joined these senior intellectuals in espousing democracy.[120] Thus, the generation gap among the modernists was overcome, and the spirit of May 4, 1919 returned to China. Mannheim wrote: "It occurs frequently that the nucleus of attitudes particular to a new generation is first evolved and practiced by older people who are isolated in their own generation (forerunners), just as it is often the case that the forerunners in the development of a particular class ideology belong to a quite alien class."[121] James Wood and Wing-Cheung Ng also found—in their research on U.S. student activists—that participation in activism appears to improve relations between the generations.[122]

It seems that these older intellectuals provided a double connection, one between the generations and the other between China and the Western world. For example, Fang Lizhi traveled widely in the West and was deeply influenced by what he had learned from his experience there. However, Fang was not the only Chinese professor who made frequent trips to the West. By 1986, more than nine hundred faculty members and students from Fang's university had been sent abroad to visit and more than two hundred foreign scholars had visited Keda.[123] Through these senior scholars, Chinese university students learned much about the West, stimulating their intellectual curiosity, as well as their depression over China's underdevelopment. Fang delivered a simple message to the students: China was far behind other countries in the world because of the failures of socialism. He said that the Chinese culture was not just backward in a particular respect, but in all things. Fang maintained that nothing short of an "all-around openness" and democracy could overcome Chinese backwardness. The burden of establishing democracy was on the shoulders of the university student generation. It was reported that students "transcribed [Fang's] talks by hand, and sent them on to friends and student groups all across China."[124]

The third characteristic of the 1986–1987 student movement concerned the state's response, which subsequently contributed to the 1989 outburst. The reactions of the Dengist state to the student unrest of 1986–1987 starkly exposed the effeteness of the Party-state. Insofar as their treatment of the students was concerned, Deng and his associates were unable to break free of Maoism. Mass campaigns were organized, both the "hard" (threatening) and "soft" (persuading) versions of them. The first type was exemplified by the "Anti-Bourgeois Liberalism" campaign and the second type was seen in the revival of the Maoist campaign of emulating Lei Feng. On the second type of these campaigns, Andrea Worden wrote: "Attempts to convince young China of Lei Feng's continued relevance, undoubtedly meet with contempt and despair."[125] At a Party-sponsored conference on "combating bourgeois liberalism" in January 1987, a number of the participants maintained that there was no "common language" between the CCP and university students. A propagandist complained at the conference: "You talk to them [students] in terms of the Marxist methodology and concepts, and they reply to you in terms of current Western methodology and concepts."[126] Completing the Maoist-like response to student disaffection, the Deng administration sent some students to the countryside to do the so-called social practice. By its own actions, the Dengist state perpetrated state-student polarization and enhanced the probability of another student outburst.

In the final analysis, the 1986–1987 student demonstrations opened the door for the 1989 movement. The Anhui students and their followers made others aware of the tremendous mobilization potential existing among university students. The demonstrators in 1986–1987 clearly exposed the cultural chasm between the Dengist state and the students. The students also provoked a split among Party-state leaders. One leader who showed some sympathy for the students was Hu Yaobang, head of the CCP. The dismissal of Hu in 1987 was yet another piece of evidence highlighting the absence of a "common language" between the Party-state and the students.

1989 Pro-Democracy Movement [127]

The 1989 pro-democracy movement differed from all previous student movements (with the exception of the mass outburst on April 5, 1976, at Tian'anmen Square) in that it was provoked by the perceived *closing*, and not the opening, of opportunity, as is often emphasized in Western studies of social movements. With the death of Hu Yaobang, students were grimly reminded of their marginal and outcast status. Prior to the start of the movement, students felt stifled and thwarted—both at the national level (caused by Hu's dismissal in 1987) and at the personal one.

Some of the statements made by the student leaders of the 1989 movement provided evidence that the perceived closure of opportunity played a part in starting the protest. For example, the following letter was written by Wang Dan, the most prominent student leader in the 1989 movement, shortly before the start of the protest. The letter was addressed to the president of Beida and signed by fifty-six students. Wang's letter began by contrasting the free atmosphere at Beida during the time of the May 4, 1919, movement with the present. Beida then was under the leadership of the famed liberal educator Tsai Yuan-pei [Cai Yuanbei]. Wang's letter stated:

> [We should] recall that seventy years ago university president Tsai Yuan-pei carried out the policy of "governing the university democratically." There was freedom in ideas and academic pursuit then. All kinds of schools of thought and trends existed at Beida. Many of our nation's fine talents with illustrious careers later were cultivated in this brilliant environment. To this day, we are still longing for and proud of the democratic spirit of Beida in the past. It is painful for us to say that, seventy years

later, the Beida tradition of freedom of speech and democracy was discontinued. This is manifested in the many restrictions on the freedoms of students to organize associations, academic forums, public lectures, and salons without any legal basis. We cannot but feel that the restrictions are responsible partly for the trends among students, such as preoccupation with the TOEFL examination, playing mahjong, or getting into business. Although there are other social causes for these fads, they are closely related to the restrictions on students' intellectual freedom.[128]

Chai Ling, who emerged as a forceful leader in the final stage of the student movement (also one of the last student leaders to leave Tian'anmen Square before the entry of troops), told a Chinese writer on the eve of the massacre:

> Before this movement, I thought that study was useless; science was useless; and our country was hopeless. People from all walks of life—workers, petty traders, and official profiteers—did not think that there was much hope for our country. Science and technology must be turned into productive force. But without the guarantee of political democracy then all these were useless.[129]

That anticipated career frustration was one of the strongest motivations for the 1989 student rebellion is also shown in the leading role that graduate students played in the protest (see Table 4.5 below). As John Dunn put it, "most men . . . rebel as a final gesture of misery, not as an expression of optimism about the future."[130]

Table 4.5 Social Background of Student Leaders, June 1989

Name	Age	Academic major	Father's occupation
Chai Ling	22	Educational Psychology (graduate student)	Army doctor
Feng Congde	23	Remote sensing (graduate student)	Teacher
Liu Gang	28	Physics (graduate student)	Cadre
Sheng Tong	21	Biology	Translator
Wang Chaohua	30	Literature (graduate student)	Professor
Wang Dan	20	History	Professor
Wuer Kaixi	21	Education	Cadre
Zhou Yongjun	22	Political science	Cadre

Sources: An informant provided data for Feng Congde and Wang Chaohua; the rest is based on reports in *Jen Min Pu Hui Wang Chi* (Hong Kong: Chi Che Hsi Hui, 1989).

The mood of the students prior to the demonstration was characterized by anger and despair. The entire movement—from April to June 1989—displayed an expressive character. The precipitating factor was mourning for a deceased populist leader (similar to the riot at Tian'anmen Square on April 5, 1976). The rise of Chai Ling as the most charismatic student leader was also a strong indication of the expressive character of the movement. Chai was skilled in arousing an emotional response from the protesters.[131] Yet another indication of the expressive nature of the 1989 movement was the young age of the student leaders. Table 4.5 lists the age and social background of the most prominent activists. Compared with the Democracy Wall activists (see Table 4.2), the leaders of the 1989 movement were significantly younger. The average age of the Democracy Wall activist was thirty, whereas that of the prodemocracy movement in 1989 was twenty-three.

The fate of the 1989 movement was practically sealed by several structural conditions. The most fundamental one was simply the low number of modernists in China, as exemplified by the small percentage of urban population in the country. The state could draw from the vast countryside an almost inexhaustible source of repressive force. Another structural constraint of the student movement was social segmentation. The rapid social change in the post-Mao period displayed a heterotropic character: going off in many directions.[132] The social classes in China have not congealed. The third structural limitation was that urban living was still predominantly dependent on the state. Autonomy of socioeconomic existence was at its early stage in the late 1980s. There was no basis yet for a civil society. The impact of these limitations on the pro-democracy movement of 1989 may be better understood by comparing it to social movements in a democratic system.

In a study of the social movements in West Germany from 1965 to 1989, Ruud Koopmans suggested a three-stage sequence. In the initial stage, the protesters relied on the novelty factor. That is, they surprised the state by daring to mobilize and confront it. At this stage, the demonstrators did not rely on any well-structured organization—the emphasis was on spontaneity. The movement was likely to succeed at the initial stage since the elites were likely to split or engage in dispute over how to deal with the protest. In the second stage, the protesters emphasized the size factor. The increased size of the movement required a more structured organization than before, and the role of professional organizers in holding the movement together became crucial. The consequence of organizational development was a moderation of the movement's goals and means. Coalition with other groups in the society also tended to make the movement moderate. The government encouraged the moderation trend by negotiating with and making concessions to the movement. Thus, the moderates in the movement became eventually integrated into the political main stream. But, the radicals separated themselves from the movement at this point. In the last stage, the radicals used militant means to continue the movement. They suffered the consequence of social isolation and the movement disintegrated.[133]

Due to structural constraints, the 1989 student pro-democracy movement in China succeeded in consummating the first stage only. The developments in the second stage were different from the movements in West Germany. At the second stage of the pro-democracy movement, its size did increase significantly. Special organizations emerged among the students, but they pushed the movement to the radical end. As a Chinese scholar recalled, "At Tiananmen square [in mid-May] the protest movement got to the stage when the more radical one was, the more likely he or she would be made a leader."[134]

Two other factors were equally important in increasing the radicalization of the movement: the government's unyielding attitude and moral support from other interest groups. The persistence of the protest and the resort to a hunger strike by the students rallied more groups to the students' side. They included journalists, the literary circles, "Democratic Parties," various workers' groups (including even part of the ACFTU), and the official Communist Youth League.[135] However, these organizations merely jumped on the revolutionary bandwagon. As Timur Kuran pointed out, protestors in a highly repressive state gathered support by breaking people's ordinary "preference falsification." More and more people became aware of the fact that their opposition to the regime was shared. The consequence of that was making the movement more radical.[136]

In the Chinese case, while the student movements were radicalizing, the revolutionary bandwagon was superficial. No Chinese organization was autonomous and bold enough to form a social compact with the students and each other. Each organization addressed the state on its own, in the traditional form of remonstrance to the emperor. That is to say, even while sharing a common opposition to the state, the Chinese protestors remained socially segmented. No group in the 1989 movement really believed that the state would incorporate any of them into the political mainstream. The pro-democracy movement merely provided another display of the polarized relationship between the state and the students and the sectionalism in Chinese society.

Student Attitudes After the Massacre

The brutal crackdown by the state did little to change the basic attitudes of the students. The unrest among the intellectual youth was caused by overall national conditions and as long as these conditions remained, students' attitudes were unlikely to change fundamentally. Opinion polls of the students after the massacre prove my point.

In a March 1990 poll of eight Beijing universities (conducted by the State Commission on Higher Education and the municipal office of the Beijing CCP), the majority of students did not approve of the government's characterization of the pro-democracy movement as a "counterrevolutionary riot." The students' own depiction of the movement stressed the expressive character of the protest. In their opinion, the movement in April–June 1989 was "an emotional expression of dissatisfaction on the part of the masses towards corruption and unfair work assignments."[137] Only 6.4 percent of the students agreed with the government that the student opposition movement was caused by "bourgeois liberalism." After the bloody suppression on June 4, 1989, the students were naturally cautious. Only 9 percent of them were willing to be active participants in another movement. Most of the students were at least temporarily indifferent to politics, half of them having no political-party affiliation.

More surveys of student attitudes in the early 1990s confirmed that several fundamental youth values had emerged clearly in the early 1980s. They were self-centeredness, materialism (or utilitarianism), and living only for the present.[138] Disinterest in the official ideology persisted, as expected. The Communist Youth League paper admitted candidly in a report on March 1994 that a survey found only 7.7 percent of the students questioned have a firm faith in socialism. Among graduate students, disbelief in socialism was more pronounced. More than a quarter of the graduate students expressed a lack of faith in socialism, compared with 9.3 percent for scientists and technicians, and 5.4 percent for undergraduates. Graduate students also had a more positive attitude toward the student movement (94.8 percent) than undergraduates (66 percent). The students' resentment of widespread corruption persisted and they lamented the fact that political reform always lagged behind economic reform.[139]

Deviance and pathology among university students seemed to be on the increase. A 1994 survey by the State Education Commission and the Youth League reported: "The number of law-breaking and discipline-violating cases was four or five times that in the previous year."[140] Mental health problems among the students rose significantly in the late 1980s and early 1990s. A study of an unnamed university found that the number of students' dropping out of school due to mental health problems increased by 60 percent from 1989 to 1991 and 75 percent from 1991 to 1992.[141] The 1994 study by the State Education Commission and the Youth League also reported that, at a college of engineering in Beijing, "34.3 percent of students have psychological illness to varying degrees, far surpassing the average level (16 percent) in the colleges across the country two years ago."[142] Apparently, both before and after the 1989 student protest, student discontent and stress were not confined to a few "oddballs," as some observers had suggested.

But student mood changed quickly and the young adapted to external conditions. There was evidence of a generation gap between the veterans of the student movements in the late 1980s and those that came later. The younger student generation may be more economically, than politically, minded from now on.[143] The government is also deliberately diverting students' attention from politics to economics. The Communist Youth League helped establish a new mass organization for young people, called the China Youth Association for Economic Development (CYAED). The chief purpose of CYAED was to assist the youth in establishing private businesses.[144]

This radical adjustment of the Communist Youth League is perhaps modeled after the experience of the Chinese Nationalist youth league in Taiwan. The Chinese Youth League for Anti-Communism and National Salvation in Taiwan was established in the 1950s by the government. As Taiwan's economic development took off, the Taiwanese youth league gradually transformed itself into a development-oriented association. The league opened special classes to teach entrepreneurship to aspiring young people and established its own industrial parks. I interviewed a number of successful Taiwanese business executives who received loans from the youth league to start their businesses. The Communist Youth League in the PRC might be undergoing the same secularization or de-politicalization process. In the meantime, the Party-state in the PRC is also contributing to the individualistic and pragmatic trends among the students. In 1994 the Chinese government announced that it was considering termination of the past policies of not requiring tuition from students and assigning jobs to graduates. Soon, Chinese university students would have to pay their own tuitions and find their own jobs after graduation.[145]

Whether the Chinese government succeeds in diverting the students now depends on economic development. If the government is successful and Chinese students' political activism subsides from here on, then the student movements throughout the 1980s may be remembered as a reflection of the inherent tension in epochal change. However, if the socioeconomic change currently going on in China is thwarted for some reason, then student activism will surge again. Repression might buy time for the authorities but cannot substitute for a policy of long-term political, social, and economic progress.

Notes

1. *Communist China: The Politics of Student Opposition*, trans. Dennis J. Doolin (Stanford, Calif.: Hoover Institution, 1964), p. 64.

2. Sheng Tong, with Marianne Yen, *Almost a Revolution* (Boston: Houghton Mifflin, 1990), p. 134.

3. Lin T'sui-feng, *Chung-kuo Min-jen T'sai-fang-lu* [Interview with famous Chinese] (Hong Kong: Ming Pao Chu-pan-she, 1992), p. 74.

4. Jeffrey N. Wasserstrom, *Student Protests in Twentieth-Century China* (Stanford, Calif.: Stanford University Press, 1991).

5. Karl Mannheim, "The Problem of Generations," in *The New Pilgrims: Youth Protest in Transition*, ed. Philip G. Altbach and Robert S. Laufer (New York: David McKay, 1972).

6. Ibid., p. 122.

7. A. Doak Barnett, *China on the Eve of Communist Takeover* (New York: Praeger, 1963), chapter 4.

8. *Communist China: The Politics of Student Opposition.*

9. Anita Chan, Stanley Rosen, and Jonathan Unger, eds., *On Socialist Democracy and the Chinese Legal System: The Li Yizhe Debates* (Armonk, N.Y.: M. E. Sharpe, 1985).

10. James D. Seymour ed., *The Fifth Modernization*, (New York: Human Rights Publishing Group, 1980); and Roger Garside, *Coming Alive* (New York: McGraw-Hill, 1981).

11. So far the best account of a participant in the 1989 movement is Sheng Tong, *Almost a Revolution*. Other major works include: Chu-yuan Cheng, *Behind the Tiananmen Massacre: Social, Political, and Economic Ferment in China* (Boulder: Westview Press, 1990); Roger V. Des Forges, Luo Ning, and Wu Yen-bo, eds. *Chinese Democracy and the Crisis of 1989: Chinese and American Reflections* (Albany, N.Y.: State University of New York Press, 1992); Michael Fathers and Andrew Higgins, *Tiananmen: The Rape of Peking*, ed. Robert Cottrell (London: Independent, 1989); Lee Feigon, *China Rising: The Meaning of Tiananmen* (Chicago: Ivan R. Dee, 1990); George Hicks, ed., *The Broken Mirror: China after Tiananmen* (Chicago and London: St. James Press, 1990); Yi Mu and Mark V. Thompson, *Crisis at Tiananmen* (San Francisco: China Books and Periodicals, 1989); Suzanne Ogden, Katherine Hartford, Lawrence Sullivan, and David Zweig, eds., *China's Search for Democracy: The Student and Mass Movement of 1989* (Armonk, N.Y.: M. E. Sharpe, 1992); Michel Oksenberg, Lawrence R. Sullivan, and Marc Lambert, eds., *Beijing Spring, 1989: Confrontation and Conflict* (Armonk, N.Y.: M. E. Sharpe, 1990); and Jonathan Unger, ed., *The Pro-Democracy Protests in China: Reports from the Provinces* (Armonk, N.Y.: M. E. Sharpe, 1991).

12. Samuel N. Eisenstadt, "Generational Conflict and Intellectual Antinomianism," in *The New Pilgrims*, ed. Altbach and Laufer, p.146.

13. *Cheng Ming*, no. 198 (April 1, 1994): 30.

14. Erik H. Erikson, *Young Man Luther* (New York: W. W. Norton and Company, 1962), especially chapter 2.

15. Chen Yusheng, "Chen Yi Tongzhidi Jingyu" [The warning words of Comrade Chen Yi], *RMRB*, August 22, 1983, p. 5; for an account of the effect of Zhou's and Chen's views, see Tung Chi-Ping and Humphrey Evans, *The Thought Revolution* (New York: Coward-McCann, 1966), especially part 3.

16. Qian Xuesheng, "Yu Hong Yu Zhuan Wei Geminliye Erpangdenggaofeng" [To be both red and expert, so to reach new heights for the revolution], *Zhongguo Qingnian Bao* [China Youth News], June 3, 1965.

17. Chin Chien-li, *Pei-kuo Chien-wen* [Odyssey in North China] (Hong Kong: Union Press, 1973), p. 472.

18. Sheng Tong, *Almost a Revolution*.

19. George Sherman, "Soviet Youth: Myth and Reality," in *The Challenge of Youth*, ed. Erik H. Erikson (New York: Doubleday and Company, 1965); and

Vladimir Shlapentokh, "Attitudes and Behavior of Soviet Youth in the 1970s and 1980s: The Mysterious Variable in Soviet Politics," in *Research in Political Sociology*, vol. 2, ed. Richard G. Braungart and Margaret M. Braungart (Greenwich, Conn.: JAI Press, 1986).

20. This concentual framework is informed by Neil J. Smelser, *Theory of Collective Behavior* (New York: Free Press, 1962), chapter 2.

21. Louis Kriesberg, *Social Conflicts* (Englewood Cliffs, N.J.: Prentice-Hall, 1982), p. 31.

22. Robert C. North, with the collaboration of Ithiel de Sola Pool, "Kuomintang and Chinese Elites," in *World Revolutionary Elites*, ed. Harold D. Lasswell and Daniel Lerner (Cambridge, Mass.: MIT Press, 1966), p. 396.

23. Tim McDaniel, *Autocracy, Modernization, and Revolution in Russia and Iran* (Princeton: Princeton University Press, 1991), p. 6.

24. Lowell Dittmer, "The Legacy of Mao Zedong," *Asian Survey* 20, no. 5 (May 1980): 552–573, especially on Mao's impact on organizations; see also Li Rui, *Mao Zedongde Gongguo Shifei* [Merits and demerits of Mao Zedong] (Hong Kong: Cosmos Books, 1993).

25. David Apter and Tony Saitch, *Revolutionary Discourse in Mao's Republic* (Cambridge, Mass.: Harvard University Press, 1994).

26. Robert E. Lane, *Political Man* (New York: Free Press, 1972), p. 252.

27. Bo Yibo, *Ruogan Zhongda Juece Yushijiandi Huigu*, [Memoir of decisions of several major policies], vol. 1 (Beijing: Zhonggong Zhongyang Dangxiao Chubanshe, 1993), p. 1164.

28. For a general discussion on the different patterns of education between upper and lower classes, see Samuel N. Eisenstadt, *From Generation to Generation* (New York: Free Press of Glencoe, 1964), esp. chapter 4.

29. Ralph H. Turner and Lewis M. Killian, *Collective Behavior* (Englewood Cliffs, N.J.: Prentice-Hall, 1972), p. 287.

30. Liu Binyan, *Liu Binyan Baogao Wenxuexuan* [Selections of Liu Binyan's journalistic works] (Beijing: Beijing Chubanshe, 1981), p. 329.

31. Arnold A. Rogow and Harold D. Lasswell, "The City Boss: Game Politician or Gain Politician," in *Political Corruption*, ed. Arnold J. Heidenheimer (New York: Holt, Rinehart, and Winston, 1970), p. 433.

32. *RMRB*, February 6, 1983, p. 1.

33. *Mao Tsetung Ssu-hsiang Wan-sui*, no. 2 (Beijing, 1969; reprint Washington, D.C.: Center for Chinese Research Materials, 1969) pp. 230–231.

34. André Malraux, *Anti-Memoirs* (New York: Holt, Rinehart, And Winston, 1968), pp. 379–389.

35. Edgar Snow, *The Long Revolution* (New York: Random House, 1972), p. 221.

36. Ibid., pp. 221–222.

37. Turner and Killian, *Collective Behavior*, p. 304.

38. Bruno Bettelheim, "The Problem of Generations," in *The Challenge of Youth*, ed. Erik H. Erikson (New York: Doubleday and Company, 1965), pp. 80–81.

39. Jo Freeman, "Resource Mobilization and Strategy: A Model for Analyzing Social Movement Organization Actions," in *The Dynamics of Social Movements*, ed. Mayer N. Zald and John D. McCarthy (Cambridge, Mass.: Winthrop Publishers, 1979), p. 172.

40. William A. Gamson and Emilie Schmeidler, "Organizing the Poor," *Theory and Society* 13, no. 4 (July 1984):567–583.

41.   Bert Klandermans, "New Social Movements and Resource Mobilization: The European and the American Approach Revisited," in *Research on Social Movements: The State of the Art in Western Europe and the USA*, ed. Dieter Rucht (Boulder: Westview Press, 1991), pp. 17–44.

42.   Friedhelm Neidhardt and Dieter Rucht, "The Analysis of Social Movements: The State of the Art and Some Perspectives for Further Research," in *Research on Social Movements*, ed. Rucht, p. 428.

43.   Sidney Tarrow, "Comparing Social Movement Participation in Western Europe and the United States: Problems, Uses, and a Proposal for Synthesis," in *Research on Social Movements*, ed. Rucht, pp. 412–413; and Herbert Kitschelt, "Resource Mobilization Theory: A Critique," in *Research on Social Movements*, ed. Rucht, p. 334.

44.   Verta Taylor, "Social Movement Continuity: The Women's Movement in Abeyance," *American Sociological Review* 54, no. 5 (October 1989):761–775.

45.   Jeffrey C. Goldfarb, "Social Bases of Independent Public Expression in Communist Societies," *American Journal of Sociology* 83, no. 4 (January 1978):927.

46.   Roger Garside, *Coming Alive* (New York: McGraw-Hill, 1981), chapters 8–11.

47.   Charles Tilly, "Repertoires of Contention in American and Britain, 1750–1830," in *The Dynamics of Social Movements*, ed. Zald and McCarthy, p. 141.

48.   Sidney Tarrow, "'Aiming at a Moving Target': Social Science and the Recent Rebellions in Eastern Europe," *PS: Political Science and Politics* 24, no. 1 (March 1991):12–19.

49.   Bruce Fireman and William A. Gamson, "Utilitarian Logic in Resource Mobilization Perspective," in *The Dynamics of Social Movements*, ed. Mayer N. Zald, John D. McCarthy (Cambridge, Mass.: Winthrop, 1979), pp. 34–35.

50.   Bert Klandermans, "The Formation and Mobilization of Consensus," in *From Structure to Action: Comparing Social Movement Research Across Cultures*, vol. 1, ed. Bert Klandermans, Hanspeter Kriesi, and Sidney Tarrow (Greenwich, Conn.: JAI Press, 1988), p. 175.

51.   Tarrow, "Comparing Social Movement," p. 412.

52.   The best account of how the students used informal means of recruitment in the 1989 pro-democracy movement is still Sheng Tong, *Almost a Revolution*.

53.   Karl-Dieter Opp and Christiane Gern, "Dissident Groups, Personal Networks, and Spontaneous Cooperation: The East German Revolution of 1989," *American Sociological Review* 58, no. 5 (October 1993):676.

54.   Bert Klandermans and Dirk Oegema, "Potentials, Networks, Motivations, and Barriers: Steps Toward Participation in Social Movements," *American Sociological Review* 52, no. 4 (August 1987):530.

55.   Eric L. Hirsch, "Sacrifice for the Cause: Group Processes, Recruitment, and Commitment in a Student Social Movement," *American Sociological Review* 55 (April 1990):245.

56.   Mancur Olson, *The Logic of Collective Action* (Cambridge, Mass.: Harvard University Press, 1975).

57.   Bert Klandermans, "Mobilization and Participation: Social-Psychological Expansions of Resource Mobilization Theory," *American Sociological Review* 49, no. 5 (October 1984):583–600; Fireman and Gamson, "Utilitarian Logic"; and Opp and Gern, "Dissident Groups."

58.   *North China Daily News*, February 26, 1949.

59.   Yuan Han-ch'ing, "Wo Suo Kán-tao-ti Ta-hsüeh ch'ing-nien Ssu-hsiang-shang-ti I-hsieh-wen-t'i" [Some of the problems in the minds of university youth that I have observed], *Hs'ueh-hsi* 1, no. 3 (November 20, 1949):36–37; and Fei Hsiao-tung, "Lun Ts'un-chi-shu Kuan-tian," [On pure-skill standpoint] *Hsüeh-hsi* 2, no. 3 (April 1950):20–21.

60.   Hu Yu-pang [Hu Yaobang], "Raise Your Vigilance and Consciousness" (speech presented at the sixteenth Congress of Chinese Students, August 6, 1955), *Zhongguo Qingnian*, no. 17 (September 1, 1955), in *Extracts from China Mainland Magazine (ECMM)*, no. 17, pp. 49–58.

61.   "Controversy Over Young Writer's Story," *Survey of Mainland China Press (SCMP)*, no. 1497, pp. 4–5.

62.   *Selected Works of Mao Zedong*, vol. 5 (Beijing: Foreign Languages Press, 1977), p. 405.

63.   The Hong Kong newspaper *Ming Pao* had published a series of reports on Lin Xilin in 1983, when she was finally allowed to leave China for France; see reports in *Ming Pao*, August 17 and 22; September 11, 12, 13, 15, and 17, 1983.

64.   Chin Chien-li, *Pei-kuo Chien-wen*, pp. 429–430.

65.   Seymour Martin Lipset, "University Student Politics," in *The Berkeley Student Revolt*, ed. Seymour Martin Lipset and Sheldon S. Wolin (New York: Doubleday and Company, 1965), p. 4.

66.   Chin Chien-li, *Pei-kuo Chien-wen*, p. 436.

67.   *Communist China: The Politics of Student Opposition*, p. 27.

68.   Taylor, "Social Movement Sontinuity, " p. 761.

69.   Ibid., pp. 765–772.

70.   Anita Chan, *Children of Mao: Personality Development and Political Activism in the Red Guard Generation* (Seattle: University of Washington Press, 1985), p. 103; also Tung Chi-ping and Evans, *The Thought Revolution*, p. 177.

71.   Bettelhelm, "The Problem of Generations," p. 83.

72.   Shi Xiaozhu, "Qingnian Xuesheng Mianqiande Liangeronglu" [The two furnaces in front of young students], *Zhongguo Qingnian* [China Youth], no. 18 (September 16, 1964):5. Also Susan L. Shirk, *Competitive Comrades* (Berkeley: University of California Press, 1982).

73.   Anita Chan, "Dispelling Misconceptions About the Red Guard Movement: The Necessity to Re-examine Cultural Revolution Factionalism and Periodization," *Journal of Contemporary China*, 1, no. 1 (Fall 1992):61–85.

74.   For Yu's entire thesis, see *Siwu Luntan* [April Fifth Forum], no. 13 (1979).

75.   For more discussion on this group of youngsters, see Thomas P. Bernstein, *Up to the Mountains and Down to the Villages: The Transfer of Youth from Urban to Rural China* (New Haven: Yale University Press, 1977).

76.   Mannheim, "The Problem of Generations," p. 118.

77.   Ibid., p. 119.

78.   See "Shenwulien Ti Cheng-chih Chu-chang Ho Yen-lun" [The political platform and opinions of Shenwulien], 5 parts, *Tsu Kuo* [China Monthly] (Hong Kong), nos. 83–87 (February–June 1971).

79.   Klandermans and Oegema, "Potentials, Networks, Motivations," p. 519.

80.   *RMRB*, April 6, 1976.

81.   For an in-depth study of a group of such discarded youth, see Richard Madsen, *Morality and Power in a Chinese Village* (Berkeley: University of California Press, 1984).

82.   Martin K. Whyte and William L. Parish, *Urban Life in Contemporary China* (Chicago: University of Chicago Press, 1984), especially chapter 8.

83.   For the distinction between the two types of grievances, see Mayer N. Zald, "The Continuing Vitality of Resource Mobilization Theory: Response to Herbert Kitschelt's Critique," in *Research on Social Movements*, ed. Rucht, p. 349.

84.   "Black Monday in Peking," *Far Eastern Economic Review*, April 16, 1976, p. 10.

85.   *China News Analysis*, no. 1039 (May 7, 1976); Zhou Weimin, "Bai Hua" [White flowers], *Beijing Zhichun* [The Spring of Beijing], no. 4 (April 2, 1979); and Sheng Tong, *Almost a Revolution*, pp. 24–27.

86.   Bi Dan, "Minzhuqian Zonghengtan" [On the scale of Democracy Wall], *Kexue Minzhu Fazhi* [Science, Democracy, Rule of Law], no. 15 (June 20, 1979).

87.   Wei Jingsheng, "A Dissenter's Odyssey Through Mao's China," *New York Times Magazine*, November 16, 1980; Liu Huigang, "Wo Wei Shen-me Tou-shen Min-chu Yung-tong?" [Why do I commit myself to the movement for democracy?], *Hai-wai Hsüeh-jen* [Overseas Scholars] (Taipei), no. 103 (February 1981).

88.   *Siwu Luntan* [April Fifth Forum], no. 3 (1980).

89.   There have been a number of works published in English on these and I shall mention just a few: Gregor Benton, ed., *Wild Lilies: Poisonous Weeds* (London: Pluto Press, 1982); Kjeld Erik Brodsgaard, "The Democracy Movement in China, 1978–1979: Opposition Movements, Wall Poster Campaigns, and Underground Journals," *Asian Survey*, 21, no. 7 (July 1981):747–774; David S.G. Goodman, *Beijing Street Voices* (London: Marion Boyars, 1982); and James D. Seymour, ed., *The Fifth Modernization* (New York: Human Rights Publishing Group, 1980).

90.   Miriam London and Ta-ling Lee, "The Young Democratic Movement in China," *Wall Street Journal*, August 11, 1981.

91.   *RMRB*, December 26, 1977.

92.   Chen Jo-hsi, "Min-chu-ch'iang Ho Min-pan-k'an-wu," [Democracy Wall and publications by the people], *Hai-wai Hsüeh-jen*, no. 106 (May 1981):32.

93.   Lin Nan, "Zhongguo Zhengzhi Daigou," [The political generation gap of China] (Hong Kong), *Ching Ming*, no. 32 (June 1980):37.

94.   The Beijing students' election activity is described in Wei Ming, "Chung-kuo Hsin-i-tai-ti Cheng-chih-chia," [The new generation of politicians in China] (Hong Kong), *Ch'ih-shih Nien-tai* [The Seventies], February, 1981, pp. 15–20; on Shanghai students, see *New York Times*, November 29, 1980; on the controversial election in Changsha, see Chung Lei, "Hunan Hsueh-sheng Cheng-min-chu Fang-kuan-liao-ti-hsin-tong" [Hunan students' pro-democracy and antibureaucratic action], *Ch'ih-shih Nien-tai* [The Seventies] (Hong Kong), December 1980, pp. 19–20, and *New York Times*, October 15, 1980.

95.   *Ming Pao* (Hong Kong), May 1, 1981.

96.   Sherman, "Soviet Youth: Myth"; and Shlapentokh, "Attitudes and Behavior."

97.   For a first-hand report on the attitude of Chinese youth, see Tani E. Barlow and Donald M. Lowe, *Chinese Reflections: Americans Teaching in the People's Republic* (New York: Praeger, 1985). The best Chinese study on the youth problem,

especially the phenomenon of generation, is Zhang Yunjie and Zhen Yuanzhong, *Di Si Dai Ren* [The people of the fourth generation] (Beijing: Dongfang Chubanshe, 1988).

98.　Chen Baopin, "Xiegei Womendifubei" [Letter to our father's generation], *Zhongguo Qingnian* [China Youth], no. 12, (1980):18.

99.　Li Wen, "Womenliangdairen Yiqiweishehuizhuyi Shiyefendou" [Our two generations work together to realize the socialist cause], *RMRB*, April 28, 1981, p. 3.

100.　Max Weber, *Economy and Society: An Outline of Interpretive Sociology*, vol. 1, ed. Guenther Roth and Claus Wittich (New York: Bedminster Press, 1968), pp. 246–249.

101.　*Deng Xiaoping Wenxuan, 1975–1982* [Selected works of Deng Xiaoping, 1975–1982] (Beijing: Renmin Chubanshe, 1983), pp. 157 and 236.

102.　Lu Ren, "Duiqingnian Jiazhiguan Duoyuanhua Qinxiangde Fengxi" [An analysis of the tendency toward value pluralism among the youth], *Sheuixue* [Sociology], no. 1 (1986):13–15.

103.　Lu Yun, "Ch'a-hsieh, Ching-tso, Tsai Tien-an-men," [Shoe shinning and sitting in at Tian'anmen] *Cheng Ming*, June, 1988, pp. 12–14.

104.　Ma Lixin, "A Cure for Educational Ills," *China Daily*, March 24, 1989, p. 5.

105.　Wang Ningjun, "Education Failing Its Test," *China Daily*, March 16, 1989, p. 5.

106.　"Exodus of Young College Teachers in Beijing," *China Daily*, April 4, 1989, p. 4.

107.　Wang Ningjun, "Education Failing Its Test."

108.　Zhao Zhixiang, Wu Yan, Liu Dixin, and Lu Chao, "Guanyudaxueshengde Renshengguan Zhuangkuang He Tediandiyanjiu" [A study on university students' outlook on life], *Shehui Kexue Chanxian* [Social science front], no. 1 (1984):119.

109.　My discussion is based mainly on the report in the Hong Kong journal *Cheng Ming*, entitled "The Campus Upheaval That Shook Chungnanhai" (November 1985), which was translated in *Inside China Mainland* (Taipei), published by the Institute of Current China Studies, January 1986, pp. 1–5. For news reports in English on this protest, see John F. Burns, "China Fights Student Protest Against 'Open Door'," *New York Times*, November 27, 1985, p. 4; and "China: Protests by Students Challenge Deng Policies," *Los Angeles Times*, December 5, 1985, pp. 18–19.

110.　"The Background Factors to the Peking University Student Demonstrations," *Wide Angles*, (Hong Kong), no. 158 (1985), as translated in *Inside China Mainland* (Taipei), January 1986, p. 9.

111.　Luo Rongxin, Zhou Qing, Bi Quanzhong, and Xiao Guangeng, "Ningjie Shangpinjingjide Xili" [Welcoming the baptism of commodity economy], *RMRB*, March 19, 1989, p. 5; Hu Junkai and Zhao Yining, "University Students and Higher Education," *Beijing Review* 30, no. 8 (February 23, 1987):23.

112.　Cheng Yuan, "Daxueshengde Wuqu Yushehuidiwudao" [The mistaken areas of university students and the mistaken guidance of the society], *RMRB*, September 6, 1989, p. 5.

113.　*New York Times*, December 10, 1986, p. 7.

114.　The most complete chronology and news summary of the demonstrations that is available to me is "A General Report on Student Unrest," *Inside China*

Mainland, (Taipei), February 1987, pp. 1–5. The article by Schell on Fang Lizhi gave the figure of twenty cities; see Orville Schell, "A Democrat in the People's Republic," *Atlantic*, May 1988," p. 43.

115.   Edward A. Gargan, "Students in China Ending Marches For Extensive Democratic Changes," *New York Times*, December 31, 1986, p. 7.

116.   Edward A. Gargan, "Chinese Demonstrations Subside After Warnings From Authorities," *New York Times*, December 23, 1986, pp. 1 and 4.

117.   Schell, "A Democrat in the People's Republic," p. 37.

118.   Su Shaozhi, "Zhengzhi Tizhigaige Yu Fandui Fengjianzhuyiyingxiang" [Political structural reform and opposition to the impact of feudalism], *RMRB*, August 15, 1986, p. 5.

119.   "Symposium on the Theory of Political Structural Reform," *Beijing Review* 29, no. 46 (November 17, 1986):14–15.

120.   "China Peeks Warily Past the Open Door to the West," *New York Times*, December 28, 1986.

121.   Mannheim, "The Problem of Generations," pp. 123–124.

122.   James L. Wood and Wing-Cheung Ng, "Socialization and Student Activism: Examination of a Relationship," in *Research in Social Movements, Conflicts, and Change,* ed. Louis Kriesberg (Greenwich, Conn. JAI Press, 1979.), pp. 21–43.

123.   Schell, "A Democrat in the People's Republic," p. 39.

124.   Ibid., p. 41.

125.   Andrea Worden, "Lei Feng and I," *Yale-China Review* 1, 0.1 (Spring 1993):29.

126.   "Qizhixianminde Fangdui Zichanjieji Ziyouhua" [Take a clear-cut stand in opposing bourgeois liberalism], *Hongqi*, no. 3, (1987):25.

127.   For descriptions of the movement, see Note 11 of this chapter, for references. I shall not describe the actual movement here.

128.   "Pei-ta Sho-chang Ch'ang-tao Hsiao-yuan Min-chu-hua-ti Ta-tzu-pao" [The first wall poster advocating democracy on campus at Beijing University], in *Jen Min Pu Hui Wang Chi* [The people will not forget] (Hong Kong: Chi Che Hsi Hui, 1989), p. 340.

129.   This is part of the interview that Chai Ling had with Chinese writer Ching Pei-li from Hong Kong on June 3, 1989, which was later broadcast in the Mandarin program of the British Broadcasting Corporation. The full text of the interview was published in the U.S. edition of the Taipei-based newspaper *Chung-yang Jih-pao* [Central Daily News], June 18, 1989, p. 4.

130.   John Dunn, *Modern Revolutions*, 2d ed. (Cambridge, England: Cambridge University Press, 1989), p. 246.

131.   Sheng Tong, *Almost a Revolution*, pp. 237–238.

132.   On the concept of heterotropicism, see Karl W. Deutsch, "The System Theory Approach as a Basis for Comparative Research," *International Social Science Journal* 37, no. 1 (1985):15.

133.   Ruud Koopmans, "The Dynamics of Protest Waves: West Germany, 1965 to 1989," *American Sociological Review* 58, no. 5 (October 1993):637–658.

134.   Lin T'sui-feng, *Chung-kuo Min-jen*, p. 70.

135.   *RMRB*, May 18, 1989.

136.   Timur Kuran, "Now Out of Never: The Element of Surprise in the East European Revolution of 1989," *World Politics* 44 (October 1991).

137.   *Ming Pao*, (Hong Kong), June 14, 1990, p. 18.

138.   Xi Mi, "Old Ideas Losing Appeal for Headstrong Youth," *China Daily*, April 7, 1994, p. 4.

139.   Paul Mooney, "Survey Views Young People's Opinion of Socialism," *Eastern Express*, (Hong Kong), March 31, 1994, in FBIS, *CHI/DR*, March 31, 1994, p. 39.

140.   *Tangtai*, (Hong Kong), no. 39 (June 15, 1994), in FBIS, *CHI/DR*, June 16, 1994, p. 26.

141.   Xue Libin and Sun Zhongxiu, "Qianxi Dangdai Daxuesheng Xinlijibin" [A preliminary analysis of the mental health problems among university students], *Shanxi Daxue Xuebao (Zhexue Shehuikexue Ban)* [Bulletins of Shanxi University (Philosophy and Social Sciences Edition)] 16, no. 3 (March, 1993):104–108.

142.   *Tangtai*, (Hong Kong), no. 39 (June 15, 1994), in FBIS, *CHI/DR*, June 16, 1994, p. 27.

143.   *South China Sunday Morning Post*, (Hong Kong), June 5, 1994, in FBIS, *CHI/DR*, June 6, 1994, pp. 16–17.

144.   *China Daily*, July 19, 1994; and FBIS, *CHI/DR*, July 19, 1994, p. 17.

145.   *Xinhua*, April 29, 1994, in FBIS, *CHI/DR*, May 2, 1994, pp. 29–30.

5

ETHNIC SEPARATISM

Without great Hanism [Chinese-ism], no local nationalism.

—Xinjiang native, 1957[1]

National separatism is the chief threat to Xinjiang's stability.

—Song Hanliang, Secretary of Xinjiang CCP, 1993[2]

The activities of 'Pan-Mongolism' have been aggravated abroad and class struggle still exists to a certain degree in China. We are facing a fairly complicated struggle in political and ideological spheres.

—Wang Qun, Secretary of Inner Mongolia CCP, 1994[3]

The antisplittist situation we are now facing is . . . still a severe one, and the mission we have to carry out is a formidable one.

—Raidi, Deputy Secretary of Tibetan CCP, 1994[4]

The reactions of Chinese peasants, workers, and students to the state may be termed "politics at the margin of the decisionmaking process." Another aspect of mass politics in China concerns the political attitudes and behavior of the ethnic minorities who inhabit China's borderland. Their politics stems from being both at the decision making and physical margins of China. But regardless of ethnic identity, the essence of mass politics in China today is the assertion of the people at the margin. Their demands and reactions have become a crucial factor in the "high politics" of the Party-state in Beijing. As the epigraphs have shown, ethnic separatism is a major concern of Chinese leaders in the 1990s. This chapter reviews the political opinions and reactions of different ethnic groups in China from the inception of the PRC to the present. Before I discuss the public opinion of the minorities, a brief analysis of the major conditions of ethnicity in China is in order.

General Characteristics of Ethnicity

Officially, there are fifty-six "nationalities" *(minzu)* in China, with the Han or Chinese nationality as the core group. According to the national census of 1990, there were a total of 91,200,314 non-Han peoples in China, who constituted 8 percent of the population.[5] But, as both overseas Chinese and U.S. anthropologists have pointed out, the official Chinese term for "nationality"—*minzu*—is highly problematic. According to Steven Harrell:

> So what ultimately makes a group a *minzu* is that the government, more precisely the Minzu Commission . . . says it is one. The Government orig-inally classified *minzu* ostensibly according to the four kinds of character-istics [common territory, a common language, a common economic base and a common psychological makeup], but in fact must have considered other factors such as self-identity and ease of administration, and felt free to ignore self-identity as well if either administrative convenience or the four kinds of characteristics got in the way.[6]

Chinese anthropologist Hsieh Jiann (at the Chinese University of Hong Kong) went so far as to maintain that in some cases, the Chinese state followed no standard at all in designating *minzu*.[7] If the government had included "group feeling" or "ethnic self-identification" in its criteria of designating different "nationalities" in China, then the total number of these people would be much larger than the present fifty-six. According to Chinese sociologist Fei Xiaotong, who participated in the Chinese gov-ernment's initial designation of nationalities, the government at first asked the ethnic minorities of China to provide their own designations. Based on these, the total number of ethnic minority groups in China was approximately 400, of which 260 were in the province of Yunnan.[8] Map 5.1 shows the regions where the ethnic minorities reside today. Figure 5.1 further illustrates the inter-ethnic relationships in China.[9] The dotted lines of four autonomous regions—Inner Mongolia, Ningxia Hui (Muslim), Xinjiang Uighur, and Tibet—and the Korean Autonomous Zhou (district) in Jilin Province represent outside orientations.

The people in Inner Mongolia feel a close kinship with the citizens of the People's Republic of Mongolia to the north. The Muslims in Ningxia always maintain a strong religious identification with the Muslims in the Middle East. The Uighurs and Kazaks in Xinjiang identify themselves not only with Muslims elsewhere but, politically, also with the central Asian

Map 5.1 Ethnic Minority Areas in China

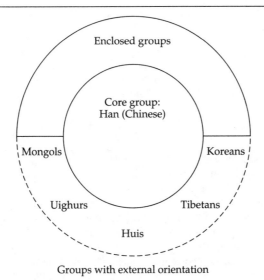

Figure 5.1 Pattern of ethnic composition in China

states of the former Soviet Union. Insofar as Tibet is concerned, both culturally and politically, it feels closer to India than to China. Today, Tibet looks to the West for support of its perennial desire for independence. The Koreans in Jilin naturally have a sense of kinship with the Koreans in the neighboring North Korea. The rest of the minorities, especially the numerous small groups in the Southwest, may be termed "enclosed ethnic groups." However, this does not mean that the southwestern ethnic groups are physically confined to China. In fact, a number of the minorities, such as the Miaos, Zhuangs, Dais, and Shans, settled throughout China and Southeast Asia. But those outside of China have not formed nation-states, so there is not a discernible irredentism among the ethnic communities in the southwestern provinces of China.

The second problematic aspect of the government's presentation of ethnicity in China concerns the size of areas where the ethnic minorities reside. The typical official version states that the minorities, with only 8 percent of the population, occupy approximately 60 percent of the national land area.[10] In reality, Chinese colonization of these borderlands has been extensive. Table 5.1 shows the proportions of ethnic minorities in the five autonomous regions. In three of the five regions, the Chinese are already in the majority (Inner Mongolia, Guangxi Zhuang, and Ningxia Hui). In Xinjiang, substantial Chinese immigration after 1949 significantly reduced the proportion of the minorities among the population. In Tibet, the Chinese appear to be a small minority because they are con-

Table 5.1 Percentages of Non-Chinese Population in Five Autonomous Regions

Region	1949–1964	1992
Inner Mongolia	15 (1956)	18.93
Guangxi Zhuang	37.91 (1953)	38.62
Tibet	97.07 (1964)	97.06
Ningxia	33.55 (1953)	33.76
Xinjiang	76 (1949)	62.02

Sources: The figures for 1949–1964 are from: Sun Jingzhi, Nei *Monggu Zizhiqu Jingji Dili* [Economic Geography of Inner Mongolia Autonomous Region] [Beijing: Kexue Chubanshe, 1956]; Huang Xianlin and Mo Datong, eds., *Zhongguo Renkou-Guangxi Fengce* [China's Population-Guangxi], (Beijing: Zhongguo Caizheng Jingji Chubanshe, 1988); *Zhongguo Renkou-Xizang Fengce* [China's Population-Xizang] (Beijing: Zhongguo Caizheng Jingji Chubanshe, 1986); *Zhongguo Renkou-Ningxia Fengce* [China's Population-Ningxia] (Beijing: Zhongguo Caizheng Chubanshe, 1988); *Zhongguo Renkou-Xinjiang Fengce* [China's Population-Xinjiang] (Beijing: Zhongguo Caizheng Chubanshe, 1990). The figures for 1992 are from *Zhongguo Tongji Nianjian* [Statistical Yearbook of China, 1993] (Beijing: Zhongguo Tongji Chubanshe, 1993), p. 69.

centrated in urban areas. In 1982, the Chinese constituted 39 percent of the urban population in Tibet.[11] In 1993, Ronald Schwartz estimated that the Chinese proportion of Tibet's urban population had reached 50 percent or more.[12]

A wide divergence in the degree of ethnic incorporation among different groups offers a third noteworthy aspect of ethnic politics in China. Don Handelman classified ethnic incorporation into four types (from least to most incorporated): category, network, association, and community.[13] The least incorporated is the ethnic *category*. At this level, ethnic distinction is based simply on its difference from other groups. The ethnicity of the ethnic category depends on individual appropriate behavior and is maintained by family socialization. The next degree of ethnic incorporation in Handelman's typology is the ethnic *network*. "This concept suggests that people will regularly interact with one another in terms of an ethnic membership set."[14] A further development in ethnic incorporation leads to the formation of an ethnic *association*, which seeks to advance the interests of an ethnic group. The highest degree of ethnic incorporation is that of the ethnic *community*. "This kind of collectivity has, in addition to ethnic networks and shared political organization, a territory with more or less permanent physical boundaries."[15]

Table 5.2 adapts Handelman's classification to the ethnic groups in China. The Manchus, Zhuangs, and Huis (Muslims) outside of Ningxia are examples of ethnic categories. They maintain their ethnicity at an individual level. The Manchus have been so integrated into the everyday lives of the Chinese that they exist primarily as a legal category. This is evidenced in the relative ease that the Manchus claim or disclaim their ethnic identity as they see fit. For example, the number of Manchus in China suddenly rose by 128 percent from 1982 to 1990. This is because of the new, post-Mao nationality policy that grants special privileges to

Table 5.2 Types of Ethnic Incorporation in China

Ethnic category	Network	Association	Community

Manchus
Huis
Zhuangs
	Huis	Huis	1. Nationalistic
			   Tibetans, Uighurs,
			   Huis, Mongols
			2. Primordial
			   Koreans, Miaos,
			   Yis
			   (All groups in
			   the southwestern
			   region)

Note: The ethnic groups in each category are examples; they do not constitute a complete list.

minorities, such as exemptions from the "one child" birth-control policy and affirmative action in education and employment. The new licences prompted many Manchus to reclaim their nationality. Before, they had assumed the Han identity to protect themselves from Mao's persecution.[16] The Huis outside of Ningxia have lived among the Chinese for a century or so but they maintain their ethnicity through the customs of the pork taboo and endogamous marriage.[17] The Zhuangs of Guangxi make up the largest ethnic minority in China and have been substantially integrated into Chinese culture. Under the Nationalist government, Guangxi was not regarded as an ethnically separate area. It was the PRC that designated Guangxi an autonomous region.

Handelman's "ethnic network" and "ethnic association" are more meaningful in the urban context of advanced industrial countries in the West than in the predominantly rural Chinese context. Most of the ethnic groups in China live in their own communities in the peripheral areas. The Huis are perhaps the most notable—forming networks and associations outside the Ningxia Autonomous Region. The incorporation of ethnic minorities in China thus displays a dichotomous pattern—either *category* or *community*. The predominant form of incorporation in China is ethnic community, which may be divided into two types. The first type consists of proto-nation-states, such as Tibet, Xinjiang, Ningxia, and Inner Mongolia. The people in these four areas acquired the following three essential conditions of a nation-state in varying degrees before the Communist takeover in 1950:[18]

1.   a bounded geographic area;
2.   centralized and complex governmental and administrative structures, an incumbent regime which controls, monitors, or otherwise regulates economic, military, political, and social affairs; and
3.   an attitudinally, culturally, or ethnically homogeneous population which is legitimately or effectively governed by the incumbent regime.

Obviously, Tibet before 1949 was the closest to a full-fledged nation-state. The pre-1949 governmental structures in Xinjiang, Ningxia, Qinghai, and Inner Mongolia were much less complex and centralized than those in Tibet. They were also more penetrated by the Chinese government than was Tibet. But all of them enjoyed a substantial degree of regional autonomy, until the birth of the PRC.[19] The southwestern ethnic groups (in western Hunan, Guizhou, Yunnan, and Guangxi) established the primordial type of community. A differentiated state structure did not evolve in these groups in either the nineteenth or twentieth century. The communities are characterized by a strong sense of their ethnic distinction and mass participation in shared activities. They have historically evolved local elites but not separate state structures. Those residing in the plains also have been culturally influenced by Chinese immigrants.[20] Ensuing discussions will show that the degree of ethnic incorporation has implications for the ways the different ethnic groups reacted to the Chinese Party-state.

However, regardless of the degree of incorporation, the ethnic minority areas are, as a whole, industrially underdeveloped. Table 5.3 shows that in 1991 average per capita output (output of agriculture, industry, construction, transportation, and commerce) of the nine provinces or regions (Inner Mongolia, Gansu, Qinghai, Ningxia, Xinjiang, Tibet, Guizhou, Yunnan, and Guangxi) where the ethnic minorities are concentrated was 2,187 yuan, as compared with 3,731 yuan in the rest of the

Table 5.3 Average Per Capita Output of Chinese Provinces or Regions in 1991

Province/Region	Value (in Chinese yuan)
Hebei	3,280
Shanxi	3,044
Inner Mongolia	2,789
Liaoning	6,418
Jilin	3,781
Heilongjiang	4,173
Jiangsu	6,183
Zhejiang	5,994
Anhui	2,219
Fujian	3,589
Jiangxi	2,332
Shandong	4,567
Henan	2,414
Hubei	3,249
Hunan	2,399
Guangdong	5,962
Guangxi	1,916
Hainan	2,686
Sichuan	2,356
Guizhou	1,484
Yunnan	1,947
Tibet	2,005
Shaanxi	2,525
Gansu	2,388
Qinghai	2,573
Ningxia	2,731
Xinjiang	3,647

Source: Zhongguo Tongji Nianjian [Statistical Yearbook of China, 1993] (Beijing: Zhongguo Tongji Chubanshe, 1993), pp. 54 and 83.

Table 5.4 Illiteracy Rates in Ethnic Minority Regions, in 1991

National average	20.61%
Inner Mongolia	20.42
Guangxi	16.62
Yunnan	35.02
Tibet	70.40
Gansu	36.73
Qinghai	38.55
Ningxia	31.36
Xinjiang	18.92

Note: Figures are for those above six years of age.

Source: Zhongguo Tongji Nianjian [Statistical Yearbook of China, 1993] (Beijing: Zhongguo Tongji Chubanshe, 1993), p. 86.

nation. In other words, the ethnic areas' average per capita social output value in 1991 was 58 percent of the value in Chinese provinces. Table 5.4 presents the rate of illiteracy among the population over six years of age. Except for Guangxi, Xinjiang, and Inner Mongolia, the rest of the regions have higher than the national average of illiteracy (20.61 percent). Impressionistic information indicates that the higher literacy rates in Guangxi, Xinjiang, and Inner Mongolia are primarily due to the large presence of educated Chinese in these areas. As mentioned in Chapter 2, the poverty areas of China are concentrated in the "old revolutionary base, ethnic minority, and border areas" *(lao, shao, bian)*. The notable exception is the Korean minority in the northeastern province of Jilin; it has the lowest illiteracy rate in China (7 percent)[21]. One might also add that the "cultural distance" between the Koreans and the Chinese is perhaps the least among all the ethnic groups (with the possible exception of the "invisible" Manchus).

So far, my discussion of the conditions of the minorities pertains to their endogenous characteristics. But ethnic politics is essentially about interaction among the various groups, especially between the minorities and the dominant (or core) group. In this regard, the most noteworthy characteristic of ethnic politics in China is the long duration of inter-ethnic communication in Chinese history. Today, Chinese scholars employed by the government are wont to emphasize the integrative aspect of Chinese ethnic relationships.[22] But the disintegrative aspect of China's ethnic history is as prominent as the integrative aspect. Ethnic relationship in China is dualistic.

When a strong state emerged in Chinese history, it tended to carry out what Harrell called a "civilizing project" to make the ethnic minorities accept the Chinese way of life. Long before the Communists implemented "socialist transformation" among the ethnic groups after 1949, traditional Chinese governments sought to "Confucianize" the various non-Chinese races. But, according to Sinologists in the West, the traditional "civilizing projects" of the Chinese state were an expression of "culturalism," not racism. "This culturalist ideology maintained that the high civilization of the Central Kingdom was something that was learned rather than inborn, and thus that anyone, regardless of birth or race, could acquire."[23] This interpretation is perhaps an accurate representation of the perspectives of the Chinese elite. One wonders if the minorities who were the targets of the "civilizing projects" also perceived the Chinese acculturation programs in nonracial terms.

To accomplish a balanced analysis of the ethnic relationship in Chinese history, one must also pay attention to the protracted conflicts and wars between the Chinese and other ethnic groups. The core of the mythical origin of the Chinese race stresses ethnic conflicts. The legendary common ancestor of the Chinese—Huang Di (the Yellow Emperor)—was said to have fought and defeated Chi Yu, the leader of the Miao tribe. This was regarded as the first war fought between the Chinese and a foreign race.[24] Since then, alien conquests of China (like those by various Mongolian and Turkic tribes from the north) were a conspicuous part of its history.

Of equal importance to the alien rule of China were ethnic rebellions. They usually occurred during regime transition, such as between the Ming and Qing dynasties in the seventeenth century, the Qing and the Republic in late nineteenth century, and the Nationalist and Communist regimes in mid-twentieth century. Large-scale uprisings by the Huis happened throughout nineteenth century. The Miaos in Guizhou revolted against the Manchu dynasty in 1795.[25] The Uighurs and Kazaks in Xinjiang organized separatist revolts in 1943 and 1947–1949 against the Nationalist government. Consequently, the CCP had to fight its way into Xinjiang in 1949. By then, Tibet was virtually independent, having long expelled or defeated the Manchu troops there. The Nationalist regime was never able to extend its control to Tibet. Hence, when the Communist forces entered Tibet in 1950, they had to contend with Tibetan government and armed forces, not Nationalist forces. Whether one stresses the integrative or disintegrative aspect of the Chinese ethnic relationship, an incontrovertible fact is that both the "civilizing projects" and inter-ethnic wars of the past contributed to a heightened sense of ethnicity among the Chinese and the ethnic minorities.

In modern times, ethnic relationships in China have been aggravated by a noticeable rise in Chinese racism. The main cause of this change is racism from the West. According to Frank Dikotter: "The transition from cultural universalism to racial nationalism [in China] took place in an age dominated by Western racial theories. The tension accumulated by the superiority-inferiority complex of the Chinese vis-à-vis Western racial arrogance was often released in depreciative descriptions of the colored people."[26] The overall effect of all these is a sharpened ethnic conscious-ness among all the groups in China, the Han in particular. This is a potent force for conflict, especially when the dominant Chinese race developed a strong state and an ideological style of politics after 1949.

In summary, the ethnic politics of China after 1949 are, to a large extent, determined by the endogenous and interactive factors discussed previously and the post-1949 policy of the PRC. Table 5.5 relates these fac-tors to the different reactions of major ethnic groups. The time frame for the first three endogenous factors—state formation, external orientation, and tradition of conflict with the Chinese state—spans the period from the mid-nineteenth century to 1949. Thus, although some groups in the southwest might have fought Chinese states in the past, the conflict occurred too long ago to influence their present reaction to Chinese rule.

The time frame of the last two variables in Table 5.5 encompasses the post-revolutionary period. The Party-state's treatment of ethnic minor-ities is interpreted here as producing either a high or low degree of cultural discontinuity among the various peoples. However, in both Inner Mongolia and the southwestern provinces, ethnic groups either are isolated from or have mingled with the Chinese for a long time. Thus the effects of post-1949 "socialist transformation" are mixed. The Mongols who reside in the few urban centers in Inner Mongolia are culturally almost indistinct from the Chinese.[27] In terms of their relationship with the Chinese, ethnic groups in southwest China, particularly the Zhuangs, are similar to the urbanized Mongols. On the reactions of dif-ferent ethnic groups, internal war refers to highly organized (relatively speaking) political violence with widespread popular participation, designed to overthrow the regime. By turmoil is meant "relatively spon-taneous, unorganized political violence with substantial popular partici-pation, including violent political strikes, riots, political clashes, and localized rebellions."[28]

Table 5.5 shows that when a minority nationality has attained a high degree of ethnic consciousness (with a degree of state formation, external orientation, and a tradition of conflict with the Chinese), then "socialist transformation" is likely to have a highly discontinuous effect on the lives of the masses. Given its ethnic identity and internal organization, such a group will resort to persistent resistance to Chinese rule. Otherwise, in the cases of some southwestern groups, even though they might have experienced a high degree of discontinuity in their lives after 1949, they are not likely to have the capability to wage a war of resistance against the Chinese state.

Like those of various Chinese groups, the reactions of ethnic minori-ties to the CCP political revolution changed from period to period. On the whole, one may divide the reactions of minorities into three kinds and three periods. In the 1950s, as exemplified in the "local nationalism"

Table 5.5 Patterns of Ethnic Reaction to Chinese Rule

	State formation	External orientation	Tradition of conflict	Degree of discontinuity	Reaction to Chinese rule
Tibetans	+	+	+	High	Internal War
Uighurs	+/−	+	+	High	Turmoil
Huis	+/−	+	+	High	Internal War/Turmoil
Mongolians	+/−	+	−	High/Low	Nonviolent Protest
Zhuangs	−	−	−	Low	Integration
Southwestern Groups	−	−	−	High/Low	Nonviolent Protest

phenomenon of the Hundred Flowers campaign in 1957, the attitudes of minorities may be called "reactive ethnicity." According to several scholars on ethnic politics, reactive ethnicity refers to an emergence of ethnic solidarity as "a reaction of the culturally distinct periphery against exploitation by the center."[29] From 1958 to 1977, the ethnic opposition movement in China was in "abeyance," as a result of the state's repression. However, minor localized disturbances did occur in this period. The third period extends from 1978 to the 1990s and is characterized by heterotropicism, that is, reactive-ethnicity, ethnic competition, and "mutual cooptation" between the state and ethnic minorities occurring simultaneously. The last reaction—"mutual cooptation"—is suggested by Harrell and pertains particularly to the ethnic groups in the southwest. It means, "The state assimilates the local elites to ensure the success of state projects while the locals appropriate the people, money, and goals of state projects to serve their own ends."[30]

Reactive Ethnicity in the 1950s

Reactive ethnicity in the 1950s was caused mainly by two policies of the state: establishment of the so-called autonomous areas (region, district or *zhou*, county, and township) and collectivization of economic life ("socialist transformation") among the minorities. The first measure meant the extension of Chinese bureaucratic control under the guise of granting "autonomy" to the ethnic minorities. This measure necessarily interfered with time-honored boundaries and jurisdictions. The groups that were affected the most by the establishment of the "autonomous" areas were the traditional elites. The second policy—collectivization—impinged directly on the everyday lives of both the elites and the masses of various ethnic groups in China. As Weber pointed out, "the belief in ethnic affinity has at all times been affected by outward differences in clothes, in the style of housing, food and eating habits, the division of labor between the sexes and between the free and unfree" and that "these things concern one's conception of what is correct and proper and, above all, of what affects the individual's sense of honor and dignity."[31] While the CCP regarded the "socialist transformation" of the minorities as a "civilizing project," the ethnic groups saw it as dishonoring and obliterating their distinct cultural identity.

As mentioned earlier, the political revolution of the CCP in the 1950s drove even the segmented and disorganized Chinese peasants to revolt. The ethnic minorities, especially those in the north, were more prepared than any Chinese group to take collective action against the state. The minorities were unified by a common cultural (religious) identity and led by a theocratic leadership. It is not surprising that the Huis in Qinghai and Ningxia were the first ones to rebel in 1952–1953. At least one traditional Muslim leader in Ningxia organized his uprising in the guise of a *jihad*.[32] Before the uprising, rumors circulated widely among the Huis that a major calamity was going to fall upon them and that the "world was coming to an end."[33] The revolt was triggered by the CCP's gerrymandering of the Ningxia Hui Autonomous Region. The traditional Muslim leadership in the area responded by staging an uprising.

In the early 1950s, other revolts by the Huis were provoked by collectivization. Two of these occurred in the separate communities of Henan and Hebei. The Chinese Muslims perceived serious threats to their identity caused by the "socialist transformation." The land of the mosques was taken over by the collectives, and the Huis' time-honored tradition of commerce was being abolished by the CCP's policy of a state monopoly over purchase and sale. The Communist political propaganda also threatened the Huis' own efforts at the socialization of the young. Above all, collectivization and Marxist indoctrination meant that the Chinese Muslims would be indistinct from the Chinese thereafter. As Weber put it, the sense of ethnic honor is a specific honor of the masses, so the revolts by the Huis in the early 1950s were genuinely "people's wars." The leadership was provided by the *imams*; young Huis who had joined the CCP or the Communist youth league and assumed the role of cadres also participated in the resistance.[34] The revolts by the Huis in 1952–1953 were but the first of three waves of Hui people's rebellions against the CCP Party-state.

The grievances that the Hui people harbored against the Chinese state were shared by all ethnic groups. During the Hundred Flowers campaign, almost all the minorities loudly criticized the CCP for its racist policy and behavior. The CCP in turn accused critics from the ethnic groups of committing the sin of "local nationalism." There were two focuses in the complaints by the ethnic groups during the Hundred Flowers campaign. The first one concerned the system of "autonomous" areas. The native elites from among the minorities accused the CCP of hypocrisy, as real power was always in the hands of the Chinese agents in their areas. The Chinese Communist Party, claimed these ethnic leaders, belonged to the Han Chinese. The Uighurs and Kazaks in Xinjiang were inspired by their counterparts in the former Soviet Union and demanded the right to form their own republics. In 1957, the second focus of "local nationalism" dealt with the same serious concern for cultural survival of the ethnic minorities that the Huis had already expressed in 1952–1953. There was almost a ground swell of opposition by the minorities against collectivization. The small scattered races in the southwest were particularly sensitive to their cultural survival. They were among the first to undergo collectivization. From them came sayings such as: "Cooperatives are suited to the *Han* nationality but not to the minority nationalities," and "Cooperativization [*sic*] of agriculture and unification of . . . grain purchase and sale have destroyed our traditions, our customs and our national characteristics."[35]

The Mongols and the various groups in Xinjiang faced an additional threat to their physical and cultural survival—massive Chinese immigration. The population of Xinjiang increased from 5.2 million in 1955 to 7 million in 1960, due to a large influx of Chinese immigrants.[36] Demobilized Chinese soldiers were sent to Xinjiang and organized into "Production and Construction Corps" that monopolized mining in the region.[37] The vast grassland of Xinjiang and Inner Mongolia was being destroyed by Chinese farming and industrial projects. The Mongols and the Uighurs wanted a clear division of territory between them and the Chinese; they even demanded expulsion of the Chinese from their land.

Although the most articulate spokespersons of the ethnic minorities in 1957 were the old elites, it was clear that they had mass support, especially from the young.[38] Various CCP leaders in charge of minority nationality affairs—some were ethnic collaborators—declared that ethnic nationalism in 1956–1957 had "reached a dangerous point."[39] For example, Saifudin, a Xinjiang native coopted by the CCP, reported the situation in his homeland as follows (translation not mine): "Since the socialist transformation, . . . local nationalism has been renewed among the national minorities, particularly among the intellectuals. The growth is remarkable in some places and has become the most dangerous ideological trend at the present time."[40] According to Liu Geping, the Muslim head of the Commission on Nationalities of the National People's Congress, separatist movements in 1957 were particularly strong among Mongolians, Muslims, Uighurs, and even the Koreans.[41]

The second wave of Hui rebellion occurred soon after the 1957 "local nationalism" episode. In Ningxia, the old issue of jurisdiction over the Hui autonomous region flared up again. Subsequently, a group of high-ranking Hui leaders was accused by the Chinese government of organizing a "parochial" opposition group.[42] There was apparently an armed rebellion by the Muslims in Gansu and Qinghai in 1958, which required the Chinese army to suppress it. The extent of army repression was such that twenty-two years later, in 1980, the government expressed a mild regret over the excesses committed by the army.[43]

In the 1957 "local nationalism" episode, the Tibetans seemed to be quiescent. That was because the Chinese government had not yet carried out "socialist transformation" in Tibet. But within two years, in 1959, the massive Tibetan revolt took place, which resulted in the Dalai Lama's escape to India. The rebellion began in the eastern periphery of Tibet. It was triggered by the Chinese policy of making the Tibetans carry out class struggle against their native upper class and undergo collectivization.[44] Thus, like the Muslims, the Tibetans readily mobilized to wage a "people's war" against the CCP.

Abeyance, 1958–1977

Like its reaction to the Chinese masses, the Chinese government's response to the manifestation of "local nationalism" by the various ethnic groups was repression, not conciliation. As the ensuing discussion will show, the mobilization potential of ethnic opposition was maintained not by any special agency of the minorities but by the state's repressive policy. It was the common cultural identity or consciousness among the various ethnic groups in China that kept alive their spirit of resistance.

After the outburst of "local nationalism" in 1957–1959, the CCP carried out an aggressive and coercive "civilizing project" among the ethnic groups, in which their customs were subject to "reform." During the severe economic crisis following the failure of the Great Leap Forward (1959–1962), Beijing's pressure on the ethnic groups temporarily eased off. But at the same time, because of massive famine in China (approximately 20 to 30 million Chinese peasants died of starvation), there was a great influx of Chinese refugees into Xinjiang and Inner Mongolia in 1959–1962. In 1959 alone, the number of Chinese immigrants in Xinjiang increased by approximately 820,000.[45] In 1960, an estimated 945,000 Chinese immigrants descended upon Inner Mongolia.[46] The coercive "civilizing" policy of Beijing and the large influx of Chinese immigrants provoked resistance by the ethnic groups in Xinjiang. The most notable event was the flight of approximately 60,000 Kazaks to the former Soviet Union in February 1962, perhaps one of the largest mass escapes in such a short time in the history of the world.[47] Three months later, there was a large demonstration by Uighur youth in Ining, one of the centers of anti-Chinese revolt in 1947–1949. The protestors denounced Chinese control of the regional government and Chinese immigrants' taking jobs away from the local people. The Chinese army suppressed the demonstrators by firing into the crowd.[48]

The Cultural Revolution escalated the Chinese state's repression of ethnic minorities.[49] The Maoists sought to obliterate ethnicity by advocating the primacy of class struggle. A decade of destruction of ethnic cultures followed. Indigenous literary works were banned and religious institutions were shut down. It was during this period that the Maoists subjected even the few remaining ethnic collaborators to persecution. These included the Mongolian leader Ulanfu (Ulanhu) who was dismissed from the Party secretaryship in 1966 for his alleged "local nationalism." The Uighur leader of Xinjiang, Saifudin, was held responsible for the mass defection of the Kazaks in 1962; he was forbidden to return to Xinjiang and ordered to remain in Beijing in 1970. The Lamaist leader of Tibet, Panchen Lama, who had always collaborated with the CCP since 1950, was accused of "opposing the people, the fatherland and socialism" in 1964 and imprisoned thereafter until Mao's death. In 1962, Ngapoi Ngawang Jigme, another Tibetan leader who had loyally served the CCP since 1950, was confined to his residence in Beijing. He was accused of criticizing the Chinese army's brutal suppression of the rebellion in Tibet in 1959.[50] At the same time, Mao dismissed and punished all the high-ranking Chinese officials who had executed the Party's conciliatory policy toward the old elites among the ethnic peoples in the early 1950s.[51] The Maoists seemed to think that they could totally dispense with the ethnic minorities.

The minorities did not acquiesce to the harshness of the Cultural Revolution. In 1969 the Tibetans in Lhasa staged a spontaneous revolt against the excesses of the Cultural Revolution. The details of this rebellion are not known but the target of the rebels seemed to be the Chinese army, which had supported the violent actions of the Red Guards. (One source stated that most of these Red Guards were young Tibetans educated by the Chinese.) About one hundred Chinese soldiers were reportedly killed in this spontaneous rebellion in 1969.[52] According to Schwartz, in 1969 there was also a rebellion by the peasants of Tibet against impending communalization of land. Chinese troops were reported to have suppressed the revolt with brutality. Subsequently, "a number of underground groups sprang into existence" among the Tibetans during the Cultural Revolution.[53]

In the following years, as the Maoists pursued their policy of liquidation of ethnic cultures and customs, Muslims in a small village in Yunnan were driven to revolt, with tragic results. In 1979, the official *People's Daily* referred to it as the "Shadian Incident" but provided little factual information about it. The report admitted that the Chinese authorities, under the influence of the left-wing leaders in Beijing, had insulted the Muslims. "A very serious incident" then ensued in July 1975.[54] However, Dru Gladney was able to gather some details about the occurrence, which was provoked by factional fighting among village youths. The Chinese army supported the radicals who forced Muslim religious leaders to eat pork and imitate pigs. After repeated petitions to the central government produced no settlement, the Huis in the village took up arms to defend themselves. Whereupon, the Chinese army bombarded the village using artillery and jet fighters. The whole village was destroyed and approximately 1,600 Huis were massacred.[55]

With this kind of state repression, there was no need to have any special interest group to sustain the will of the minorities to resist Chinese rule. The liquidation policy of the Chinese government performed the function of holding ethnic mobilization in abeyance; all it required for the mobilization to resume was a period of reduction in state control. It was thus inaccurate for a U.S. scholar on Chinese ethnic affairs to claim that "on balance, the Cultural Revolution appeared to have resulted in loss of ethnic group cohesion and a concomitant increase in the level of integration of minorities."[56]

Those minorities who were not organized as efficiently as the Huis and the Tibetans resisted Chinese rule in the 1970s by adopting a single form of amorphous social action—the refusal to learn either the Chinese language or Chinese-designed native languages. In 1977 officials of the Central Institute for Nationalities, Beijing's chief academy for training ethnic cadres, admitted that even ethnic Party members and cadres did not learn Chinese. Consequently, they could not transmit important government instructions to the masses because the information was announced only in internal meetings by Chinese cadres who had not bothered to learn ethnic languages.[57] Deng's administration finally terminated the Maoist policy requiring minorities to learn either Chinese or Chinese-designed native languages.

Heterotropic Ethnicity, 1978–1995

After the death of Mao, the Chinese government adopted an accommodative approach toward ethnic minorities. However, Deng's strategy was to institute a trade-off between granting the minorities a degree of cultural autonomy and obtaining their cooperation. Toward those ethnic groups that have a theocratic tradition, such as the Huis, the Dengist state sought to exchange cultural autonomy for religious revivalism. In Xinjiang, Ningxia, and Qinghai, where the Muslims are concentrated, the Chinese government advocated and even subsidized cultural revivals but kept religion under close political supervision. In Tibet, the Chinese government tried to separate religion and politics. The CCP maintained that it was not opposed to the Dalai Lama as a religious leader of the Tibetans, but it would not allow him to assume political leadership.

In the meantime, the Chinese state continued its "civilizing project" among the minorities but advertised it behind the new facade of economic development. All provinces were now "equal" before this developmental strategy. That is, each province or region must rely on its own resources and design its own strategy for development. There may be rich provinces and poor provinces but not "superior" or "inferior" ones. A handful of elites coopted from ethnic groups were appointed to state positions. The proportion of ethnic minority delegates in the National People's Congress (18.6 percent) currently exceeds the percentage of minorities in the population. All these measures enabled the Deng administration to proclaim (through the coopted Uighur leader Ismail Amat) that "the relationship of nationalities in China is now characterized by equality, unity and mutual help."[58] Nevertheless, the reactions of ethnic communities were different from those portrayed by the official spokesperson [59]

In general, the attitudes of ethnic minorities in the post-Mao years underwent a three-phase developmental sequence. The first phase was marked by a cultural and religious renaissance. The second phase was characterized by a rise in ethnic consciousness, as a result of cultural restoration. The third phase was distinguished by a resurgence of ethnic separatist movements in Tibet, Inner Mongolia, and Xinjiang.

From Cultural Revival to Separatism

The Deng administration was behind the rapid cultural restorations in ethnic communities in the 1980s. In Tibet, between 1980 and 1993, the state spent US$23 million in repairing 1,600 temples and monasteries. A thousand copies of Buddhist texts were printed for local use. The Tibetan Buddhism Institute trained 3,000 monks and nuns.[60] The government also allocated over US$1 million to renovate more than 150 Buddhist temples and Christian churches in Yunnan.[61] Throughout the Muslim regions of China, mosques were reopened and renovated. More importantly, parochial schools were re-established, now that ethnic groups are allowed to use their own original languages. The Uighurs in Xinjiang and the Huis all over China prefer parochial schools, where their children learn the Koran, to state-operated secular schools.

The right to use native languages also gave the minorities the incentive to own mass media, especially in Inner Mongolia, Ningxia, and Xinjiang. In 1994, the government claimed that in Xinjiang, "any minority nationality with a population of more than 100,000 . . . has its own radio and television stations."[62] Similar to what happened in the Chinese countryside where clans and clan authority were restored, the power of religious leaders was also reestablished in ethnic minority areas. This led further to the reinstatement of traditional marriage rules in Muslim areas. A renewal of contact with Muslim countries in the Middle East brought external assistance, in the form of grants and loans, to rebuild cultural and religious landmarks in Hui areas.[63] Naturally, this cultural and religious renaissance greatly enhanced ethnic consciousness among all groups.

The raised ethnic consciousness produced a short-term effect— increased ethnic segregation. Huis in China told Gladney that there was reduced contact between them and the Chinese, due to their greater devotion to religious worship and a reawakened sense of faithfulness to religious teachings. In the meantime, growing commercialism in China gave rise to a trend among Chinese writers to portray the minorities as exotic and sexual in order to enhance the sale of their works. In this stereotyping of the minorities, Gladney also saw a way for the Chinese to affirm their own identity.[64]

This trend of heightened ethnic consciousness, however, contributed to racial conflict. Moreover, there was an increase in religious sectionalism resulting in reduced communication among Chinese Muslims of different sects.[65] A tragic incident occurred in Ningxia in May 1993 when rival factions of the Zheherenye sect engaged in armed fights. Although the Chinese army quelled the internecine fight, forty-nine people were killed.[66] It seems that this heightened sense of ethnicity was partly caused by dispensation with "preference falsification," which people were forced to practice under the repressive Maoist regime. Enhanced ethnic consciousness and weakened social control by the state soon led to ethnic strife, as seen in several collective protests by the Huis. These included: (1) the 1985 demonstration by Xinjiang students in Beijing, objecting to China's testing of atomic weapons in Xinjiang; (2) the 1988 Xinjiang university students' protest against insulting graffiti on their campus; (3) the 1989 Muslim student march in Beijing, protesting against a book that was said to have defamed their religion; and (4) the 1993 Muslim riot in Qinghai, again over an insulting book.[67] One may regard this Hui militancy in the 1980s and 1990s as the third wave of Muslim rebellion against Chinese rule since the early 1950s.

For Deng's administration, certainly the most ironic result of its accommodative policy toward ethnic minorities was the resurgence of separatist movements in Tibet, Xinjiang, and Inner Mongolia throughout the late 1980s and early 1990s. However, it is not out of the ordinary, socio-psychologically speaking, that political reform, after a long period of repression, creates an opportunity for oppositional sentiment to surface. The three ethnic communities of China—Tibetans, Xinjiang Uighurs, and the Mongols of Inner Mongolia—displayed varied manifestations of separatism, due mainly to the different endogenous factors presented in Table 5.5, especially the varying degrees of state formation.

Tibetan separatism is the archtype of a nationalistic secessionist movement. According to Schwartz, from 1987 to 1992, there were 140 demonstrations against Chinese rule and for Tibetan independence. More importantly, the leaders of these demonstrations were no longer the traditional elites; they were young monks and nuns from the countryside, educated in the newly opened monasteries.[68] The Chinese government reports describing the political conditions in Tibet in the 1990s openly admitted that native CCP cadres were sympathetic to the independence movement. The "basic units" of the Tibetan CCP could not be relied upon by the Chinese government.[69] Tibetan separatism has become a "national" cause with a massive following. In this sense, the Tibetan independence movement is in the same league as the famous mass resistance by Norwegians against Nazi occupation during World War II, the uprising by the people of Northern Ireland against the British, and the war of the Palestinians against Israel in the West Bank.[70]

Four factors account for the effective mobilization of Tibetans. The first one is a high degree of cultural identity among Tibetans, which is institutionalized in an elaborate system of symbols, consisting of myth, signs, and icons.[71] Lamaism is the myth in which all Tibetans deeply believe. The signs that serve to transmit the myth are everywhere in Tibet—the numerous temples, monasteries, and the Tibetan flag. Finally, the icons—those signs that bear a physical resemblance to aspects of the myth—are hierarchically presented in Tibet: Dalai Lama, the monks, and the nuns. Second, the unique cultural-religious identity of Tibetans clearly sets them apart from the Chinese. There is, thus, a sharp "we–they" division between the two groups. Third, Tibetans have a network or infrastructure that is integrated with their everyday lives, which both eases communication among them and counters Chinese control measures. Schwartz mentioned networks among the youth and the cadres. The monks naturally use the monasteries as their network. The popular religious activities, which the Chinese government is publicly committed to respect, serve as a legitimate forum in which Tibetans can express their views and mobilize collective actions.[72]

Finally, the Tibetans' resistance against the Chinese focuses on values, not material gains. It is a struggle of wills. The Chinese state's command of superior coercive force is of limited use in such a contest of wills. In 1994, there were reports that the Chinese government is considering a major change in its policy toward Tibet. In response to the unreliability of Tibetan CCP cadres, the new policy is reportedly advocating an increase in the proportion of Chinese cadres in the "basic units" of the Tibetan government. The allowed proportions of Chinese cadres would increase to 40 or even 70 percent of all cadres in the Tibetan administration. This internal CCP document stated that what is worrisome is not separatism but the fence-sitting attitude of the cadres.[73]

The separatist movement in Xinjiang is comparatively weaker than that in Tibet for two primary reasons. The first one is the diversity of ethnic groups in Xinjiang. There are forty-seven different ethnic groups in the region, most of them living in segregated communities. They do share the same Islamic faith and the same dislike of the Chinese. However, racial pluralism may have caused the separatist movement in Xinjiang to become badly splintered. After the 1988 student demonstration against racism on a university campus, a Uighur official revealed that there were seven Uighur exile groups secretly fomenting secessionism in Xinjiang. They were known as: "Eastern Turkish National Salvation Committee," "Eastern Turkish National Revolutionary Front," "Eastern Turkestan Charity Funds," "Kazak Turk People Charity Funds," "New Eastern

Turkish Residents' Association," "World Islamic Federation," and "Eastern Turkestan, Mongolian, Manchurian, and Tibetan Peoples' Federation Committee." The CCP was said to be most concerned with an exile group in Turkey that was led by a former Uighur official, named Aisha, who had collaborated with the Nationalist government before 1949. These separatist groups can count on a degree of mass support in Xinjiang. In 1988 it was reported that among Xinjiang CCP cadres, there were views such as (translation not mine): "The formulation that 'Xinjiang has been part of China since the ancient past' lacks historical basis" and "The idea that 'the *Han* nationality is inseparable from minority nationalities, and that minority nationalities are inseparable from the *Han* nationality' lacks theoretical basis."[74]

The second reason for the weakened separatist movement in Xinjiang is the heavy penetration by Chinese immigrants. This factor is highlighted by the serious uprising of the people of the Kizilsu Kirghiz Autonomous *Zhou* in April 1990. The revolt occurred in the Baren township, near the city of Kashgar in southern Xinjiang, where the population was made up mostly of ethnic minorities. The Chinese tend to concentrate in the northern part of Xinjiang, as shown in Table 5.6. The three traditional centers of revolt against Chinese rule before 1949—Ili, Tacheng, and Altay—are now predominantly Chinese cities. Consequently, ethnic unrest shifted to areas like Kashgar in southern Xinjiang where the Chinese are still in the minority. In a geographical pattern similar to that of the workers' and peasants' unrest in 1992 (see Chapter 3), the size or density of the population served as the mobilization force that stirred revolts by the minorities of Xinjiang. Like the Tibetan resistance, religion served as a cementing force in the Baren uprising. The incident happened during a religious festival and was said to have been triggered by the government's closure of a mosque and its ban on the construction of new mosques and Islamic schools. A riot ensued and a Chinese army of 1,000 strong was sent in to suppress it. By the government's own account, twenty-two people were killed.[75]

Today, Xinjiang remains in a restless state. The various separatist groups in the area seemed to have coalesced into two large groups. The radical one that advocates revolution is known as the "People's Revolutionary Front of the United Nationalities of East Turkestan." Its leader is Yucubek Mukhlisi. The moderate group—which seeks a nonviolent way to achieve independence—is dominated by the Uighurs. The group is called "Freedom Party of the Uighurs" and is led by a man named Ashir Vakhidov.[76] Although the separatists in Xinjiang were less unified than the Tibetans, they were more extreme in their actions. A terrorist bomb attack took place in Xinjiang in June 1993. Ismail Amat, Xinjiang's collaborationist leader, declared in November 1993 that the government "should effectively prevent infiltration by hostile forces"; he hinted that the native cadres were politically unreliable.[77] Similar to the

Table 5.6 Distribution of Uighurs and Han Chinese in Xinjiang in 1982 (in percentage)

	Uihgurs	Han Chinese
Total	40.48	40.41
Northern Region		
Urumqi City	10.93	75.63
Karamai City	14.04	78.83
Shihezi City	0.88	96.17
Turfan District	70.83	22.32
Hami District	20.00	68.09
Changji Hui Autonomous *Zhou*		
Ili District[a]	23.96	42.91
Tacheng District[a]	5.02	59.24
Altay District[a]	2.20	47.74
Boertala Mongolian		
Autonomous *Zhou*	13.39	65.01
Bayingeleng Autonomous		
Zhou	35.03	54.23
Southern Region		
Aksu District	76.28	22.00
Kirgiz Autonomous *Zhou*	64.90	4.90
Kashgar District[b]	90.77	7.70
Khotan (Hetian)	96.37	3.53

[a]Old areas of revolt

[b]Recent area of revolt

Source: Zhong Chongjing, ed., *Zhongguo Renkou-Xinjiang Fengce* [China's Population-Xinjiang], (Beijing: Zhongguo Caizheng Jingji Chubanshe, 1990), p. 288.

situation in Tibet, the center of unrest in Xinjiang shifted to the impoverished rural areas in the southern part of the territory. In late 1994, the head of the Xinjiang CCP Committee, Wan Lequan, made a special visit to the southern area and urged local leaders to make a concerted effort to promote economic development.[78] In the meantime, Xinjiang news media continuously complained of a lack of discipline among local cadres.[79]

Whereas the strong desire for separatism in both Tibet and Xinjiang has been known for a long time, the appearance of separatism in Inner Mongolia in the 1990s—hitherto known as "a model autonomous region"—shows how ineffective the CCP's policy of ethnic integration has been.[80] Inner Mongolia was the first "autonomous region" established by Beijing in 1947, even *before* the founding of the PRC. The CCP had extended its political influence to Inner Mongolia as early as 1925, barely four years after the Party's birth. A "Revolutionary People's Party of Inner Mongolia" (*Nei Menggu Renmin Gemingdang*) was fostered by the

CCP in that year. In the 1930s, a Communist guerrilla force, led by a Mongolian Communist named Ulanfu, operated in the region, fighting against the Nationalist authorities there. After the end of World War II, the CCP orchestrated several forms of "autonomous people's governments" in Inner Mongolia to undermine the Nationalist government. After the founding of the PRC, Ulanfu was regarded as Beijing's most illustrious leader of ethnic minority origin.[81] To Beijing, the Mongols in Inner Mongolia seemed to be "in good hands." But the Maoists' liquidationist policy toward the minorities alienated both Ulanfu and the Mongols in general.

During the Cultural Revolution, former members of the 1925 Revolutionary People's Party suffered terribly at the hands of the Red Guards. In 1979, Deng politically rehabilitated 2,000 Mongolian victims of the Cultural Revolution.[82] In 1983, as a gesture of atonement, Deng's administration made Ulanfu the vice-president of the PRC. But, by then, a militant dissident movement had already come into existence. In 1991, Beijing arrested members of two organizations for their pro-independence activity; the groups were the Ih Ju League National Culture Society and the National Modernization Society. Beijing accused the Mongolian dissidents of trying to unite with the neighboring Mongolian People's Republic.[83] In the following year, some exiles from Inner Mongolia formed the General Coordination Committee of Inner Mongolian Rejuvenation Movements in Ulan Bator, capital of the Mongolian People's Republic. The committee claimed to have 2,000 members, half of them in Inner Mongolia. One dissident leader expressed the following opinion which must have reflected the views of many of his fellow Mongols in China: "Our economy is based on colonialism. Our land is rich, but the Chinese take our resources and leave us poor. We see that! And there's been pressure from immigrants. We're now a minority in our own land. Life for our people is worse than ever."[84] In 1994, the head of the Inner Mongolian CCP Committee claimed that "western hostile forces" were conducting a campaign of "westernization and disintegration" against Inner Mongolia.[85]

The conflicts in Inner Mongolia were primarily caused by domestic problems. The massive Chinese colonization of the area probably also brought the Chinese political culture of corruption to the people of Inner Mongolia. An incident occurred in April 1994 during which 4,000 cadres organized a petition campaign against the regional government for its corrupt deeds. Premier Li Peng had to go to Inner Mongolia to mediate the dispute.[86] Although Inner Mongolian authorities later denied the incident, subsequent developments tended to verify it.[87] For example, the head of the CCP Committee in Inner Mongolia and his deputy were relieved of their duties in August 1994.[88] While visiting Inner Mongolia about the same time, Hu Jintao, member of the CCP Politburo, called on the regional government "to improve the quality of government leaders at all levels, and select and promote excellent young cadres."[89]

Along with the militant separatism in Tibet, Xinjiang, and Inner Mongolia, the rest of the northwestern borderland of China was experiencing its share of turmoil. Ethnic conflicts were alive and well among the Huis in Ningxia and the Tibetans, Mongols, and Huis in Qinghai. In October 1993, a demonstration involving 12,000 Muslims and their *imams* took place in the capital of the Ningxia Hui Autonomous Region. The demonstrators reportedly called for "an end to Chinese rule."[90] In Qinghai, the government-operated newspaper, *Qinghai Daily*, reported in February 1994:

> Small numbers of evildoers are still carrying out acts of sabotage. They are fabricating rumors to confuse and poison people's minds and are using all sorts of dirty tricks in a vain attempt to sabotage the stable and united political situation, in which people of various nationalities throughout the province are engaged in a united struggle *which is not easily won.* (emphasis added)[91]

Development as Panacea

While Mao Zedong wished to dispose of the ethnic problem by stressing the primacy of class struggle, Deng Xiaoping sought ethnic quiescence through emphasis on economic development. "We have discovered that the nationality question is in fact a question of development," said a native leader of Inner Mongolia in 1994.[92] After Deng assumed power in 1978, the Chinese government allocated a considerable sum to the minority areas, particulary Tibet, to initiate developmental projects. Since then, the various ethnic groups in China have been in the early stages of what some anthropologists call the typical "race relations" cycle, which "would lead from isolation through competition, conflict, and accommodation to assimilation."[93] Available evidence indicates that ethnic communities in China are primarily in the first phase—breaking out of isolation. Some instances of competition and conflict already have been discerned. My discussion here will focus mainly on these early phases of the race-relation cycle, with an emphasis on the potential for conflict. Whether development will eventually overcome separatism cannot yet be ascertained.

First of all, almost all the ethnic regions in China are rich in raw materials, especially in the North and Northwest. Southwestern communities, such as Yunnan, are rich in commercial crops. To tap these resources, modern transportation is necessary. Since the 1980s, many of the ethnic communities have been constructing roads and railways to end their historical isolation. Tibet now has 22,000 kilometers of highway, a modern airport, and a telecommunications network, which connect the region with other parts of China and the world.[94] A resource-rich area, such as

Xinjiang, has been able to obtain loans from the World Bank to build modern highways.[95] In the minority areas of the southwestern provinces, there have also been vigorous efforts to build roads and highways to connect the various ethnic groups.[96] But these modern infrastructures also destroy the environment and threaten the traditional way of life in the grasslands in the Northwest. I have already mentioned one Mongolian dissident's complaint addressing the Chinese destruction of the pastures in Inner Mongolia. In July 1991, there was a demonstration in the capital city of Xining by Tibetans in Qinghai. Thirty demonstrators gathered in front of the municipal government and held up placards saying: "Return to us our land of snow; return to us our land of grass; we are on the verge of starvation."[97]

Second, economic development is likely to offend the ideological beliefs among some ethnic elites, such as those of the Tibetans. The Chinese government is even encouraging Tibetan Lamas to engage in commercial work.[98] In December 1994, a stock exchange center was opened in Lhasa, the Tibetan capital. Given Tibet's theocratic values and institutions, new commercialism might clash with Tibetans' anti-chrematistic tradition. In a 1994 report by the head of the Tibetan CCP Committee, Chen Kuiyuan, I found the following statement, indicating opposition of economic reform at high levels (translation not mine):

> However, if all party members stick to the old practice of reading only Chairman Mao's books and stubbornly defend his conclusions, if our thinking remains on the same level as before the Third Plenary Session of the 11th CCP Central Committee, and if we do not arm ourselves with Comrade Deng Xiaoping's theory on building socialism with Chinese characteristics, our party's fate will not necessarily be better than that of the Soviet Communist Party.[99]

Apparently, opposition to developmentalism also came from the Lamaist establishment. In an inspection tour of eastern Tibet in November 1994, Chen Kuiyuan hinted at this problem: "Some people do not really understand the true essence of Buddhism, pay no attention to happiness in real life, and pursue the so-called happiness of the next life, which does not exist at all."[100]

Third, economic development in minority communities also means increased contact with the Chinese and other ethnic groups. Since almost all the ethnic areas are industrially underdeveloped, they need technical aid or cooperation from the advanced provinces in the east. From 1985 to 1993, officials of Tibet and the inland Chinese provinces signed agreements for over six hundred economic and technical cooperative projects; in turn, 2,000 Chinese skilled technicians were sent to Tibet.[101] In 1994, the government of Inner Mongolia reported that in the past year alone, it "completed 1,147 economic cooperative items and 462 technological cooperative projects" with other provinces.[102] Yunnan signed twenty-eight economic cooperative projects with Shanghai in 1994.[103] In Guangxi, various ethnic groups were reported to have organized cooperative councils among themselves, building modern roads and establishing local markets.[104] These inter-ethnic contacts are bound to increase opportunities for disputes and conflicts. At the least, cross-ethnic exchanges and cooperative efforts make the poorer ethnic regions conscious of the disparity between theirs and the more advanced provinces. The governor of Qinghai said to a Chinese reporter in 1994: "the market forces worsen Qinghai's ability in closing the [regional] gap."[105]

The situation in Xinjiang is even more susceptible to conflict, due partly to an influx of Chinese migrant workers who were attracted to the area by the availability of land and employment. The Xinjiang regional government reported that there were 300,000 (Chinese) migrant workers in the area in 1994, majority of them from Sichuan. The report described one situation as follows:

> There is a production team on a vegetable farm in the southern part of the Taklimakan desert that consists of 430 members, all of whom are migrant workers. Zheng Bangjun came to Xinjiang from Sichuan's Qiuling County. As soon as he found a plot of land for development in the Tarim basin in 1987, he immediately helped move six of his eight brothers and sisters to this place.[106]

Given the history of the Xinjiang people's resentment of Chinese immigration, these new migrant workers from Sichuan provide an obvious potential for renewed conflicts between the Xinjiang natives and the Chinese. In Tibet, there already were reported instances of Tibetan protestors attacking and burning Chinese-owned stores in Lhasa.[107] Schwartz wrote that Tibetans felt excluded from economic growth, the benefits of which were appropriated by the Chinese (as Tibetans perceived it). Tibetans did not give the Chinese government any credit for the improved living conditions they had gained after 1978.[108]

Fourth, in almost all the economic development plans prepared for ethnic communities, a prominent role is allocated to foreign trade and international tourism. A large volume of foreign trade and significant numbers of tourists attracted to one's province constitute new status symbols among the various provinces and regions of China. The Xinjiang government proudly reported in 1994: "Three hundred and sixty-three foreign-funded enterprises were approved in 1992, and foreign capital of $243 million was utilized, an increase of 86.9 percent" and "in 1992, Xinjiang received 241,000 tourists from home and abroad, earning foreign exchange of $40 million, an increase of 12.16 percent."[109] Statements like these are routinely found in every regional government's annual report.

In addition, traditional trade centers on the borders between Tibet and India and between Xinjiang and the central Asian states have now been opened for commerce. A 1994 report from Tibet states, "The Yamagrong Border Trade Fair, which had been suspended for 33 years, and other traditional border markets were restored."[110] In a reopened traditional border market town in southern Xinjiang, a Chinese reporter found all kinds of shops, including (most significantly) video shops.[111] Thus, news and all kinds of information from the world outside of China can now be transmitted to China through these border towns. The minorities of China may be better informed about the world than the multitude of Chinese peasants in China's interior. All these foreign contacts strengthen ethnic consciousness for some groups, such as the Huis. They learn about the religious activities of fellow Muslims in the Middle East. Western tourists, business professionals, and publications also serve to "put China in its place" in the world. Tibetans and other ethnic minorities now realize how "backward" China is among the nations of the world.[112] The CCP is no longer able to maintain its old presumption of superiority among the minorities. Consequently, the will to maintain the cause of separatism among some ethnic groups might be strengthened by foreign contacts. The effects of Western knowledge on the university students of China have already become obvious.

Fifth, experience in Western countries shows that modernization tends to increase ethnic competition with the core group. Economic development increases homogeneity within an ethnic region and endows local authorities with additional resources. These in turn facilitate mobilization on a large scale.[113]

Finally, in the early phase of rapid economic growth, ethnic areas may become enclaves for outcasts. There are several contributory causes for this phenomenon: being on the border of China, living in a mixed population, alienation from Chinese rule, and a degree of local autonomy. In China, organized crimes have become a serious problem in Inner Mongolia, Ningxia, Xinjiang, and Yunnan. Because of the large number of Chinese immigrants in Inner Mongolia, most of whom are able-bodied males, abducting and trafficking of women are notoriously frequent crimes.[114] An active market in fake pharmaceuticals has also been discovered in Inner Mongolia. These inferior medicines are made elsewhere in China and then brought to Inner Mongolia for sale.[115]

In Xinjiang, due to its rapid economic growth, criminals prey on major routes of communication. The southern agricultural areas of Xinjiang are also plagued by social disorder. A special conference was held in Xinjiang's capital, Urumqi, in August 1994. The focus was on how to deal with rural social order. The communiqué of the conference in part stated (translation not mine):

Areas and spots to be managed are areas along railways and highways, rural villages and towns, military regiment production-construction farms, areas where urban and rural areas meet, factories and mines, areas around oilfields, rural fair trades, farmers' markets, border ports, and rural areas where social order is in chaos. Troublemakers, fierce fighting, train and road bandits, murderers, robbers, rapists, violent criminals, gangs, theft rings, and other serious criminal offenses are the targets of the crackdown.[116]

As for the southwestern province of Yunnan, its proximity to the so-called Golden Triangle for illegal drug production in Burma made the province a center of drug smuggling.[117] One might see the criminal activities in these ethnic minority areas with the same perspective that one regards the disorder in China's rural areas (Chapter 2). They represent a way for marginal people to overcome their disadvantages in a competitive market. No matter how one interprets the social disorganization in the minority areas, there is a potential for inter-ethnic strife. At the least, endemic crimes in these regions tend to reinforce racial stereotyping. Moreover, the example of the civil war between the Russian government and the breakaway republic of Chechnya in 1994 is a reminder of how the label "a criminal republic" facilitates a government's bloody crackdown on an ethnic minority region.

In the final analysis, development as a panacea for ethnic problems is extremely problematic. Several U.S. scholars specializing in ethnic politics have pointed out that ethnic strife is cultural or subjective in nature. The solution lies in politics, not in economics. Walker Connor stated: "But the tendency for ethnonational groups to aspire to greater autonomy, while being prepared to settle for something short of full independence, does underline the fact that a solution to ethnic heterogeneity must ultimately be found in the political sphere and not in the economic one."[118] Elise Boulding also put it well: "Increased national wealth is not all that is needed in dealing with the groups that foster separatism; if it were, then the rich nations of Europe would not have separatist movements."[119] What is at issue is self-worth and self-realization for the minorities. As the "local nationalism" episode in 1957 has proven, ethnic groups in China (or, for that matter, elsewhere in the world) felt that the government threatened their ethnic identity and that its promise of autonomy was a sham.

Today, the Dalai Lama does not insist on a full national independence for Tibet and he disavows violence.[120] He seems to be genuinely concerned about the cultural and social effects of increasing commercialism and Chinese immigration in Tibet. The Dalai Lama's primary concern is Tibet's distinct cultural or ethnic identity.[121] But it is Deng Xiaoping's grand (or illusive) strategy for the Chinese and the ethnic minorities alike to exchange a higher standard of living for a participatory political system. The failure of this strategy for the university students of China has already been discussed. There is even less reason to think that Deng's strategy would work among the Tibetans, Mongolians, and Uighurs. As suggested by Harrell, developmentalism may be working among some ethnic groups in the southwestern provinces of China, where there is no demand for separatism. These scattered ethnic groups might complain about Chinese racial chauvinism, but they still "see the possibility of participating in local development and construction through channelling government initiatives to local advantage."[122] However, to do so, these ethnic groups must learn the Chinese language and operate in the wider Chinese society. Moreover, these southwestern groups might well be on their way to completing the "isolation ... assimilation" cycle. Nevertheless, the north and northwestern groups, whose desire for separatism is strong, must wait for the Chinese government to realize that political issues must be solved politically, not economically.

Notes

1. *SCMP*, no. 1881, p. 23.
2. FBIS, *CHI/DR*, August 9, 1993, p. 50.
3. FBIS, *CHI/DR*, April 7, 1994, p. 33.
4. FBIS, *CHI/DR*, May 25, 1994, p. 56.
5. *Zhongguo Baike Nian Jian, 1991* [Encyclopedia of China, 1991] (Beijing: Zhongguo Da Baike Quanshu Chubanshe, 1991), p. 396.
6. Steven Harrell, "Ethnicity and Kin Terms Among Two Kinds of Yi," *Special Issue on Ethnicity and Ethnic Groups in China, New Asia Academic Bulletin* 3 (1989):181. I am grateful to Professor Harrell for supplying me this and other publications by him.
7. Hsieh Jiann, "Wen-hwa Jen-t'ung, Tsu-ch'un Jen-t'ung Yu Min (Kuo) Tsu Chu-yi: Yi Chung-kuo-ti To-yuan-hsin Wei-li," [Cultural and ethnic identity and nationalism: As exemplified in the pluralism of China], in *Min-tsu Chu-yi Yu Chung-kuo Hsien-tai-hwa* [Nationalism: Its interaction with modernization in China], ed. Liu Qinfeng (Hong Kong: Chinese University of Hong Kong Press, 1994), p. 160.
8. Fei Xiaotong, *Minzu Yu Shehui* [Nationality and society] (Tianjin: Renmin Chubanshe, 1985), pp. 1–4.
9. The design of the chart is adapted from J. Milton Yinger, "Ethnicity in Complex Societies: Structural, Cultural, and Characterological Factors," in *The Uses of Controversy in Sociology,* ed. Lewis A. Coser and Otto N. Larsen (New York: Free Press, 1976), p. 202.
10. For a recent statement, see Cheng Zhaoxin, "Guanyu Minzudiqu Difanggongye Fazhande Shikao," [Thoughts on the industrial development in ethnic minority areas], *Gongye Jingji* [Industrial Economy], no. 5 (1992):157–165.
11. Liu Riu, ed., *Zhongguo Renkou-Xizang Fengce* [Chinese population–Tibetan] (Beijing: Zhongguo Caizheng Jingji Chubanshe, 1989), p. 285.
12. Ronald D. Schwartz, *Circle of Protest: Political Ritual in the Tibetan Uprising* (New York: Columbia University Press, 1994), p. 204.

13.   I am following the discussion in Thomas Hylland Eriksen, *Ethnicity and Nationalism* (London: Pluto Press, 1993), pp. 41–45.

14.   Ibid., p. 42.

15.   Ibid., p. 43.

16.   Meiqiu Jiang, "The Structure of Nationalities and the Future Federal System in China" (in Chinese), *Papers of the Center for Modern China*, no. 8 (June, 1991):21.

17.   For a thorough and comprehensive description of the lives of the Huis in China, see Dru C. Gladney, *Muslim China: Ethnic Nationalism in the People's Republic* (Cambridge, Mass.: Council on East Asian Studies, Harvard University, 1991).

18.   According to Lee E. Dutter, "Theoretical Perspectives on Ethnic Political Behavior in the Soviet Union," *Journal of Conflict Resolution* 34, no. 2 (June 1990):314.

19.   For descriptions of the politics in these areas, see A. Doak Barnett, *China on the Eve of Communist Takeover* (New York: Praeger, 1963), chapters 12–18.

20.   See, for example, Steven Harrell, "Ethnicity, Local Interests, and the State: Yi Communities in Southwest China," *Comparative Study of Society and History* 32, no. 3 (1990):515–548. Also, Hsieh Jiann, "A Study on Directed Sociocultural Change of the Samei in Yunnan (1949–80)," (in Chinese), in *Proceedings of the Conference on Modernization and Chinese Culture* (Hong Kong: Faculty of Social Science and Institute of Social Studies, Chinese University of Hong Kong, 1985), pp. 85–98.

21.   *China Daily*, November 9, 1994.

22.   See, for example, Chen Yuning and Tang Xiaofang, "Zhonghua Minzu Ningjuli Xinchende Lishiyaosu" [The essential elements of the fusionary forces of the Chinese nationality], *Xinhua Wenzhai* [New China Digest], no. 6 (1993):56–59.

23.   Steven Harrell, "Linguistics and Hegemony in China," *International Journal of Society and Language*, no. 103 (1993):98; see also Steven Harrell, "Introduction: Civilizing Projects and the Reaction to Them," in *Cultural Encounters on China's Ethnic Frontiers*, ed. Steven Harrell (Seattle: University of Washington Press, 1994).

24.   Lin Hui-hsiang, *Chung-kuo Ming-tsu-shih* [History of the Chinese nationality], vol. 1 (Taipei: Commercial Press, 1965), pp. 101–107.

25.   For ethnic revolts in the first two transitions, see Iwakichi Inaba, *Shincho Zenshi* [A history of the Qing dynasty] (Tokyo, 1914), translated by Tan T'ao under the title *Ch'ing-ch'ao Ch'uan-shih* (Taipei: Chung-hua Shu-chu, 1960), chapters 45, 51, 52, 75, 76, and 77.

26.   Frank Dikotter, "Group Definition and the Idea of 'Race' in Modern China (1793–1949)," *Ethnic and Racial Studies* 13, no. 3 (July 1990):429.

27.   William Ronald Jankowiak, "Huhhot: An Urban Profle" (Ph.D. diss., University of California at Santa Barbara, 1986.)

28.   Ted Robert Gurr, *Why Men Rebel* (Princeton: Princeton University Press, 1970), p. 11.

29.   François Nielsen, "Toward a Theory of Ethnic Solidarity in Modern Societies," *American Sociological Review* 50, no. 2 (April 1985):133.

30.   "Ethnicity and Development in Southwest China," *Precis*, (M.I.T. Center for International Studies), 5, no. 1 (Winter 1993–1994):15.

31.   Weber, *Economy and Society*, vol. 1, p. 391.

32. P. H. McNair Jones, "China's Muslim Region," *Far Eastern Economic Review,* September 14, 1961, pp. 492–494.

33. *SCMP,* no. 1640, pp. 14–20; and *RMRB,* December 19, 1980, p. 4.

34. See, for example, *SCMP,* nos. 1728, 1764, 1770, and 1779; also *Guangming Ribao,* May 29, 1958.

35. "Responsible Nationality Cadres Criticized Local Nationalism at CCP Yunnan Provincial Congress," *RMRB,* December 15, 1957, in *SCMP,* no. 1689, p. 19.

36. Zhou Chongjing, ed., *Zhongguo Renkou-Xinjiang Fengce* [China's Population-Xinjiang] (Beijing: Zhongguo Caizheng Jingji Chubanshe, 1990), p. 68.

37. See the testimony of a former Chinese student in Xinjiang in *Current Scene* 1, no. 18 (November 18, 1961):5.

38. For reports from different areas, see *SCMP:* (1) On Inner Mongolia, nos. 1656, 1718, 1725, 1733, and 1813; (2) On the Huis, nos. 1640, 1699, 1728, 1764, 1770, and 1779; (3) On Xinjiang, nos. 1652, 1661, 1672, 1689, 1718, 1726, 1764, 1873, and 1998; and (4) On Guizhou and Guangxi races, nos. 1672, 1689, 1718, and 1813.

39. "Minorities Affairs Commission Holds Forum to Discuss Nationalism Problems," *NCNA,* November 22, 1957, in *SCMP,* no. 1672, pp. 4–5; "Local Nationalism Criticized by Cadres of the Nationalities Affairs Commission," *NCNA,* January 17, 1958, in *SCMP,* no. 1699, pp. 1–2; Yang Ching-jen, "Fan-tui Ti-fang Ming-tsu-chu-i" [Opposing local nationalism], *Hsüeh Hsi,* no. 5, 1958, pp. 18–21.

40. "Saifudin Censures and Refutes Local Nationalism," *RMRB,* December 26, 1957, in *SCMP,* no. 1689, p. 7.

41. Liu Ke-p'ing, "A Socialist Education Against Local Nationalism Among the National Minorities," *SCMP,* no. 1698 (January 24, 1958), p. 4.

42. Jones, "China's Muslim Region," p. 493.

43. *RMRB,* December 19, 1980, p. 4.

44. P. H. McNair Jones, "Tibet Drags Its Feet," *Current Scene,* October 1959–April 1961, pp. 288–293.

45. Zhou, *Zhongguo Renkou-Xinjiang Fengce,* p. 68.

46. Liu Jingping and Zheng Guangzhi, eds., *Nei Menggu Zizhiqu Jingji Fazhan Kailun* [A general discussion of the economic development of Inner Mongolia], (Huhehot: Nei Menggu Renmin Chubanshe, 1979), p. 526.

47. Zhou, *Zhongguo Renkou-Xinjiang Fengce,* p. 153; *RMRB,* January 18, 1979, p. 3.

48. Daniel Tretiak, "China's New Frontier Trouble," *Far Eastern Economic Review,* October 10, 1963, pp. 60–62.

49. June Dreyer, "China's Minority Nationalities in the Cultural Revolution," *China Quarterly,* no. 35 (July-September, 1968), pp. 96–109.

50. Xiaoyuan Gao, "Regional Autonomy of Minorities Under Centralized Control" [in Chinese], *Papers of the Center for Modern China,* no. 8 (June 1991):10–11; also Carey Winfrey, "Tibetan Spiritual Leader: The Panchen Lama," *New York Times,* February 25, 1978.

51. "National Minorities," *China News Analysis,* no. 831 (February 12, 1971):1.

52. Ilsa Sharp, "Beware the Little People," *Far Eastern Economic Review,* August 20, 1970, pp. 13–14; Bill Heaton, "Revolt of the Liberated Serfs," *Far*

Eastern Economic Review, November 14, 1970, pp. 22–24; Chiang Yung, "Dalai Tai-piao-tuan Ho-hsi-tsang-cheng-mien-mu" [The delegation of Dalai and the truth about Tibet], *Ch'ih-shih Nien-tai* [The seventies] (Hong Kong), May 1980, pp. 13–16. Chinese scholar Xu Mingxu reported that the violent Red Guards were mostly Tibetans, see Xu Mingxu, "Xizangwenti: Lishi Xiangzhuang Yu Weilai" [The Tibetan Issue: History, Present and Future], *Papers of the Center for Modern China,* no. 12 (October 1991):10.

53. Schwartz, *Circle of Protest,* p. 13.

54. *RMRB,* September 11, 1979, p. 1.

55. Gladney, *Muslim China,* pp. 137–140.

56. June Teufel Dreyer, *China's Forty Millions* (Cambridge, Mass.: Harvard University Press, 1976), p. 268.

57. "Study 'On the Ten Major Relationships' and Do a Good Job in Nationality Language Work," *Guangming Ribao,* March 25, 1977, in *SCMP,* no. 6326, p. 60.

58. FBIS, *CHI/DR,* November 28, 1994, p. 36.

59. For a general description and interpretation of the results of Deng's policy toward the minorities, see June Teufel Dreyer, "Ethnic Minorities in Mainland China Under Teng Hsiao-p'ing," in *Forces for Change in Contemporary China,* ed. Bih-jaw Lin and James T. Myers (Taipei: Institute of International Relations, National Chengchi University, 1992), pp. 251–262. I take exception to Dreyer's assessment that Mao's policy toward the minorities was successful, to a certain extent, in integrating the ethnic groups, while Deng's policy achieved more disintegration than integration.

60. *China Daily,* October 7, 1994, p. 4.

61. *China Daily,* February 21, 1992, p. 4.

62. FBIS, *CHI/DR,* November 17, 1994, p. 56.

63. Gladney, *Muslim China;* and Hu Yang, "Xinjiang's Experience: Conflicts and Compromise in China's Nationalities," (in Chinese) *Modern China Studies,* no. 1 (1994):82–91.

64. Dru C. Gladney, "Representing Nationality in China: Refiguring Majority/Minority Identities," *Journal of Asian Studies* 53, no. 1 (February 1994):92–123.

65. Gladney, *Muslim China,* pp. 119 and 302.

66. FBIS, *CHI/DR,* February 22, 1994, p. 63; and *New York Times,* February 20, 1994.

67. *New York Times,* December 24, 1985; FBIS, *CHI/DR,* October 27, 1988, pp. 51–53; *New York Times,* May 13, 1989; and FBIS, *CHI/DR,* October 12, 1993, pp. 24–26.

68. Schwartz, *Circle of Protest,* pp. 1, 84, 100, and 101.

69. FBIS, *CHI/DR,* June 6, 1994, pp. 77–80; and FBIS, *CHI/DR,* October 3, 1994, pp. 76–80.

70. On the case of the Norwegians, see Paul Wehr, *Conflict Regulation* (Boulder: Westview Press, 1979).

71. For a general analysis of the symbols, see Harold D. Lasswell, "Key Symbols, Signs and Icons," in *Symbols and Values: An Initial Study,* ed. Lyman Bryson, Louis Finkelstein, R. M. MacIver, and Richard McKeon (New York: Conference on Science, Philosophy, and Religion in Their Relation to the Democratic Way of Life, 1954).

72. Schwartz, *Cirle of Protest*, pp. 125, 163, 184, 207, 214–217, and 224–225.

73. *Chung-kuo Shih-pao* [China Times], December 21, 1994, citing information sources based in Hong Kong and New Delhi.

74. Kung Yen, "Ethnic Relations Tense in Xinjiang as Students Demonstrate and Pamphlets Circulate," *Ming Pao*, (Hong Kong), October 26, 1988, p. 10, in "Ethnic Confrontation in Xinjiang Reported," FBIS, *CHI/DR*, October 27, 1988, pp. 51–52.

75. *New York Times*, August 14, 1993; and also a digest of the government's internal report on the incident in the Hong Kong journal *Cheng Ming*, April 1994, pp. 32–34.

76. *Chung-kuo Shih-pao* [China Times], August 25, 1994. The source of this report came from Moscow.

77. FBIS, *CHI/DR*, November 10, 1993, p. 24.

78. FBIS, *CHI/DR*, December 7, 1994, pp. 61–63.

79. FBIS, *CHI/DR*, December 7, 1994, pp. 64–66.

80. Zhou Enlai called Inner Mongolia "a model autonomous region" in 1959; see FBIS, *CHI/DR*, May 11, 1994, p. 77.

81. See the entry on Ulanfu in Donald W. Klein and Anne B. Clark, *Biographic Dictionary of Chinese Communism, 1921–1965*, vol. 2 (Cambridge, Mass.: Harvard University Press, 1971), pp. 880–885.

82. *RMRB*, February 9, 1979, p. 3.

83. Sheryl WuDunn, "2 Dissident Mongol Groups Are Suppressed by Chinese," *New York Times*, July 28, 1991, p. 6.

84. Nicholas D. Kristof, "Restlessness Reaches Mongols in China," *New York Times*, July 19, 1992, E3.

85. FBIS, *CHI/DR*, April 7, 1994, p. 34.

86. *Cheng Ming*, no. 200 (June 1994), in FBIS, *CHI/DR*, June 6, 1994, pp. 20–22.

87. *Wen Wei Pao*, July 12, 1994, in FBIS, *CHI/DR*, August 4, 1994, pp. 57–58.

88. *RMRB*, August 18, 1994; and *Neimenggu Ribao* [Inner Mongolia Daily], November 20, 1994, in FBIS, *CHI/DR*, November 30, 1994, p. 54.

89. FBIS, *CHI/DR*, August 17, 1994, p. 18.

90. *Cheng Ming*, no. 194 (December, 1993):18.

91. *Qinghai Ribao*, February 17, 1994, p. 1, in FBIS, *CHI/DR*, March 3, 1994, p. 89.

92. FBIS, *CHI/DR*, August 4, 1994, p. 57.

93. Eriksen, *Ethnicity and Nationalism*, p. 19.

94. *China Daily*, July 27, 1994.

95. FBIS, *CHI/DR*, September 8, 1994, p. 74; *China Daily*, November 12, 1994.

96. FBIS, *CHI/DR*, May 17, 1994, p. 68.

97. *Chung-kuo Shih-pao* [China Times], September 25, 1991, p. 9.

98. FBIS, *CHI/DR*, August 8, 1994, pp. 42–43.

99. FBIS, *CHI/DR*, October 3, 1994, p. 77.

100. FBIS, *CHI/DR*, December 2, 1994, p. 55.

101. FBIS, *CHI/DR*, June 14, 1994, p. 63.

102. FBIS, *CHI/DR*, May 23, 1994, p. 70.

103. FBIS, *CHI/DR*, December 6, 1994, p. 55.

104. FBIS, *CHI/DR*, May 17, 1994, p. 68.

105. *China Daily,* June 6, 1994, p. 4.

106. FBIS, *CHI/DR,* May 27, 1994, p. 84.

107. Schwartz, *Circle of Protest,* pp. 158–159.

108. Ibid., pp. 197 and 203.

109. FBIS, *CHI/DR,* April 13, 1994, p. 67.

110. FBIS, *CHI/DR,* May 27, 1994, p. 67.

111. FBIS, *CHI/DR,* February 22, 1994, p. 64.

112. Schwartz, *Circle of Protest,* p. 201.

113. Joane Nagel and Susan Olzak, "Ethnic Mobilization in New and Old States: An Extension of the Competition Model," *Social Problems* 30, no. 2 (December 1982):127–143; and Nielsen, "Toward a Theory."

114. FBIS, *CHI/DR,* June 17, 1994, pp. 48–49.

115. FBIS, *CHI/DR,* August 5, 1994, pp. 51–52.

116. FBIS, *CHI/DR,* August 9, 1994, p. 71.

117. For a recent report, see FBIS, *CHI/DR,* December 2, 1994, pp. 58–59.

118. Walker Connor, *Ethnonationalism* (Princeton: Princeton University Press, 1994), p. 84.

119. Elise Boulding, "Ethnic Separatism and World Development," in *Research in Social Movements, Conflicts, and Change,* vol. 2, ed. Louis Kriesberg (Greenwich, Conn.: JAI Press, 1979), p. 277.

120. *Eastern Express* (Hong Kong), March 10, 1994, in *FBIS, CHI/DR,* March 11, 1994, pp. 45–46; *Yomiuri Shimbun* (Tokyo), September 20, 1994, in FBIS, *CHI/DR,* September 21, 1994, pp. 67–68.

121. See Dalai Lama's lengthy interview with the reporters of the Taiwan newspaper *Chung-kuo Shih-pao* [China Times], August 30, 1993, p. 3. In the interview, the issue that stunned the Dalai was the Taiwan reporter's account of Tibetan youths' being influenced by Western music and dance in Lhasa.

122. Steven Harrell, "Differential Educational Achievement in a Back Corner of China: A Local Success-Story with Control Groups." I am grateful to Professor Harrell for making this unpublished paper available to me.

6

CONCLUSION: PUBLIC OPINION, POLITICAL CULTURE, AND PROSPECTS FOR CIVIL SOCIETY IN CHINA

Communism was not defeated by military force but by life, by the human spirit, by conscience.

—Havel[1]

Throughout this book, I have been tracking and analyzing the effects of Chinese public opinion from 1949 to the present. I hope this work succeeds in demonstrating that there has been "public opinion" in the PRC since the 1950s, albeit of the uninstitutionalized kind. From the descriptions and analyses in the previous chapters, it is clear that the total effect of the CCP's political revolution in China since 1949 was a sharpening of the state-society division. Due to its own strong group consciousness, the CCP strengthened each social group and even heightened individual awareness of interests.[2] Since the essence of opinion dynamics in the PRC is the rise of group awareness, I find anthropologists' insights into ethnicity particularly applicable to the analysis of Chinese public opinion and mass political culture. Like that of ethnicity, the locus of public opinion in China is everyday interaction. However, in the case of public opinion, it is interaction between the masses and the Party-state. Chinese public opinion emerges and is made politically significant through state-society encounters and the people's ways of coping with the demands and challenges of the state. Similar to the study of ethnicity, the analysis of public opinion in China entails a focus on dynamics rather than statics.[3] In the ensuing discussions, I shall comment on how public opinion contributes to a mass political culture in China and the latter's implications for the possibility of a civil society.

Public Opinion and Political Culture

As mentioned earlier, one school of anthropology proposes that inter-ethnic relations typically undergo the process of: isolation–competition–conflict–accommodation. After making necessary adjustments, one can see that the state-society interaction in China from 1949 to the present has gone through a similar process, although with one crucial variation. There is an intervening phenomenon between conflict and accommodation: political culture. As a result of dealings with the Party-state, a mass political culture emerged among Chinese peasants, workers, students, and ethnic minorities. The fate of Deng's policy of accommodation is crucially determined by the mass political culture. The revised state-society interaction process is presented in Figure 6.1. At first, both the state and Chinese society were isolated from each other. The CCP developed its peculiar political culture and power apparatus in the periphery of China before 1949. The post–1949 encounter between the CCP Party-state and the various social groups resulted in either competition or conflict. Peasants, workers, and ethnic minorities competed with the state for the means of subsistence and the fruits of labor. Students and minorities were in conflict with the Party-state over ideology, mobility, and participation. Until the death of Mao, the state's responses to the demands and opinions of various groups were consistently uncompromising.

The state-society relationship under Mao was marked more by conflict escalation than de-escalation. By the time Deng Xiaoping changed the state's reaction to accommodation, a mass political culture had been born. Two primary characteristics of this culture are occasionalism and sectionalism. The first means every group (or person) attempts to maximize its (or his/her) short-term interest while a specific occasion allows it. The second means every group deals with the state independently of other groups. The root of occasionalism lies in the massive distrust of the state, along with that of sectionalism and social segmentation (made worse by the state's pervasive bureaucratic control).

The Chinese masses do not trust the accommodation policy of Deng's regime to last. Their chief response is "involution"—the intensification of each group's time-tested response to the state. Some, such as peasants in the interior and cohesive ethnic minorities, use the opportunity provided by Deng's accommodation policy to return to their pre–1949 isolation and particularism. As one Chinese Muslim told Gladney: "No matter which political winds blow, I am going to stick to Islam—the Quran doesn't change its mind."[4] Others, such as workers and part of the peasantry, strengthen their competition with the state over goods and services, as exemplified by widespread corruption and outright rebellions (or migra-

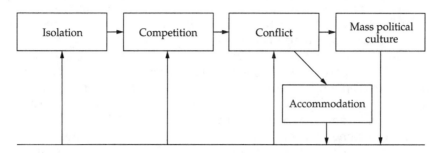

Figure 6.1   Pattern of state-society interaction in China, 1950–1994

tion) of peasants. The students and some minorities have taken up their pre–1949 mass demonstrations and separatist movements once more.

One might then ask how Chinese public opinion is transformed into political culture. First of all, the dividing line between public opinion and political culture is very narrow. Both are born of everyday interaction with the state. On the surface, public opinion is more transient and specific than political culture, but opinions regarding political or public affairs are the raw materials of which any particular political culture—more permanent and generalized than public opinion—is made. Every encounter between an individual and the state produces some kind of response or opinion from both parties. Insofar as the Chinese public is concerned, various groups aggregated their opinions over time into consistent ways of treating the state. Thus a mass political culture was born. I shall refer to this process as the aggregation pattern of opinion-to-culture evolution. Another pattern appears through reinforcement of an existing political culture. If an individual's or group's experience with a new or different state tends to conform to the person's or group's existing view of the state, then each opinion readily reinforces or solidifies the time-honored political culture. In the PRC, both patterns of opinion-to-culture evolution seem to have been in operation.

With respect to the aggregation pattern, the mid-1950s marked the nodal point. The political revolution that the CCP forced upon Chinese society had already generated a complex of state-society competiton (for example, over land and food with the peasantry) and conflicts. But by all accounts, China's masses still harbored a degree of wishful thinking toward the CCP. As one former student recalled, that so many bright university students participated actively in the Hundred Flowers campaign of 1957 was due to their trust in the CCP. They believed that the Party was sincere in inviting critical public opinion and carrying out reforms.[5] The

Party's subsequent intransigent stand, as exemplified in the 1958 Anti-Rightist campaign, served as the turning point in Chinese opinion evolution. From then on, the masses of China adopted various modes of amorphous social actions to oppose the Party-state.

On the reinforcement pattern of opinion-to-culture evolution in China, it is important to point out that an alienated mass political culture already existed when the CCP assumed power in 1949. In the 1920s, the famed scholar and social commentator Liang Ch'i-ch'ao [Liang Qichao] enumerated eight characteristics of the Chinese people's attitude toward the state and one another. They were: survivalism (that is, feeling lucky to have escaped unscathed), inurement to violence, a propensity to internecine conflicts, falseness-and-craftiness, egocentricity, myopia, fearfulness, and volatility. One may regard these as eight different expressions of anomie that were caused by the lack of stability and universal values in society. Liang attributed this distinct mass political culture of China to a dictatorial political tradition, repression by tyrants, a high frequency of destructive wars, poverty, and a deficiency in education and learning.[6] Now, after twenty-eight years of chronic instability and repression under Mao's rule, the cultural characteristics suggested by Liang in the 1920s are still much in evidence. For example, Thomas Gold found that personal relations in China since the Cultural Revolution were characterized by "instrumentalism," "commoditization," and an acute awareness of "Us-and-They" division.[7] As I mentioned in my discussion of student politics, in 1989 Beida students were angered and depressed by the "grab-and-run" mentality of the masses. All these are but different expressions of occasionalism and social segmentation.

But there is another dimension to political cultural continuity in China from the 1920s to the present. That is, the members of the CCP were themselves socialized in the uncivil environment of early modern China, which Liang Ch'i-ch'ao commented upon so pointedly. Thus, the Chinese Communist movement embodied tendencies toward alienation and segmentation. The members of the CCP, particularly its national leaders, do not identify the Chinese nation with more than their own corporate interests. Toward the end of Mao's rule, separation between the Party-state and Chinese society went one step further. The corporate interests of the CCP and the universal values of the Chinese nation were incorporated within one man—Mao. In other words, the CCP rule and the alienated mass political culture of the Chinese formed a vicious circle.

The culture of occasionalism and sectionalism contributed significantly to the "heterotropic" character of the social change in the post-Mao period. I have borrowed the term "heterotropic" from Karl Deutsch and Richard Merrit. "Hetero" means different, and "tropic" means going in various directions. Deutsch explained that in *Alice in Wonderland* there was someone who "rode off furiously in several directions."[8] Post-Mao

Chinese society is, in effect, doing just that. The reversion to a market form of economy and the rapid growth in eastern parts of China released strong centrifugal forces in Chinese society. Newly risen phenomena, such as migration, differentiation within groups, and regional disparity in growth, made the anomic quality of mass Chinese political culture even more salient than in the past.

Prospects of Civil Society

The Chinese political culture of occasionalism and sectionalism has serious implications for the possibility of a civil society in China. Until now, Western scholars' discussion of the yet-to-be-constituted civil society in China tended to gloss over political culture. One group of Sinologists examined Chinese history to find any semblance of a "public sphere" in traditional China. On the whole, they found none.[9] Another group began with the Tian'anmen massacre of June 1989. The writers of this school are optimistic about the prospect of a civil society emerging in China.[10] They see in the student movement and the reappearance of many voluntary groups in Chinese society during the post-Mao period evidence of the germination of a civil society. But there are also some skeptics who pointed out that the concept of civil society is alien to the Chinese way of thinking.[11] In summary, Sinologists tend to either take a structural approach to civil society or, once more, stress intellectuals rather than the masses of Chinese. Several comments about these arguments are in order.

First, civil society should not be understood solely as a structural concept, as those who searched for a "public sphere" in traditional China seemed to have done. If civil society simply means an arena where state power is absent and social actions predominate, then one finds "civil society" even in the most despotic political systems. Thirty years ago, Karl Wittfogel referred to this autonomous sphere in "oriental despotic" states as a "beggars' democracy."[12] Historians who looked for a "public sphere" in pre-modern China mistook the surface for the substance. As for those who found an incipient civil society in the pro-democracy movement, it is questionable to regard mass demonstration as a functional equivalent to civil society.[13] Mass protests signal the absence of a civil society; they represent politics of incivility, rather than civility. Moreover, the major characteristics of student movements—volatility, factionalism, and formlessness—are the opposite to those of a civil society. The reappearance of many voluntary groups in China during the 1980s is perhaps nothing more than a "beggars' democracy."[14]

The Dengist state finally recognized what Wittfogel called "the law of diminishing administrative returns." The urban Chinese are now allowed to form what one Chinese writer called "small interest groups," such as dancing clubs, karaoke singing groups, and housing exchange associations. These groups sprang up spontaneously and their membership was based on affective bonds, such as those among classmates, co-workers, alumni, veterans, neighbors, and relatives. They were multifarious in purpose and structurally formless.[15] They may be seen as the urban equivalent of clans and secret societies in rural China. All of them were primarily *Gemeinschaft* in character. One may include *Gemeinschaft* groups in a civil society, as T. H. Rigby does.[16] But the real function of a civil society—subjecting the state to the purview of public opinion—is to be carried out by *Gesellschaft* organizations. In the Chinese context, these "small interest groups" tend to substitute or preempt *Gesellschaft*, as Chinese history demonstrates.

The essence of a civil society is not just the right to be left alone to fulfill one's individualistic and socializing needs. Almost all writers agree that civil society means purposeful organization, which forces the state to serve society. Rigby wrote: "If civil society is to flourish, it must not only be in symbiotic relationship with the political order, but must substantially *colonize* it and remake it in its own image."[17] In Habermas's conception, the main task of a civil society is to promote critical public debate of state affairs.[18] Here, Habermas made civil society and an institutionalized public opinion one and the same. Both mean a deliberate and conscious attempt to transform the state into an agency of society (that is, society in the universalistic sense). As John Keane forcefully put it, "Civil society should become a permanent thorn in the side of political power."[19]

Based on the European and North American historical experience, the foundations of a civil society are urbanization, literacy, a middle class, independent associations, and an institutionalized public opinion. The middle class is the most crucial social component of a civil society. Both Habermas's discussion of a liberal public sphere and Speier's analysis of the history of public opinion in the West stressed the middle class as the social base of democracy.[20] Above all, for civil society to emerge there must be a stable and safe environment for the development of a market-centered society. Reinhard Bendix, John Bendix, and Norman Furniss stressed long-term commitment as the basis of forming civil society. They wrote: "One building block of civil society thus consists of a person's (and/or his family's) cumulative commitments. The other consists of the organizational safeguards that help protect an individual (and/or family's) interests in the cumulative life chances he has (or they have) obtained."[21] Decisions made by the organizations and institutions in civil society tend to be for the long term. Only a stable economic and social environment could guarantee an individual's or institution's long-term commitment.

Implicit in the theory of civil society is the notion that the state coexisting with a civil society must be of a certain type. According to Franz-

Xaver Kaufmann, civil society in most continental European nations had to extract itself from an absolute state and a feudal order.[22] For independent associations to come into being (thus giving birth to civil society), the state must accept the principle of individual autonomy and equality as the basis of the polity.[23] The stability upon which a civil society rests is based on the rule of law. Only under this type of political order can "a citizen. . . find redress against any other (including officers of the state) for breaches of law and where such redress is constitutionally guaranteed."[24]

Civil society is also founded on a cultural condition. That is the spirit of civility—a behavioral, not structural, concept. As Adam Seligman pointed out, "Civility, the mutual recognition of each individual's innate human dignity and membership in the political community is, as Edward Shils has argued, at the heart of civil society and, in his words, 'at bottom the collective consciousness of civil society.'"[25]A number of writers have pointed out that both former and ongoing socialist states are lacking in the political and cultural conditions required for a civil society. Politically, the principle of individual autonomy and equality as the basis of the polity is not accepted by these governments. Socially, the individual is often subordinated to primary or primordial groups such as clans and ethnic communities. Moreover, there is a pervasive sense of mistrust among the people.[26] Robert Miller described it as "an incidious moral relativism, bordering on moral anarchy and cynicism." Economically, there is "a mass psychological preoccupation with basic security of employment and egalitarianism in wages."[27]

Now it seems clear that the Chinese tradition of authoritarian governments, frequent wars of destruction, the predominantly agrarian social composition, social segmentation, and mass poverty are all serious impediments to the possible emergence of a civil society. My study of the reactions of the peasants, workers, students, and ethnic minorities in China fully corroborates Seligman's and Miller's observations about the various obstacles to a civil society in socialist states. Occasionalism, segmentalism, and separatism do not prepare China for a civil society. The crucial point about these attitudes is that once they have been formed, they are able to exist independently of the original reality that gave birth to them. The masses of China see Deng's accommodation as just another occasion of a temporarily receding state for them to "grab and run." Among university students and intellectuals, there exists the idea of an independent public opinion or the citizens' right to discuss state affairs. However, the tragic end of the pro-democracy movement in April-June 1989 testifies to the social isolation of Chinese intellectuals and students. They essentially inherited the fate of traditional Confucian scholars and court censors, whose criticisms of the emperor often resulted in their violent death.[28] Both the traditional dissidents and the Beijing students in 1989 were dependent—politically, socially, and economically—on the state. In the context of an overwhelming rural social environment, literacy, philosophy, and, nowadays, scientific and technological knowledge were valuable only in court- or state-centered high culture. Thus, the social isolation of Chinese students and intellectuals enabled the state to dispose of them as it saw fit.

Some writers are hopeful that the rising number of new entrepreneurs in China may increase the probability of a civil society.[29] As this study has shown, compared with other groups, the new private entrepreneurs are more participation-inclined. Their ranks have been growing rapidly. From 1978 to 1992, the total number of self-employed in China increased fifty-six times (from 150,000 to 8,380,000).[30] In 1994, however, these new businessmen constituted no more than 3 percent of all employed Chinese and 5 percent of the state's revenue (in 1992).[31] Moreover, the entrepreneurs also are strongly affected by regionalism and sectionalism. They tend to concentrate in eastern and coastal cities, such as Guangzhou where the private firms accounted for 52.4 percent of the total registered capital in the city in 1993.[32] Their political perspectives are diverse. Like other groups in contemporary Chinese society, the new entrepreneurs are still reacting to their experience under the Maoist rule. Some of them are dependent on the local Party establishment for their operations.[33] A portion of the self-employed supported the students in the pro-democracy movement. But there were others who agreed with the state. The best example of private business owners' support for the Beijing massacre came from Wenzhou—the "miracle economy" in post-Mao China, where private business is the mainstay of the local economy. A number of Wenzhou business owners collectively sent donations to the troops in Beijing to show their support for the June 4 crackdown.[34] These merchants were perhaps motivated more by self-preservation than genuine support of the state's action. As Seligman observed, "Whatever else they are, the workings of a free-market are not in themselves a guarantee of a liberal society and are not sufficient preconditions for the existence of civil society."[35]

Politically, as far as the state's conception of the individual is concerned, there does not appear to be any fundamental difference between Mao's and Deng's regimes. There is no acceptance of the principle of individual autonomy and equality as the basis of polity. This is clearly evidenced in the dispute between the Chinese government and the United States concerning the human rights situation in China. The standard Chinese rejoinder to U.S. criticism seeks to nullify the concept of human rights by stressing national sovereignty and the ability of the Chinese government to provide welfare goods to Chinese citizens.[36] Apparently, the Dengist state is incapable of conceiving individuals apart from their membership in a collectivity or as subjects of the state.

It is the lack of any fundamental change in the character of the Chinese state that virtually preordained the Tian'anmen massacre. The kind of conciliatory actions that Andrew Nathan suggested, such as a dialogue between Zhao Ziyang and the students, liberal laws on the press and demonstration, and the voluntary retirement of Deng, which could have resolved the Tian'anmen crisis of April-June 1989 peacefully, required a basic alteration in the perspective of the CCP elites.[37] To carry out the actions that Nathan envisioned, Deng and his colleagues would have had to allow an independent public opinion to exist. That would have meant that the corporate interests of the CCP were not necessarily identical to Chinese national interests. Deng and the whole CCP oligarchy were not prepared to make this fundamental change in their perspective. As Deng's daughter, who wrote his official biography (hagiography), explained to a U.S. reporter, the reason for the bloody crackdown on June 4, 1989, was that in Deng's heart, "he believed he had no other alternative but to take this action and it had to be taken. If no firm action was taken, China's future would be too terrible to imagine."[38]

There is also a strict limit to the Chinese state's tolerance of voluntary associations among the people. In 1994, the government launched an aggressive campaign to crackdown on Christian activities. While in 1993, a CCP propagandist revealed that the Party was divided over how to deal with increasing activities among Christians—especially concerning "house churches" (groups of Christians meeting in private homes for worship), by 1994 the government had decided on a policy of repression.[39] At first, Beijing publicized two important rules on religion: "Control of Sites of Religious Activities" and "Provisions on the Management of Religious Activities of Foreign Nationals Within the Boundaries of the PRC."[40] Under the cover of these rules, CCP cadres carried out arrests and tortures of Christians all over China.

The targets of this campaign were two groups: those Christians who were sympathetic toward political dissidents and those who form independent churches. The head of Beijing's largest church (in Gangwashi) was arrested and accused by the government of supporting the pro-democracy dissidents.[41] Members of "house churches" and indigenous sects that were "evangelical, mystical, subjective, intuitive, apocalyptic and individual" in character were also prime targets for the state's crackdown.[42] In December 1994, the police arrested thirty-one members of a Protestant sect called "Jesus Family" in Shandong. This is a rural movement that has a long history, dating back to the 1920s. In addition to arresting the leading members, the police razed the entire village where the members of this sect were concentrated.[43] The zeal that local cadres and police showed in persecuting Chinese Christians reminds one of the mass xenophobia in China at the turn of the century, which gave rise to the Boxer Rebellion in 1900. The often abusive or violent actions of cadres toward Chinese Christians prompted even the head of the state-controlled churches to lodge complaints with the government.[44]

But the Dengist state was also affected with heterotropicism. Some of the laws that Beijing enacted are likely to facilitate the emergence of a civil society in the future. Significantly, the Chinese government felt the necessity to enact the following legislations from 1990 to 1994: Administrative Procedure Law, State Compensation Law, Law on Trade Unions, and Arbitration Law. In principle, the first two legislations allow Chinese citizens to sue the government, especially local cadres, for misdeeds. These new laws might sharpen Chinese people's consciousness of their "rights" as citizens and provide a basis for regularity and predictability in their lives. If these new laws are honored in the future, they will have marked the beginning of the end of the occasionalism that is antithetical to a civil society.

The increasing integration of the Chinese economy with the Western markets is also likely to have an effect on the character of the Chinese state. The changed world culture, especially advanced Western nations' conception of power, is likely to affect the elite perspectives in Beijing. The elderly revolutionists who still control China are students of Western and Japanese imperialism that victimized modern China. Their concept of power is negative, coercive, and political. Today, especially after the collapse of the Soviet Union and socialism in Eastern Europe, national power in the world is defined more in a positive, noncoercive, and economic way. While it is unrealistic to expect Deng and his colleagues to change their power perspective fundamentally, their successors are likely to be more responsive to the changing world culture.

These discussions lead one to suggest that the path to a civil political and social order in China is likely to follow the Hungarian type, rather than the Polish way of forming a social compact among the people. According to Janian Frentzel-Zagorska, the democratic change in Hungary in the late 1980s and early 1990s was made possible by a "grand coalition" that was economy-centered, nonconfrontational (evolutionist), and elite-centered. The Hungarian strategy was based on two assumptions: (1) the Communists will never resign from power, and (2) the only feasible way of transforming the system is to change the character of the ruling elite, rather than to replace it.[45] The Hungarian way is similar to the Taiwanese way. The autocratic and Leninist character of the Chinese Nationalist Party in Taiwan was basically changed by economic development and cultural influence from the West. Through an evolutionary process, the outlook of the Communist elites might become increasingly secular and managerial. The influence of revolutionary politics, with its proneness to use force to resolve political or social differences, would recede. In the meantime, economic transformation would lay the foundations for a civil society and would include progressive changes such as urbanization, literacy, and relatively permanent associations. Economic development will almost certainly reduce urban-rural segmentation in China. A more prosperous peasantry, whose identification is no longer confined to the clan and the village, would deprive the remnant revolutionists in the Chinese state of an inexhaustible source for political repression in China (soldiers of the PRC armed forces were recruited primarily from the countryside).

Paradoxically, however, in the interim of changing from one type of society to another, the role of the state is strengthened. Rapid social change is always accompanied by all types of anomic manifestations, as exemplified by post-Mao Chinese society. "The State was a functional response to the general disruption of once integral society," wrote Harry Eckstein.[46] The role of the state is vital in several areas. First, the state must legislate new laws and rules to pave the ground for a new integral society. Second, a strong state is needed in an era of rapid economic growth to prevent socioeconomic strife from escalating. The state must also control inflation. In contemporary economic development, foreign investment is almost unavoidable and the state is the agency to receive, regulate, and supervise economic interaction with the outside world.

At present, the Chinese state's surrogacy for an integral society meets obstructions both "from above" and "from below." From above, the revolutionary tradition of the Chinese state dies hard. The Western press has reported numerous instances of efforts by the "Left" to obstruct social change in China, such as the publication of a book entitled *Looking at China Through a Third Eye*.[47] The author of this book sought to capitalize on the anomic situation in Chinese society by advocating a reversion to Maoism, much like the way Khomeini did in the Iranian Revolution of 1978–1979. However, the more serious challenge to the Chinese state's execution of economic development comes "from below"—ethnic separatism in particular. As stated earlier, ethnic separatism cannot be resolved by economic growth, even though Deng's administration seemed to believe it could. The Tibetans, Uighurs, and Mongolians are more authentic "nations" than are the Chinese. On the one hand, economic development is likely to strengthen their desire to be independent. But all indications are that, for the foreseeable future, the Chinese state will not hesitate to use repression against ethnic separatists. Escalating violence in ethnic relationships will cause serious ruptures in China's external relations and strengthen the "hardliners" among the elites. On the other hand, while economic development definitely will not dampen ethnic desire for autonomy, it will change the character of the Chinese state. A more decentralized and limited state might eventually result from successful economic development. A solution to China's ethnic conflicts may have to wait for this profound political change to come about.

Notes

1. V. Havel, "The End of the Modern Era," *New York Times*, March 1, 1992, E15.

2. For a general and largely explorative discussion on the Chinese state and the individual, see Lucian W. Pye, "The State and the Individual: An Overview Interpretation," *China Quarterly*, no. 127 (September 1991):443–467. I take exception to Pye's assessments that there is no state-society division in China but rather a state-individual division and that the Chinese people were passive toward CCP rule. My study refutes these points. Pye is also in error concerning the youth's attitude toward Lei Feng and the internal dossiers that were a prominent issue during the Cultural Revolution.

3. My summation of public opinion and political culture is benefited by Eriksen's discussion on ethnicity; see Thomas Hylland Eriksen, *Ethnicity and Nationalism* (London: Pluto Press, 1993), especially chapter 1.

4. Dru C. Gladney, *Muslim China: Ethnic Nationalism in the People's Republic* (Cambridge, Mass.: Council on East Asian Studies, Harvard University, 1991), p. 140.

5. Chin Chien-li, *Pei-kuo Chien-wen-lu* [Odyssey in North China] (Hong Kong: Union Press, 1973), especially chapter 21.

6. Liang Qichao (Liang Ch'i-ch'ao), *Yin-ping-shih Wen-chi* [Collected essays of the Ice-Drinkers' Studio], vol. 1 (Taipei: Hsin-hsin Shu-chu, 1955), pp. 97–106.

7. Thomas B. Gold, "After Comradeship: Personal Relations in China Since the Cultural Revolution," *China Quarterly*, no. 104 (December 1985):657–675.

8. Karl W. Deutsch, "The Systems Theory Approach as a Basis for Comparative Research," *International Social Science Journal* 37, no. 1 (1985):15.

9. See the various essays in the special issue of *Modern China* 19, no. 2 (April 1993). Contributors to the discussion were: Heath B. Chamberlain, Philip C.C. Huang, Richard Madsen, Mary Backus Rankin, William T. Rowe, and Frederic Wakeman Jr.

10. Thomas B. Gold, "The Resurgence of Civil Society in China," *Journal of Democracy* 1, no. 1 (Winter 1990):18–31; David Strand, "Protest in Beijing: Civil Society and Public Sphere in China," *Problems of Communism* 39, no. 3 (May-June 1990):1–18; and Martin K. Whyte, "Urban China: A Civil Society in the Making?" in *State and Society in China*, ed. Arthus Lewis Rosenbaum (Boulder: Westview Press, 1992), pp. 77–102.

11. Barrett L. McCormick, Su Shaozhi, and Xiao Xiaoming, "The 1989 Democracy Movement: A Review of the Prospects for Civil Society in China," *Pacific Affairs* 65, no. 2 (Summer 1992):182–202; and David Kelly and He Baogang, "Emergent Civil Society and the Intellectuals in China," in *The Development of Civil Society in Communist Systems*, ed. Robert F. Miller (North Sydney, Australia: Allen and Unwin, 1992), pp. 24–39.

12. Karl A. Wittfogel, *Oriental Despotism* (New Haven: Yale University Press, 1963), pp. 108–125.

13. Mary Rankin is of the same view with regard to the pre-1949 student movements; see Mary Backus Rankin, "Some Observations on a Chinese Public Sphere," *Modern China* 19, no. 2 (April 1993):177.

14. This is especially obvious in Whyte's article; see Whyte, "Urban China."

15. Han Weicai, "Shilun Woguo Shehui Shenghuozhongde Xiaoxin Liyiqunti" [On the small interest groups in the social life in China], *Shehui Kexue* [Social Science], no. 9 (1992):39–41.

16. T. H. Rigby, "The USSR: End of a Long, Dark Night?" in *The Development of Civil Society in Communist System*, ed. Miller, p. 14.

17. Ibid.

18. Jürgen Habermas, *The Structural Transformation of the Public Sphere*, trans. Thomas Burger, with the assistance of Frederick Lawrence (Cambridge, Mass.: MIT Press, 1989), pp. 51–52.

19. John Keane, *Democracy and Civil Society* (London: Verso, 1988), p. 15.

20. Habermas, *The Structural Transformation*, pp. 51–79; Hans Speier, *Social Order and the Risks of War* (New York: George W. Stewart, 1952), pp. 323–338.

21. Reinhard Bendix, John Bendix, and Norman Furniss, "Reflections on Modern Western States and Civil Societies," in *Research in Political Sociology*, vol. 3, ed. Richard G. Braungart and Margaret M. Braungart (Greenwood, Conn.: JAI Press, 1987), p. 18.

22. Franz-Xaver Kaufmann, "The Blurring of the Distinction 'State Versus Society' in the Idea and Practice of the Welfare State," in *Guidance: Control and Evaluation in the Public Sector*, ed. Franz-Xaver Kaufmann, Giandomencio Majone, and Vincent Ostrom (Berlin: Walter de Gruyter, 1986), cited in Bendix, Bendix, and Furniss, "Reflections on Modern Western States," p. 25.

23. Adam B. Seligman, *The Idea of Civil Society* (New York: Free Press, 1992), chapter 4.

24. Bendix, Bendix, and Furniss, "Reflections on Modern Western States," p. 7.

25. Seligman, *The Idea of Civil Society*, p. 172.

26. Ibid., chapter 4.

27. Robert F. Miller, "Concluding Essay," in *The Development of Civil Society*, ed. Miller, pp. 140 and 141.

28. Lin Yutang, *A History of the Press and Public Opinion in China* (New York: Greenwood Press, 1968).

29. McCormick, Su, and Xiao, "The 1989 Democracy Movement," p. 196.

30. *Zhongguo Tongji Nianjian, 1993* [Statistical Yearbook of China, 1993] (Beijing: Zhongguo Tongji Chubanshe, 1993), p. 97.

31. *China Daily*, November 11, 1994, p. 4.

32. *Xinhua*, February 22, 1994, in *FBIS, CHI/DR*, February 23, 1994, p. 30.

33. Dorothy J. Solinger, "Urban Entrepreneurs and the State: The Merger of State and Society," in *State and Society in China*, ed. Rosenbaum, pp. 121–142.

34. *New York Times*, January 27, 1993, A4.

35. Segliman, *The Idea of Civil Society*, p. 178.

36. See, for example, "Comments on U.S. State Department Human Rights Report on China," *China Daily*, June 9, 1994, p. 4.

37. Andrew J. Nathan, *China's Crisis* (New York: Columbia University Press, 1990), pp. 193–211.

38. *New York Times*, January 13, 1995, A6.

39. Ye Xiaowen, "Luelun Xinxinshixia Minzu, Zongjiaofangmiandi Renmin Neibumaodun," [On the internal contradictions among the people in ethnic and religious spheres under the new circumstance], *Xinhua Wenzhai* [New China Digest], no. 9 (1993):10–13.

40. FBIS, *CHI/DR*, March 3, 1994, pp. 25–26; April 20, 1994, p. 29; and April 8, 1994, pp. 18–20.

41. FBIS, *CHI/DR*, September 14, 1994, pp. 22–23.

42. FBIS, *CHI/DR*, June 21, 1994, pp. 17–18.

43.   FBIS, *CHI/DR*, December 9, 1994, p. 11.

44.   *South China Morning Post*, March 4, 1994, p. 8, in FBIS, *CHI/DR*, March 4, 1994, pp. 25–26.

45.   Janian Frentzel-Zagorska, "Patterns of Transition from a One-Party State to Democracy in Poland and Hungary," in *The Development of Civil Society*, ed. Miller, pp. 41–44.

46.   Harry Eckstein, "On the 'Science' of the State," in *The State*, ed. Stephen R. Graubard (New York: W. W. Norton and Company, 1979), p. 16.

47.   FBIS, *CHI/DR*, September 7, 1994, pp. 24–26, and September 16, 1994, p. 31.

SELECTED BIBLIOGRAPHY

General Reference

Back, Kurt W. "Metaphors for Public Opinion in Literature." *Public Opinion Quarterly* 52 (Fall 1988):278–288.

Bendix, Reinhard, John Bendix, and Norman Furniss. "Reflections on Modern Western States and Civil Societies." In *Research in Political Sociology,* ed. Richard G. Braungart and Margaret M. Braungart. Vol. 3. Greenwich, Conn.: JAI Press, 1987.

Converse, Philip E. "Changing Conceptions of Public Opinion in the Political Process." *Public Opinion Quarterly* 51 (Winter 1987):S19–S24.

Eckstein, Harry. "On the 'Science' of the State." In *The State,* ed. Stephen R. Graubard. New York: W. W. Norton, 1979.

Eisenstadt, S. N. *From Generation to Generation.* New York: Free Press, 1964.

Eriksen, Thomas H. *Ethnicity and Nationalism.* London: Pluto Press, 1993.

Fantasia, Rick. *Cultures of Solidarity: Consciousness, Action, and Contemporary American Workers.* Berkeley: University of California Press, 1988.

Goldfarb, Jeffrey C. "Social Bases of Independent Public Expression in Communist Societies." *American Journal of Sociology* 83 (January 1978):920–939.

Habermas, Jurgen. *The Structural Transformation of the Public Sphere.* Trans. Thomas Burger. Cambridge, Mass.: MIT Press, 1989.

Hirsch, Eric L. "Sacrifice for the Cause: Group Processes, Recruitment, and Commitment in a Student Social Movement." *American Sociological Review* 55 (April 1990):243–254.

Key Jr., V. O. *Public Opinion and American Democracy.* New York: Knopf, 1963.

Klandermans, Bert, Hanspeter Kriesi, and Sidney Tarrow, eds. *From Structure to Action: Comparing Social Movement Research Across Cultures.* Greenwich, Conn.: JAI Press, 1988.

Kriesberg, Louis. *Social Conflicts.* Englewood Cliffs, N.J.: Prentice-Hall, 1982.

Kriesberg, Louis, ed. *Research in Social Movements, Conflicts, and Change.* Vols. 2-3. Greenwich, Conn.: JAI Press, 1979-1980.

Kuran, Timur. "Now Out of Never: The Element of Surprise in the East European Revolution of 1989." *World Politics* 44 (October 1991):7–49.

Lippmann, Walter. *Public Opinion*. New York: Macmillan, 1961.

Mannheim, Karl. "The Problem of Generations." In *The New Pilgrims: Youth Protest in Transition,* ed. Philip G. Altbach and Robert S. Laufer. New York: David McKay, 1972.

Niedhardt, Friedhelm, and Dieter Rucht. "The Analysis of Social Movements: The State of the Art and Some Perspectives for Future Research." In *Research on Social Movements: The State of the Art in Western Europe and the USA,* ed. Dieter Rucht. Boulder: Westview Press, 1991.

Pool, Ithiel de Sola. "Public Opinion." In *Handbook of Communication,* ed. Ithiel de Sola Pool et al. Chicago: Rand McNally College Publishing, 1973.

Seligman, Adam B. *The Idea of Civil Society.* New York: Free Press, 1992.

Sherman, George. "Soviet Youth: Myth and Reality." In *The Challenge of Youth,* ed. Erick H. Erikson. New York: Doubleday, 1965.

Shlapentokh, Vladimir. "Attitudes and Behavior of Soviet Youth in the 1970s and 1980s: The Mysterious Variable in Soviet Politics." In *Research in Political Sociology,* ed. Richard G. Braungart and Margaret M. Braungart. Vol. 2. Greenwich, Conn.: JAI Press, 1986.

Speier, Hans. *Social Order and the Risks of War: Papers in Political Sociology.* New York: George W. Stewart, 1952.

Turner, Ralph H., and Lewis M. Killian, eds. *Collective Behavior.* Englewood Cliffs, N.J.: Prentice-Hall, 1972.

Weber, Max. *Economy and Society: An Outline of Interpretive Sociology,* Vol. 1 and 2. Ed. Günther Roth and Claus Wittich. New York: Bedminster Press, 1968.

Yinger, J. Milton. "Ethnicity in Complex Societies: Structural, Cultural, and Characterological Factors." In *The Uses of Controversy in Sociology,* ed. Lewis A. Coser and Otto N. Larsen. New York: The Free Press, 1976.

Chinese Politics and Society

Barlow, Tani E., and Donald M. Lowe. *Chinese Reflections: Americans Teaching in the People's Republic.* New York: Praeger, 1985.

Burns, John P. "Chinese Peasant Interest Articulation." In *Groups and Politics,* ed. David S. G. Goodman. Cardiff, U.K.: University College Cardiff Press, 1984.

Chan, Anita. *Children of Mao: Personality Development and Political Activism in the Red Guard Generation.* Seattle: University of Washington Press, 1985.

Chan, Anita, Richard Madsen, and Jonathan Unger. *Chen Village.* Berkeley: University of California Press, 1984.

Chen, Ta. "Basic Problems of the Chinese Working Classes." *American Journal of Sociology* 53 (1947):184–191.

Dittmer, Lowell. "The Legacy of Mao Zedong." *Asian Survey* 20 (May 1980):552–573.

Friedman, Edward, Paul G. Pickowicz, and Mark Selden. *Chinese Village, Socialist State.* New Haven: Yale University Press, 1991.

Garside, Roger. *Coming Alive.* New York: McGraw-Hill, 1981.

Gladney, Dru C. *Muslim China: Ethnic Nationalism in the People's Republic.* Cambridge, Mass.: Council on East Asian Studies, Harvard University, 1991.

Harrell, Steven. "Ethnicity, Local Interests, and the State: Yi Communities in Southwest China." *Comparative Study of Society and History* 32 (1990):515–548.

———. "Introduction: Civilizing Projects and the Reaction to Them." In *Cultural Encounters on China's Ethnic Frontiers,* ed. Steven Harrell. Seattle: University of Washington Press, 1994.

Kelly, David, and He Baogang. "Emergent Civil Society and the Intellectuals in China." In *The Developments of Civil Society in Communist Systems,* ed. Robert F. Miller. North Sydney, Australia: Allen & Unwin, 1992.

Liang Heng and Judith Shapiro. *Son of the Revolution.* New York: Random House, 1983.

Nathan, Andrew J. *China's Crisis.* New York: Columbia University Press, 1990.

Nee, Victor. "Peasant Household Individualism." In *Chinese Rural Development: The Great Transformation,* ed. William Parish. Armonk, N.Y.: M. E. Sharpe, 1985.

Schwartz, Ronald D. *Circle of Protest: Political Ritual in the Tibetan Uprising.* New York: Columbia University Press, 1994.

Strand, David. "Protest in Beijing: Civil Society and Public Sphere in China." *Problems of Communism* 39 (May-June 1990):1–18.

Tong, Sheng. *Almost a Revolution.* Boston: Houghton Mifflin, 1990.

Walder, Andrew G. *Communist Neo-traditionalism.* Berkeley: University of California Press, 1986.

———. "Workers, Managers, and the State: The Reform Era and the Political Crisis of 1989." *China Quarterly* 127 (September 1991):467–492.

White III, Lynn T. *Policies of Chaos: The Organizational Causes of Violence in China's Cultural Revolution.* Princeton: Princeton University Press, 1989.

Whyte, Martin K. "Urban China: A Civil Society in the Making?" In *State and Society in China,* ed. Arthur Lewis Rosenbaum. Boulder: Westview Press, 1992.

Whyte, Martin K., and William L. Parish. *Urban Life in Contemporary China.* Chicago: University of Chicago Press, 1984.

Wilson, Jeanne L. "Labor Policy in China: Reform and Retrogression." *Problems of Communism* 39 (September–October 1990):44–65.

———. "'The Polish Lesson': China and Poland, 1980–1990." *Studies in Comparative Communism* 23 (Autumn-Winter 1990):259–279.

ABOUT THE BOOK AND AUTHOR

Exploring the crucial link between state and society in the PRC, this study analyzes the interaction between the Chinese Communist Party and the country's major social groups—peasants, workers, youths and students, intellectuals, and ethnic minorities—since the founding of the People's Republic. Alan Liu argues that uninstitutionalized public opinion has existed in China ever since the inception of the Communist regime and that it gradually grew powerful enough to thwart Mao's policies and programs. He contends that the government's radical post-Mao reforms emerged less from the preferences of another paramount leader—Deng—than from public opinion, which has grown too strong for the communist party either to ignore or control.

Alan P.L. Liu is a professor of political science at the University of California–Santa Barbara.

INDEX